The history of *flight*

The history of *flight*

DAVID SIMONS AND THOMAS WITHINGTON

p

This is a Parragon Publishing Book
First published in 2004

Parragon Publishing
Queen Street House
4 Queen Street
Bath BA1 1HE, UK

Editorial and design by
Amber Books Ltd
Bradley's Close
74–77 White Lion Street
London N1 9PF
www.amberbooks.co.uk

ISBN 1-40543-800-2

Printed in China

Front cover montage: Wright Flyer, 1903 © Art-Tech/Aerospace/TRH Pictures
Back: Boeing X-45A UCAV (pilotless aircraft) © TRH Pictures/Boeing

Photograph below shows Paul Cornu's 1907 'flying bicycle', the first machine
to take off vertically with a pilot and make a free flight.

Contents

introduction

Flight has gripped our imagination for as long as we have stared in wonderment at the birds and insects moving above our heads. From the mythical Vimana flying machines of ancient India to the technologically advanced stealth bombers and giant airliners of modern times, humans have pursued a tireless quest to ascend higher and travel faster in the skies and beyond.

The success enjoyed by the early pioneers of flight such as the Montgolfier and Wright brothers triggered frantic innovation and experiments. The results have allowed people to step on both the moon and foreign continents, to travel at supersonic speeds for war and pleasure, and to navigate the globe for fun and profit.

This book provides a detailed and lavishly illustrated commentary on humankind's valiant dash for the skies. From the earliest musings on aviation to the aircraft of tomorrow, it gives a detailed summary of the way aviation has shaped the modern world. It profiles the innovators who sought to roll back the boundaries of aviation through endurance, speed and danger; the use of aircraft as a weapon of war and peace; how air travel has shrunk the globe for commerce and travel; the contribution of space flight to our understanding of the earth and the cosmos; and finally, a glimpse at tomorrow and the role that aviation may play in the future.

According to aviation visionary and pilot Dick Rutan, as we look back on more than a century of flight, "it could be tempting to suggest that all the things that could be invented have been invented. But we are just on the frontier of discovery and invention. It's a very exciting time."

Left: *The Boeing B-29 Superfortress was without doubt the most complex bomber of World War II. The technological advances made during its development paved the way for a new generation of airliners after the war.*

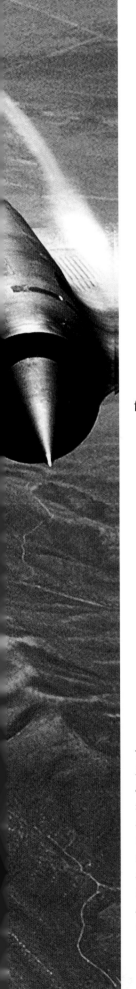

the thinkers

Flight has fascinated human beings for as long as they have been aware of the sky above them. For thousands of years we have gazed upwards with wonderment at the birds and insects that seem effortlessly to soar through the air, asking "what would it be like to fly?"

Top: *This woodcut of the flight of Daedalus and the fall of Icarus is among the earliest printed representations of human flight, dating from 1493.*
Left: *One of the end results of mankind's desire to fly faster, higher and farther is the Lockheed SR-71 Blackbird, a Cold War spyplane capable of sustained flight at more than three times the speed of sound.*

The concept of human flight exists in the mythology of almost all ancient civilizations. Deities in ancient Egypt, Mesopotamia, and Asia Minor were often depicted as having wings. One example was the supreme god, Ahura Mazda ("Lord Wisdom,") sculpted in stone in the palace of the Persian Emperor Darius I, the Great, (522–486 BC) at Susa. The winged cherubim and seraphim of the ancient Hebrews were depicted on the Ark of the Covenant.

The Greek philosopher Plato (427–347 BC) said of flight that: "the natural function of the wing is to soar upwards and carry that which is heavy up to the place where dwells the race of gods. More than any other thing that pertains to the body it partakes of the nature of the divine." Socrates, another Greek sage, took an alternative approach, believing that flight was essential if human beings were to increase their understanding of the Earth. He said: "Man must rise above the Earth—to the top of the atmosphere and beyond—for only thus will he fully understand the world in which he lives."

The importance which humans attached to flight can be traced back to the Sanskrit texts of ancient India. Sanskrit was the ancient language of modern-day India, and one

Right: *Two winged sphinxes are depicted under the emblem of Ahura Mazda which was discovered at Susa in modern-day Iran.*

sacred text, known as the *Rig Veda,* which is thought to have been written down in the third century BC, discusses various flying vehicles known as "Rathas" which seem to have been some kind of aerial carriage. Ancient Sanskrit texts also talk of vehicles called "Vimanas." These were said to be flying machines capable of extremely high speeds, with a three-person crew known as a "tribandhura." The Vimanas were said to resemble horse-drawn chariots and even had an undercarriage that could be retracted during flight. The craft were constructed from precious metals like gold, silver, or iron. Nails and rivets were used to build the Vimanas and it was said that the vehicles were not just capable of navigating the skies, but that they could travel through space towards the sun and the moon.

These ancient texts discuss two distinct categories of Vimanas. The first were the chariots which could fly with the aid of bird-like wings. The second category included large, un-aerodynamic structures which would fly in an erratic and unpredictable manner. Allusions to these machines, which are described as "an aerial chariot with the sides of iron and clad with wings," can be found in the *Rig Veda* but also in the *Mahabharata* (Great Epic of the Bharata Dynasty) and in the *Ramayana* (Romance of Rama). This last work also described a machine called a Pushpak Vimana: a double-deck, cylindrical aircraft festooned with portholes and a dome which could fly at the speed of thought, resonating the while with a "melodious sound."

By the third century BC, *Arthashastra*—a work by Kautilya, discussed aviation at length. Pilots were called "Saubhikas" or "pilots conducting vehicles in the sky—one who flies or knows the art of flying

Above: *The British-designed Harrier is the only aircraft in current military service able to undertake vertical take-offs and landings, a feat which our ancestors would surely have considered supernatural.*

Above: *This mysterious representation of a monkey, drawn in the sands of the Nazca desert in Peru, is only visible from the air. Could the civilization that created these lines have possessed flying machines?*

an aerial city." Saubha was the name of a supposed flying city belonging to King Harishchandra, the ruler of Ayodhya. Kautilya also discusses ancient "fighter pilots" known as *Akasa Yodhinah*—"persons who are trained to fight from the sky."

Another ancient Sanskrit text, the *Matsya Purana,* also talks of flying cities. These cities were said to be either mobile or stationary. They could dock together in a similar fashion to present-day spacecraft. In Bhoja's manuscript *Yuktikalpataru,* the author refers to "aerial cars," similar to the Vimanas. One recurrent theme in the depiction of the Vimanas is that they could fly vast distances across the oceans.

Other ancient civilizations also seem to have regarded flight as important. In around 2300 BC, King Etana of Mesopotamia was depicted on a cylinder seal as flying on the back of an eagle. More than 3000 years later Inca mythology talks of Manco Capae, the founder of the Inca empire, as being "winged and could fly." Some archaeologists have even argued that the ancient Nazca civilization of Peru was able to use flying machines

like those described in the Sanskrit epics. When flying above the high desert in Peru, strange mysterious lines can be seen etched into the ground. Some have suggested that these might have been some kind of ancient runway or landing strip. A more mundane suggestion is that they might have been paths running between religious sites.

Chinese experiments

In addition to the myths and legends that surround the early history of flight, there are documented examples of experiments with aviation in ancient times. In 2200 BC, the legendary Chinese Emperor Shin was said to have jumped from a burning tower wearing two large straw hats which he hoped would act as wings. These hats are still worn in parts of modern-day China and can reach 3ft (90cm) in diameter. Unlike many who would attempt similar stunts in the future, Shin landed safely.

According to some accounts, by 1766 BC Emperor Cheng Tang of the Tang Dynasty had

Left: *Daedalus encouraged his son Icarus to fly from Crete to Sicily with waxed wings attached to his arms. The consequences for Icarus were disastrous. Icarus flew too close to the sun, which melted the wax on his wings, and he plunged into the Mediterranean.*

Learning to fly—the myth of Daedalus and Icarus

Greek mythology also has its legends of flight. The tale of Daedalus and Icarus as told by the Roman poet Ovid introduces Daedalus, a Greek artisan who had been determined to fly ever since witnessing Medea, a barbarian witch, take to the skies in a chariot drawn by dragons.

While working for King Minos of Crete, Daedalus set up a secret workshop overlooking the cliffs of the island where he would spend many hours observing the flights of the eagles and gulls soaring overhead. This encouraged him to make feathered wings sealed with beeswax to carry him towards the heavens. But while Daedalus was working on his wings, King Minos ordered his arrest, accusing him of betraying the secrets of the famous Labyrinth, the legendary underground maze-complex that was the home of the deadly Minotaur—a man with the head of a bull and an appetite for humans.

As Minos' soldiers approached, Daedalus resolved to escape with his son Icarus. Father and son donned their wings. Daedalus ordered Icarus to jump off the cliffs into the sky. He warned his son not to fly too low, lest sea water wash into the wings; or to fly too high in case the sun should melt the wax that held the wings together. Icarus, full of youthful exuberance, forgot his father's advice. Flying to close to the sun, the wax on his wings melted, and he plunged spiraling into the sea. His father was luckier, making good his escape to Sicily.

Right: *A Chinese kite used for night flying, made in the shape of a fish with a lantern attached to the tail.*

in the world. Mo-tse later handed down his kite-making secrets to his protégé Lu Ban who later applied the idea to military uses like message-carrying and surveying wind conditions. Kites were also thought to be useful for warding off evil spirits. Underpinning their recreational value kites earned the Chinese name "Fengzheng"—"Feng" meaning "wind" and "Zheng" being a reference to a musical whistle made of bamboo. These instruments were attached to kites, making them whistle as they flew through the air.

Chinese kite design reportedly evolved into the construction of huge flying machines that were capable of carrying passengers. Lu Ban claimed to have developed a kite that could be used for espionage, like an early version of a spy plane. He was also said to have designed a kite: "when he worked in a place very far away from his hometown. He missed his wife very much, so he made a wooden (kite). After being redesigned several times, the wooden kite could fly. Lu Ban went home on the kite to meet his wife and returned to work on the next day." In the fourteenth century, Marco Polo, the celebrated Italian explorer, reported seeing kites capable of carrying humans during his visits to the Orient.

Chinese ingenuity, which had discovered the principles of the kite, also unlocked some of the secrets of modern-day space flight. It is thought that the Chinese were experimenting with rockets by the first century AD. These early vehicles were fuelled by a gunpowder mix of saltpeter, sulfur, and charcoal dust. The mixture was put in bamboo tubes, which were then thrown onto a fire where they would ignite, sending the rockets flying off in all directions.

But it was not until 1232 that rockets were first used on the battlefield, at a time when the Chinese and the Mongols were at war. At the Battle of Kai-Keng the Chinese put up a bombardment of rocket-propelled "arrows of flying fire." While the destructive effect of these rockets is unknown, they probably had a powerful psychological effect on the Mongols. It is thought that rocketry was developed further by the Mongols as they expanded their empire from Central Asia into Iran and further west. They were said to have used rockets under the leadership of Timur (Tamerlane) when he besieged Baghdad in 1401.

successfully built a flying machine, but he destroyed his contraption to stop anyone else learning the secrets of flight. By the third century BC, the Chinese poet Chu Yun claimed to have used an aircraft to make aerial surveys of the Gobi desert. He was said to have been especially impressed by his craft's ability to withstand harsh weather and sandstorms.

One of the outstanding Chinese contributions to the development of aviation was the invention of the kite. Flown in parks throughout the world, the kite may have owed its creation to military necessity. Mo-tse, a Chinese philosopher who lived from 468 to 376 BC, apparently designed a kite shaped like a sparrowhawk. The construction of his kite took three years—the first of its kind

Right: *Early cultures believed that only magicians were capable of flight, with the help of demons. Here the magician Simon Magus demonstrates his powers to the emperor Nero.*

Left: *John Wilkins was a founding member of the Royal Society for Improving Natural Knowledge. In 1648 Wilkins published his theories into the nature of the upper atmosphere, and proposed the use of lighter-than-air flying machines.*

Medieval Europe

As the Chinese were experimenting with rockets, some in Europe were beginning to contemplate flight and even space travel. In 66 AD a Roman magician, Simon Magus, tried to fly over Rome, but luck was not on his side. He jumped off a tower but fell into the Forum, breaking his neck. Lucian, a philosopher and writer born in Syria in 125 AD discussed a trip to the Moon in his work "A True Story," talking of a ship which "ascended to the rising moon upon a waterspout."

In 852 AD a man called Armen Firman jumped out of a tower in Cordoba. He was determined to stay aloft with a big, billowing cloak which he hoped would act as a wing. But gravity dictated otherwise and Firman came crashing to the ground, fortunately sustaining only minor injuries.

There were several other early attempts at flight in Spain. Possibly building on Firman's experiences, a doctor named Abbas ibn-Firnas decided to attempt a flight in Andalusia. He covered himself with many feathers and some accounts indicate that he might have actually got airborne and flown for some distance. But he lost stability and hit the ground hard, damaging his back badly. He blamed his failure on his lack of a tail.

It is unknown whether Oliver of Malmesbury, an English Benedictine monk (in some accounts called Eilmer of Malmesbury), was aware of Firnas's and Firman's unsuccessful ventures. But if so their mishaps did not stop him attempting to fly. Using wings attached to his arms and feet, which were said to have been inspired by those used by Daedalus, he jumped off the tower of Malmesbury Abbey, but crashed into the ground, shattering his legs. Oliver had apparently been a gifted soothsayer, predicting events yet to happen, but on that fateful day it seems that his powers failed him and he spent the rest of his life unable to walk. Like Firnas, he believed his failure was the result of not having a tail. Oliver's experiment is now immortalized in a stained glass window at Malmesbury Abbey—where he is seen standing, holding his wings—presumably depicting Oliver before his flight attempt.

Under the rule of Manuel Comnenus, Emperor of Byzantium, an unnamed Saracen used similar means to Oliver and his predecessors to get airborne. Climbing the tower of the hippodrome in Constantinople (present-day Istanbul), the man intended to use his robe, which was kept taut by a wooden frame, to act as his wings. The spectacle of the Saracen and the daring of his attempt drew a crowd of spectators, who were barely able to contain their excitement and impatience shouting: "Fly, fly, O Saracen! Do not keep us so long in suspense while thou art weighing the wind!" As soon as the wind strength seemed right the Saracen threw himself off the tower and did actually rise in the air—before crashing. He would have done well to heed the advice printed on a children's Batman costume in the 1990s which warned: "Cape does not enable the user to fly."

Bacon and Leonardo

By the thirteenth century, the theoretical musings of the thinkers were turning into something like scientific research. Roger Bacon was a scholar who made detailed observations about the principles of flight. In addition to studying alchemy, mathematics, and astronomy, he described a process for making gunpowder. He said this could be used to propel flying machines,

ships, and land vehicles. Born in 1214, Bacon had a privileged upbringing and in his early education he excelled at geometry, arithmetic, and music. By 1250 Bacon was absorbed by his studies. In *The Wonderful Power of Art and Nature* he described, among other things, the design of a flying machine: "Such a machine must be a large hollow globe of copper or other suitable metal, wrought extremely thin in order to have it as light as possible. It must then be filled with ethereal air or liquid fire and launched from some elevated point into the atmosphere, where it will float like a vessel upon the water." This was a notable departure from the previous theorists and would-be pilots who believed that wings were essential for flight. Bacon had in essence outlined

Below: *Roger Bacon, author of* The Wonderful Power of Art and Nature, *which was written in about 1260. His work outlined a prototype design for a flying machine.*

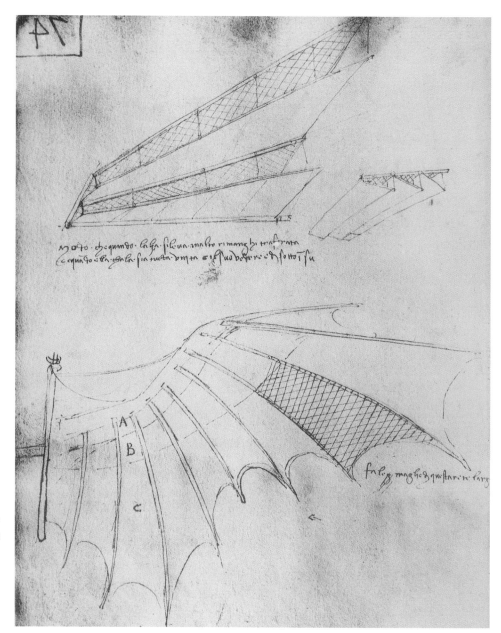

Right: *Leonardo da Vinci studied the wings of birds, and sketched his designs for mechanical wings for flying machines based on their structure.*

Far right: *Combining his knowledge of the density of air with inspiration derived from a Chinese toy, Leonardo conceived an aerial screw which would carry people aloft with a circular motion. It was the precursor of the modern helicopter.*

the principles which would later allow balloons and airships to take to the skies; stating that hot air or a gas which was lighter than air, such as helium, would be sufficient to carry a craft aloft. Several hundred years later, in 1648, John Wilkins, a founding member of the Royal Society for Improving Natural Knowledge, expanded on some of Bacon's ideas. Wilkins talked of "ethereal air" in the upper reaches of the atmosphere which was less dense than that closer to the ground, arguing that containers filled with this ethereal air would rise.

Bacon did not discount wings completely. He discussed the design of a flying machine with flapping wings—known in modern parlance as an "ornithopter." He resolved "to make flying-machines in which the man, being seated or suspended in the middle, might turn some winch or crank, which would put in motion a suit of wings made to strike the air like those of a bird."

The design of flying machines would make important advances in the fifteenth century, thanks to the drawings of Leonardo da Vinci. Although best known as an artist, Leonardo was

Helicopter. Combining his knowledge
of the density of air with...
from a C...
an aeris...
whirled for bearing people aloft, translated
the modern helicopter.

Leonardo da Vinci

fascinated by flight. From 1486, he began to make detailed drawings of flying machines, including helicopters and parachutes. Like Bacon he also ruminated on the ornithopter, designing a machine where the wings could be manoeuvred using pulleys and levers. Leonardo's ornithopter also featured a tail, a standard feature on nearly all modern aircraft. The design for this was based upon the artist's observation of birds. It featured an elevator which could move up or down, causing the aircraft to climb or dive, and a rudder which would control the side-to-side movement—a modern aircraft simply cannot fly properly without such equipment. The elevators and the rudders would be controlled by a harness which connected them to the pilot's head, which would then control the movements of the aircraft. Leonardo's error was in thinking that a human would have the strength and stamina to keep the wings flapping during the flight. This factor was later addressed in 1680 by the Italian mathematician and physiologist Giovanni Alfonso Borelli, in his book "Concerning Animal Motion" where he argued correctly that humans simply did not have the physical strength to fly like a bird.

Rockets and feathers

By the sixteenth century, despite their earlier popularity with the Chinese, Mongols, Arabs and French, rockets were out of fashion in Europe as a weapon of war, although they were still a standard feature at firework displays. This kept people such as Johann Schmidlap—a German firework maker—in business. He managed to devise a method by which a rocket could lift itself to a high

Above: Leonardo da Vinci also invented an "ornithopter"—a flapping wing aircraft. The band around the pilot's forehead is connected to the aircraft's tail surfaces. When the pilot moves his head, the tail moves too, thus controlling the aircraft in flight. Right: The sheer power and expense required to send a man to the moon would have been almost unimaginable to Renaissance philosophers such as Leonardo.

Below: *The "flying boat" designed by Francesco de Lana de Terze in 1670. The copper spheres above the hull of the boat would contain a vacuum, which would haul the craft aloft.*

altitude. The solution, Schmidlap argued, was to be found in using several rockets of diminishing sizes, which would be attached to each other. The largest rocket would be at the base of the design and would fire first, carrying the smaller rocket aloft. Once the fuel in the larger rocket was used up, the smaller rocket would ignite, reaching a higher altitude before the final rocket exploded "showering the sky with glowing cinders." This technique eventually became the basis for the huge multi-stage rockets which would be necessary to propel astronauts into space.

It would be over 400 years before Louis Bleriot's ground-breaking flight across the English Channel, but in 1507 John Damian decided to attempt a flight to France by attaching wings made of chicken feathers to his arms and jumping off the battlements at Stirling Castle in Scotland. As well as donning wings Damian, who was an alchemist, claimed that he had discovered an elixir which would allow him to take to the heavens—some accounts have speculated that Damian might have been taking hallucinogenic mushrooms at the time. Upon take-off, he immediately plunged to the ground. His fall was cushioned by a heap of pig dung and he broke his leg. He attributed his lack of success to the fact that he used chicken feathers, noting that the chicken is a flightless bird.

Across the Channel, just under thirty years later, a Frenchman called Denis Bolor attempted to fly by using wings attached to a spring mechanism. Unfortunately, a spring in one of the wings snapped, sending Bolor to his death. Hezarfen Celebi would have more luck than Damian or Bolor. Celebi had studied the drawings of Leonardo, and designed a set of wings to help him fly. In 1638 he climbed up the 183ft (42m) Galata Tower in Istanbul. He jumped off the tower and one account claims that he succeeded in flying over the Bosphorus. He was awarded 1000 gold pieces for his efforts.

Scientific beginnings

In 1660 Gaspard Schott of Palermo, Sicily, took Bacon's ideas a bit further. Schott believed that the shells of hen's eggs could be sealed and heated with solar rays. This would warm the air inside the eggs causing them to rise upwards. Other larger spheres such as: "the eggs of the larger description of swans, or leather balls stitched with fine thongs, (could be) filled with niter (saltpeter or

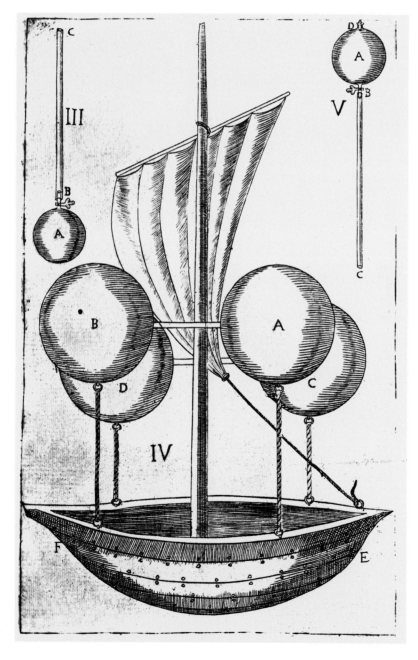

Above: *Trained birds take the traveler into space,*
landing him safely on the moon, as described in Francis
Godwin's 1638 work The Man in the Moon.

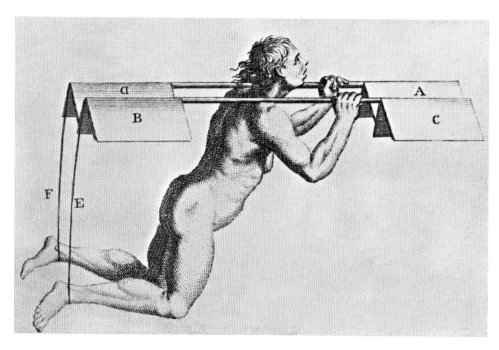

Left: *Detail of a flying machine designed by Besnier, a French artisan, which had control rods attached to the pilot's feet to control the attitude of the aircraft.*

Below: *A flying machine depicted in 1709. The influence of birds was very much in the minds of the early aviation theorists.*

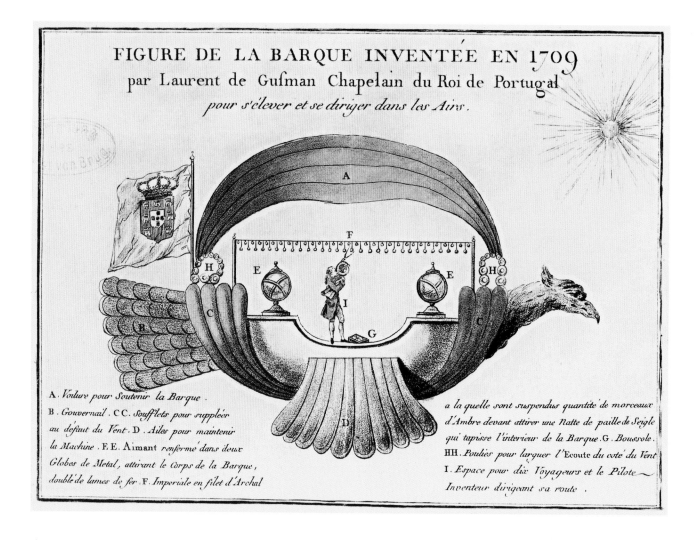

FIGURE DE LA BARQUE INVENTÉE EN 1709
par Laurent de Gufman Chapelain du Roi de Portugal
pour s'élever et se diriger dans les Airs.

A. *Voiture pour Soutenir la Barque.*
B. *Gouvernail. CC. Soufflets pour suppléer au défaut du Vent. D. Ailes pour maintenir la Machine. F.E. Aimant renfermé dans deux Globes de Metal, attirant le Corps de la Barque, doublé de lames de fer. F. Impériale en filet d'Archal*

a la quelle sont suspendus quantité de morceaux d'Ambre devant attirer une Natte de paille de Seigle qui tapisse l'intérieur de la Barque. G. Boussole. HH. Poulies pour larguer l'Ecoute du coté du Vent. I. Espace pour dix Voyageurs et le Pilote Inventeur dirigeant sa route.

potassium nitrate), the purest sulfur, quicksilver, or kindred materials which rarefy by their caloric energy" and would ascend to greater heights.

Schott's arguments were expanded in 1670 by a Jesuit priest from Rome. Francesco de Lana de Terze studied atmospheric pressure and proposed a "flying boat." But unlike Schott, Bacon, and Wilkins, he believed that his flying machine could take off using four copper spheres from which all of the air inside had been removed. Yet this presented a problem. If the copper spheres were not strong enough, they would implode because of the greater force of the surrounding exterior atmospheric pressure. Despite this, de Lana had designed the first lighter-than-air vehicle based on a careful assessment of scientific principles.

By the last years of the seventeenth century the wonder of flight was gripping scientists around the world. Bartholomeu Lourenço de Gusmão was a priest and mathematician born in Santos, Brazil, in 1685. After completing his religious instruction at the University of Coimbra in Portugal, he devoted himself to mathematics. He approached King John V of Portugal and asked to demonstrate to the monarch a flying machine he had designed which was based on a glider and called the "Passarola" (Great Bird) but it is thought that this glider never took to the skies. Suitably impressed with his efforts the King gave Gusmão a Professorship at the University of Coimbra.

Following his experiments with kites, he turned his attention to balloons. In 1709, during an audience with the King, Gusmão lit a small fire underneath a model balloon he had constructed. However, during the experiment the balloon caught fire, causing nearby furniture and curtains to ignite, although the King was too enthralled by Gusmão's discovery to take offence at the damage. Yet his efforts eventually landed him in trouble, attracting the interests of the Inquisition, who imprisoned him for sorcery. He later escaped to Toledo in Spain.

Military applications

Building on de Lana's ideas of using low pressure air to achieve flight, Joseph Galien, a Dominican professor of philosophy and theology at the University of Avignon, France, proposed in his 1755 work "The Art of Sailing in the Air" a design of aircraft which would be large enough to transport an entire army and its equipment to Africa. His idea was to build "a gigantic cube-shaped vessel of good, strong canvas of double thickness plastered with wax and tar, covered with leather and reinforced in places with ropes rigging." The entire craft would be around 6500ft (1981m) in length, and would be "larger than the city of Avignon," resembling "a fair-sized mountain." It was to be filled with lower-density air, which would allow it to float majestically through the skies.

As the scientific inquiry continued so did the daredevil flying stunts, most of which involved jumping off high buildings. In the eighteenth century the Marquis de Racqueville attempted to fly by jumping from his hotel room in Paris but crashed into a boat full of washerwomen on the Seine. Racqueville's exploits were the subject of public derision for many years to come. Although making more careful preparations than the reckless Marquis, the Abbe Deforges of Etampes in France was similarly unsuccessful. In 1772 the Abbe announced that he had invented a "Flying Gondola" which would accommodate a pilot (known as the "Gondola Conductor") and which would have room for baggage and provisions. The Gondola would travel at speeds of "thirty leagues per hour," being propelled by large oars that were designed to act as wings. A crowd assembled in Etampes to watch the Abbe's departure but, as one observer noted, "the more he worked, the more his machine cleaved to the earth, as if it were part and parcel of it."

But in June 1783, just over a decade after the Abbe Deforges' failure, the diligent work of the scientists, the early test flights of the eccentrics and the musings of the mystics finally yielded results, when the Montgolfier brothers made the first balloon flight. The dawn of aviation was breaking.

Over the next two hundred years humans would soar higher and faster than ever before, touching the surface of the moon, smashing the sound barrier and circumnavigating the globe in their flying machines. Why did these early pioneers and thinkers devote so much time and energy to flight? It is impossible to say, but one anonymous quote may give us an insight—"To most people, the sky is the limit. To those who love aviation, the sky is home."

From the art of aeronautics to the science of flight

the pioneers

In the eighteenth and nineteenth centuries, the pioneers of aviation were ridiculed for their efforts. Early balloons and gliders were slow and uncontrollable, but in the early years of the twentieth century a few brilliant scientific minds made a historic breakthrough: the first manned, powered flying machines.

Left: *After centuries of dreams the airplane was made a reality in the early years of the twentieth century. Here a Voisin biplane takes to the air in 1907.*

Top: *The first hot air balloon. At Annonay in June 1783 the Montgolfier brothers flew a paper and linen sphere carrying a sheep, a cock, and a hen.*

Throughout the eighteenth and nineteenth centuries there were two schools among the pioneers—those advocating unpowered and powered flight. Powered flight was barely a distant possibility, awaiting the design of a lightweight and practical combustion engine, when two brothers in France first noticed the effect of heat on light objects. Joseph Michel and Jacques Étienne Montgolfier were paper makers who observed the ascent of the ash and smoke of their burning waste. Intrigued, the brothers made a large sphere out of paper and linen and took it to the market place in the village of Annonay on June 4, 1783. As they lit a wool and straw fire beneath the sphere, a crowd gathered to see their balloon rise with the heat of the flames. Flight was possible.

Right: *Joseph and Jacques Montgolfier. The Montgolfier brothers pioneered the hot-air powered balloons, known as Montgolfières.*

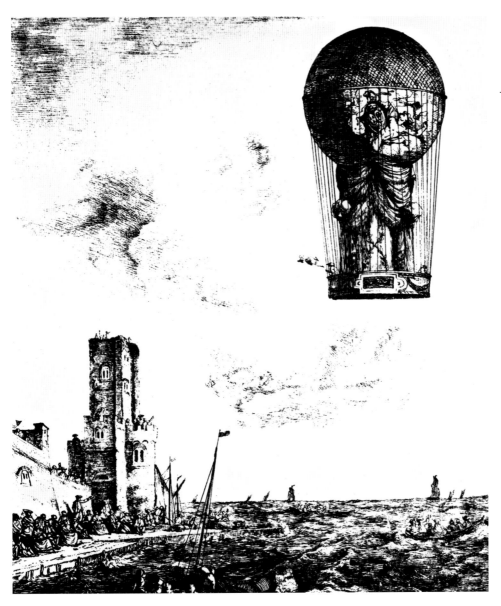

But the Montgolfier brothers had a rival—perhaps a necessary spur to their labors. Professor Jacques Alexander César Charles built and launched a hydrogen balloon in August 1783, flying for 45 minutes and covering 15 miles (24km). An air race had begun. The next month the Montgolfier brothers staged the first balloon flight to carry passengers—a cock, a sheep, and a duck. They drew a crowd of 130,000, including King Louis XVI and Marie Antoinette, to witness the ascent. The intrepid farm animals flew for just eight minutes and landed some two miles (3.2km) away.

Two types of balloon now dominated—the hot air Montgolfière and the hydrogen-filled Charlière, but it was a Montgolfière that made the first manned ascent. On October 15, 1783, François Pilâtre de Rozier climbed aboard one of the brothers' balloons and slowly rose into the air—though the balloon was still tied to the ground for safety. This was followed quickly by the first untethered, manned flight just one month later, when the Marquis d'Arlandes accompanied Rozier on a 5½ mile (9km) flight from Bois de Boulogne to Butte-aux-Cailles. The controls for this groundbreaking flight were simply a water bucket and a sponge for the onboard fire. Not to be outdone, Charles took off in December 1783 with his colleague Robert and flew from the

Tuileries Gardens in Paris to land in Nesles 27 miles (43.5km) away. At Nesles Robert got out, Charles took on some ballast and flew on for another four miles (6½km).

In the second half of 1783 France had been a center of activity for lighter-than-air craft but, as news of the Montgolfière and Charlière balloons spread, it was not long before the whole of Europe had caught the fever for balloon flight. Getting balloons airborne was easy enough now, but the problem of control persisted. A number of solutions were tried, including a flap on the balloon to allow heat to escape, propelling the balloon in the opposite direction. But for now the controllable balloon was out of reach and in the Revolutionary and Napoleonic wars the balloons used for observation and artillery spotting were always tethered.

Below: The rivals. Unlike the Montgolfières, Jacques Charles' balloons were filled with hydrogen. Charles and Robert the elder made their first flight in a Charlière balloon in December 1783.

British visions

Although experiments with lighter-than-air craft continued, they were eventually pushed into the background by the development of aircraft that were heavier than air. Sir George Cayley, the "Father of Aerial Navigation," as his admirer and follower William Samuel Henson called him, was born in 1733 across the English Channel from the Montgolfier brothers. Even at a very young age, he took great interest in flight. Cayley constructed aircraft to various designs, including a kind of helicopter in 1796 and a heavier-than-air model in 1809; and he wrote painstakingly on his "art," as he considered it. Unfortunately, the exploits of so-called "Tower Jumpers" who tested primitive parachutes, and other poor and tragically comical attempts at getting airborne, gave the real aviation geniuses a bad name. So when he wrote his *On*

Mechanics' Magazine,

MUSEUM, REGISTER, JOURNAL, AND GAZETTE.

No. 1520.] SATURDAY, SEPTEMBER 25, 1852. [Price 3*d*., Stamped 4*d*.

Edited by J. C. Robertson, 166, Fleet-street.

SIR GEORGE CAYLEY'S GOVERNABLE PARACHUTES.

Fig. 2.

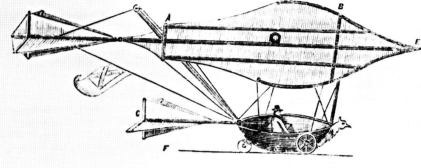

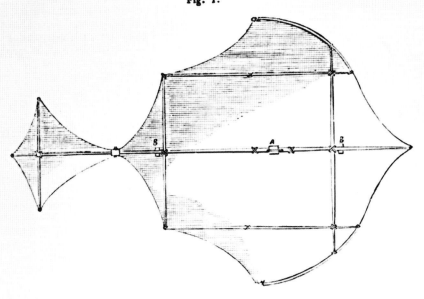

Fig. 1.

Above: Mechanics' Magazine *published many of Sir George Cayley's designs for balloons, convertiplanes, and gliders.*

Fig. 1.   **Fig. 2.**

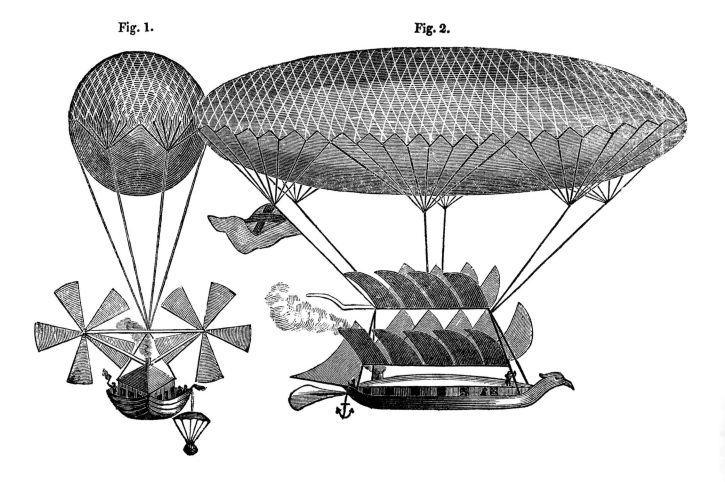

Above: *A diagram of Cayley's steam-powered dirigible.*

Aerial Navigation, first published in 1809, Cayley felt it necessary to explain his title:

"…the art of flying, or aerial navigation as I have chosen to term it for the sake of giving a little more dignity to a subject bordering upon the ludicrous in public estimation…"

And this he did. Despite the ridicule, designers had man airborne in powered heavier-than-air craft within a hundred years. Cayley's contribution was broad: he published designs for dirigible balloons, "convertiplanes," triplanes, and a glider design with full flying instructions (published in *Mechanics' Magazine* in 1852).

As already mentioned, one of Cayley's disciples was fellow Englishman William Samuel Henson. Henson was also a great visionary and proposed to open an air service called the "Aerial Transport Company" with his friend John Stringfellow. The aircraft for this air service was to be the "Aerial Steam Carriage" that Henson unveiled in 1842. It

was a feat of engineering and was the first powered heavier-than-air craft with what can be called a "modern" configuration. It was a high-wing monoplane with a 150ft (45.7m) wingspan and double-surfaced cambered wings, and was powered by twin 30hp (22.4kW) pusher (backward facing) propellers. Stringfellow was the engineer for the project and although the engine was effective, the aircraft itself was unstable and could not maintain any real momentum in flight. As a result of this failure, Henson retired from the field of aviation, while Stringfellow merely took a break. The first truly powered aircraft was Henri Giffard's airship, which flew in September 1852, powered by a 3hp (2.2kW) steam engine. The airship was not powerful enough to cope properly with contrary winds, but Giffard's design was an advance nonetheless.

Through the 1860s, aeronautic activity in Britain gathered pace. In 1866 the Aeronautical Society (later the Royal Aeronautical Society) was established, and the first aeronautic exhibition was held at Crystal Palace in London in 1868. This was chosen by John Stringfellow as the stage for the unveiling of his new aircraft. Although not a truly effective design, Stringfellow's steam-powered triplane captured the imagination of the general public at a time when Europe was taking the last steps towards achieving powered flight.

The problem of propulsion

It was the French who created the first practical airplanes with which propulsion methods could be tested. In August 1871, 21-year-old Alphonse Pénaud drew an audience that included members of the Société d'Aviation for a demonstration of his "Planophore." This monoplane featured a tailplane behind the main wings and rubber band-powered pusher propellers. Although flying just 131ft (40m), it was the first naturally stable airplane. Three years later Félix du Temple made

his first flight in a monoplane he had been working towards for 16 years. In the late-1850s du Temple had experimented with clockwork and steam-powered model aircraft. From this testing he constructed a full-size version. This was a monoplane with dihedral wings, a tailplane with a rudder, a retractable undercarriage, and a single tractor (forward facing) propeller powered by a steam engine. Although built before Pénaud's, it was not truly powered as it required a ramp for take-off and landed after it lost its momentum.

The designs in existence were good, but the powerplants were not and this was to be the case until the late 1870s. In 1876 N.A. Otto designed and built the first practical combustion engine in Germany. It used liquid fuel and did not weigh as much as the heavy steam engines then used in many aircraft designs.

Above: *William Henson's "Aerial Steam Carriage"
with which he and John Stringfellow planned to start
the "Aerial Transport Company."*

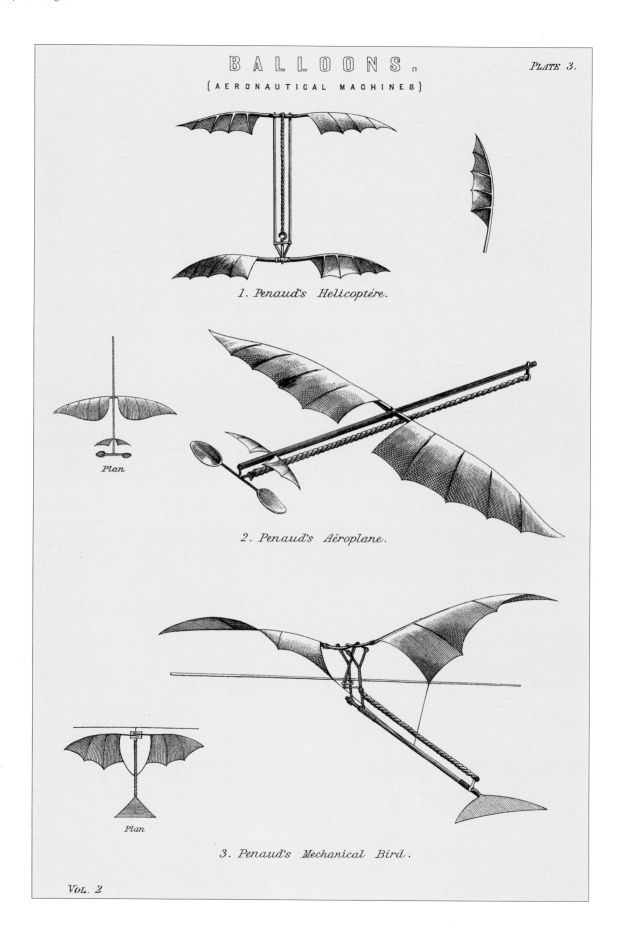

BALLOONS.

(AERONAUTICAL MACHINES)

PLATE 3.

1. Penaud's Helicoptére.

Plan

2. Penaud's Aëroplane.

Plan

3. Penaud's Mechanical Bird.

VOL. 2

Left: *Aviators made their work known through publishing their designs in journals. Here, Penaud lays out his helicoptère, aëroplane, and mechanical bird.*

Above: *Clement Ader's most famous design, the steam-powered batwing monoplane Eole.*

The world now almost expected powered flight, and many pioneers set about delivering that reality. Although Gottlieb Daimler and Karl Benz produced light petrol engines in the early 1880s this type of engine did not have an immediate impact, as designers stood by previous methods of propulsion. In 1885 Lieutenant Renard and Captain A.C. Krebs flew their airship *La France* at 13mph (21km/h). This was powered by heavy chromium chloride batteries, driving a 9hp (6.7kW) electric motor. Another important designer, Clement Ader, used a steam engine for his famous batwing monoplane, *Eole*.

Ader's success with the *Eole* was later overshadowed by his over-inflated claims. The *Eole* was a high-wing monoplane with a single tractor propeller driven by a 20hp (15kW) steam engine. On October 9, 1890, the aircraft took to the air without the aid of a ramp and so was the first airplane to take off under its own power. It flew 163ft (50m) before returning to the ground. But the later, incomplete *Avion II* and poorly performing *Avion III* were anticlimactic. Unfortunately, Ader felt he had to exaggerate his success to achieve fame and later claimed that in 1891 the *Eole* flew for 330ft (100m) and that *Avion III* flew 1000ft (305m) in 1897. The French Ministry for War refuted these claims in a 1910 publication.

Glider pioneers

Although the first take-off had been made and the first powered airplane had flown, work on airship and glider design continued. In 1889 Otto Lilienthal published *Der Vogelflug als Grundlage der Fliegekunst (Bird Flight as the Basis of Aviation)*, the same year as he tested his No.1 glider. The No.1 and No.2 gliders were monoplanes under which the pilot hung and merely moved his body position to change direction. Both of these failed, but the No.3 made a number of short flights in 1891. True success came with the No.6 in 1893, which had rounded cambered wings. So successful were Lilienthal's gliders that the No.8 became a

Above: *During the mid-1890s Otto Lilienthal built three types of biplane glider.*

production model in 1894, and in the same year his No.11 *Normal-segelapparat* (Standard Sailing Machine) made a 1200ft (366m) glide. Lilienthal also experimented with biplane gliders in his Nos.13, 14 and 15 before a crash with a No.11 in 1896 fatally broke his back.

Chanute and Langley

Although many of the early aviation pioneers were European, American Octave Chanute is credited as the first aviation historian. He contributed journal articles from 1891 to 1893 and published his *Progress in Flying Machines* in 1894, which later inspired the Wright brothers. Chanute's book was published just too early to document the exploits of fellow American Samuel Pierpoint Langley.

Langley began his life in aeronautics, like many others, by experimenting with models. At first he used rubber-powered aircraft, before using steam engines for his six *Aerodromes* numbered "0" through to "5"—though these were not great successes and were later redeveloped. The No.5 was rebuilt as a tandem wing aircraft and flew

Above: *Samuel Franklin Cody left the United States for Britain in 1889. From 1902 he was Chief Kite Instructor at the British Army Balloon Factory. Pictured is one of his man-lifting box kites.*

3300ft (1006m) in May 1896. No.4 was similarly reconstructed and renamed No.6 before making a ¾ mile (1.2km) flight in November of the same year. This effort caught the attention of the United States War Department, who offered Langley $50,000 for a manned airplane to be called the *Aerodrome A*. For this, Langley commissioned Stephen M. Balzer with building a 12hp (9kW) engine lighter than 100lb (45kg). The production began well, with a quarter-scale model flying successfully in August 1903, just before the full size version was completed.

Aerodrome A was a tandem wing airplane with the engine powering two pusher propellers. The pilot sat ahead of the engine, between the front wings. Despite the design and the money, *Aerodrome A* was a sorry failure. On October 7, 1903, it trundled down its launch ramp only to crash straight into the Potomac River. This sad effort was repeated two months later on December 8 with the same outcome. Despite this inauspicious start to the new century, true powered aircraft were almost within reach and a number of different projects were afoot.

Above: *Samuel Pierpoint Langley's* Aerodrome No.5 *prior to launch at Quantico, Virginia, in 1896.*

Orville and Wilbur Wright

Just nine days after Langley's second crash, two brothers made the first genuine powered flight. These were Orville and Wilbur Wright, who owned a bicycle shop in their home town of Dayton, Ohio. The Wright brothers were fascinated by manned flight and read all they could on developments in aviation, including Chanute's history. From this research they began experimenting with balloons and kites, and observed how the weather, especially wind, affected flight. So meticulous were the brothers that they constructed their own wind tunnel to develop gliders, and test wing shapes and aerodynamics.

The Wright brothers made all their glider experiments on the dunes around Kitty Hawk, North Carolina, because that location offered an almost constant 20mph (32km/h) prevailing wind. The first trial flights were conducted in September and October 1900 with the imaginatively named *Glider No.1*. This glider had a 18ft (5.5m) wingspan upon which the pilot lay with no control other than by shifting his body position. Through the winter of 1900-01, the brothers returned to Dayton to develop a new glider, *Glider No.2*, which they took to North Carolina in July 1901. This model had a 22ft (6.7m) wingspan and boasted curved wings for better airflow. Although they achieved longer flights with this aircraft, the curvature of the wings was too great. But the brothers were learning and progressing.

Back in the wind tunnel, Orville and Wilbur tested over 200 models and gained statistical data for their designs. *Glider No.3* was their largest glider, with a 32ft (9.7m) wingspan and a weight of 116lb (52.6kg). In September 1902 the brothers carried out 1000 glides with *No.3*, the longest lasting 30 seconds and covering 600ft (183m). This glider also featured a single movable fin to offer the pilot more control over the aircraft. Having mastered aerodynamics and basic controls, the Wright brothers were ready to take on powered flight.

In September 1903 Orville and Wilbur returned to Kitty Hawk with their *Glider No.3* and their new airplane, *Flyer*. *Flyer* (later renamed *Flyer I*) was a wooden biplane with a wingspan of 40ft (12m)—greater than any of the gliders. They had built their own hand-carved wooden propeller and a lightweight four-cylinder water-cooled in-line petrol engine specially for *Flyer*. At first, poor

weather meant that the brothers dared not take off in their powered airplane, so more tests were carried out on *Glider No.3*. The time finally came on December 14, but at the first attempt the *Flyer* crashed. Unperturbed, the Wrights invited locals down to view a second attempt three days later. Alternating piloting duties, it was Orville who clambered onto *Flyer* on the morning of December 17, 1903. In 22–27mph (35–43km/h) winds, *Flyer* took off just after 10:30 a.m. in front of five local witnesses. It took just 40ft (12m) to get airborne, but by leaving the ground history was made—*Flyer* was the first powered airplane to take off, fly, and land unassisted. Three more flights were made that day. Wilbur flew for 11 seconds and Orville for another 15 seconds before the longest and last, made by Wilbur at midday, when he flew for 59 seconds and travelled 852 ft (259m). Unfortunately, this was the last flight of the *Flyer* for some time because a gust of wind turned her over and did a good deal of damage. But for now the aircraft had lived up to its name.

Below: *Orville (left) and Wilbur Wright at home in Dayton, Ohio.*

Above: *The first ever self-propelled take-off, flight and landing by Orville Wright at Kitty Hawk, North Carolina, on December 17, 1903.*

France takes the baton

The Wright brothers continued to develop the *Flyer* design and performed public demonstrations throughout 1904 and 1905. In late 1905 *Flyer III* was the first airplane to fly circles, figures-of-eight, and bank and turn. The focus of aviation innovation was, however, switching to Europe, where a Brazilian by the name of Alberto Santos-Dumont was gaining fame. Santos-Dumont began his ventures into aviation with airship design, and on October 19, 1901, his "No.VI" circled the Eiffel Tower with a flight of 29 minutes and 30 seconds. In September 1906 he returned with his "No.14 bis" biplane and made a 200ft (61m) flight at the Bois de Boulogne, watched by a much larger crowd than had ever seen a Wright brothers flight. Santos-Dumont advocated the petrol engine over steam. His No.VI airship had been powered by a 20hp (15kW) Buchet/Santos-Dumont engine and the No.14 bis with an 24hp/18kW (later upgraded to 50hp/37kW) Antoinette engine. The engine was the new focus—airplanes could take off and fly, but the new goal was to find an engine that could take them greater distances with greater efficiency.

Engine development

The engines of the eighteenth and nineteenth centuries were either too heavy or too inefficient for powering airplanes and airships. Light, powerful petrol engines first emerged in Germany courtesy of Gottlieb Daimler and Karl Benz, but it was in France that a major breakthrough occurred at the crucial time for the new aircraft to progress. Frenchman Laurent Séguin primarily made engines for automobiles, but in the first decade of the twentieth century he turned his hand to aeronautical engines. It had already been established that the larger the front of an engine, the more drag it produced, so in-line engines were preferred. But the biggest problem was cooling the engine in flight. Séguin designed an

Below: The fastest aircraft to fly in the years before World War I, one of Bechereau's sleek and powerful Deperdussin racers.

ingenious radial engine that was cooled by the airflow as the airplane flew. With a rigid crankshaft bolted to the body of the aircraft, his "Gnôme" engine turned with the propeller, ensuring a cooling flow of air around the engine at all times. Although this rotary design was the best of its day, there were innate problems with it. There was no control over how much fuel and air reached the cylinders, which was at times inefficient. Another problem was that turning and banking could bring unpredictable results: the torque of the radial engine could wrench control of the aircraft out of the pilot's hands. But there were no better alternatives, and the Gnôme engine powered many early air racers. In 1909 Glenn Curtiss won the Gordon-Bennett race at 47mph (76km/h) with a Gnôme engine and Louis Bechereau used them to power the most aerodynamic airplanes of the era. Soon, Bechereau's Deperdussin racers incorporated the engine, controls, and pilot inside a smooth monocoque fuselage ("single-shell" in French). The best engines available plus this aerodynamic design made

Deperdussins the fastest aircraft of the pre-First World War era, as was demonstrated when Maurice Prevost won the 1913 Gordon-Bennett race averaging 124½mph (200km/h).

Séguin's Gnôme had set the standard and designers across Europe tried to catch up. In Germany, Daimler began producing a 6-cylinder in-line engine in 1911, and a year later a prize was offered as part of Kaiser Wilhelm's birthday celebrations for the best German-designed airplane engine. In Britain, as part of a military specification, H.P. Folland and Geoffrey de Havilland began work on the S.E.2 in mid-1912. This biplane was powered by a 100hp (74.6kW) Gnôme engine giving speeds of up to 92mph (148km/h). This was merely a testbed for the 1914 S.E.4 that had a 160hp (119kW) Gnôme engine, flaps on the upper and lower wings and a cowled engine as seen in the Deperdussins. In its short six-month life, the S.E.4 achieved a speed of 135mph (217km/h). The aero engine—and the fledgling aircraft industry—had come of age.

Above: *By the outbreak of World War I, the monocoque design of monoplanes and biplanes like the Deperdussin had replaced the earlier gliders and tail-first aircraft like this Santos-Dumont design.*

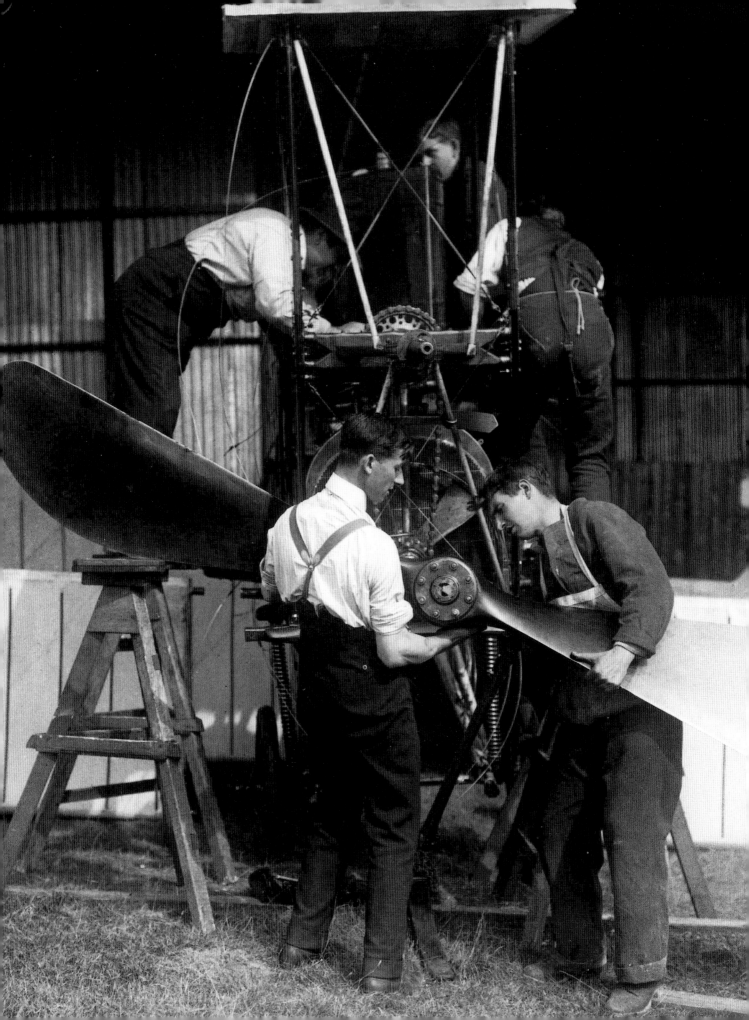

building the century's flying machines

the entrepreneurs

Many of the world's greatest airplane designers and manufacturers emerged in the early twentieth century. Driven by a passion for engineering and a love of flight, these men—including Boeing, Lockheed, Douglas, and von Zeppelin—would shape the future of aviation, and their aircraft would become household names.

Left: *Samuel Franklin Cody helping to assemble one of his aircraft in 1912.*
Top: *Count Ferdinand von Zeppelin.*

Glenn Hammond Curtiss was born in Hammondsport, New York, in 1878. Early in his life he had seen and heard of the exploits of Samuel Langley, the Wright brothers, and others and this inspired him in later years. In 1901 he opened his own bicycle business, G.H. Curtiss Manufacturing Company, which later added motorcycle construction and repairs to its activities. In 1904 Curtiss's life took a turn that made his name in aviation history when Thomas Scott Baldwin, a businessman from San Francisco, approached him to build an engine for the airship *Californian Arrow*. Baldwin was impressed by Curtiss's work and after the great San Francisco fire in 1906 he moved his business to Hammondsport so that they could work together on airship propulsion. One of their collaborative achievements was the sale of a balloon to the US Army in August 1908, the military's first aircraft.

In 1907, Curtiss joined a prestigious group called the Aerial Experiment Association (AEA) that included Alexander Graham Bell among its members. This two-year fixed-term association planned to build an aerodrome (the contemporary name for an airplane), but the intention was never mass production. With Curtiss as Director of Experiments, the AEA built four aerodromes during 1908—the No.1 *Red Wing*, No.2 *White Wing*, No.3 *June Bug,* and No.4 *Silver Dart.* A legal row broke out over a number of these airplanes. After their 1903 flight, the Wright brothers had patented certain design concepts, some of which were essential to any aircraft. All the AEA's aircraft were in violation of the Wright patent, but the *Red Wing* and *White Wing* were excused, as they were not built for commercial use. However, the *June Bug*, piloted by Curtiss, won an *American Scientific Magazine* prize for straight flight, which

the Wright brothers saw as financial gain from their ideas. The Wright patent war, as it has been called, truly came to a head outside of the AEA. After the pre-planned dissolution of the AEA in March 1909, Curtiss teamed up with Augustus Herring and built the *Golden Flyer* for the New York Aeronautical Society and, as the first airplane sold to a private buyer, was in obvious contravention of the Wright patent. In 1913 Orville won his fight (Wilbur died in 1912), but Curtiss insisted that Langley's *Aerodrome A* had been the first airplane and that the Wright patent was therefore invalid. The "war" ended during World War I when the US Aircraft Manufacturers' Association pooled all the patents to build aircraft for the war effort, while the

Below: *Glenn Curtiss taxiing his Triad amphibious aircraft on North Island in San Diego Bay in 1911.*

British Government elected to purchase both Wright and Curtiss patents for $20,000 and $75,000 respectively.

Legal disputes aside, Curtiss was clearly a brilliant pilot and designer. Before World War I he won the 1909 Scientific American Trophy, the 1909 Gordon-Bennett race, the 1910 Scientific American Trophy, the 1912 Collier Trophy for development of the hydro-aeroplane (seaplane) and the 1913 Collier Trophy for the development of the flying boat. This was no mean feat, but Curtiss was to gain even greater fame in producing aircraft for the US military, and in particular the Navy. The Army bought its first airplane, a Wright model, in 1908, before the Navy followed suit the following year. It was the Navy that Curtiss targeted in his marketing campaign, taking off and landing on Navy ships on both the West and East coasts. The real deal-

clincher was the free flight tuition of a Navy officer, offered by Curtiss in November 1910 and accepted the following month. Just six months later the US Navy bought its first two Curtiss airplanes.

As acknowledged by his two Collier prizes, Curtiss made great strides with waterborne aircraft, making the first successful hydro-aeroplane flight in January 1911. This was a conventional pusher aircraft, but his second repositioned the engine and propeller in front of the pilot as a tractor, and therefore out of the spray produced when taking off and landing. Curtiss is acknowledged as the inventor of the flying boat, the first being simply named the *Curtiss Flying Boat No.1*. The first successful flying boat was the subsequent and again obviously titled *Flying Boat No.2*, or *Flying Fish*, which first flew in July 1912. The US Navy became the prime contractor of Curtiss airplanes, and his aircraft saw

Above: *A replica of Curtiss's June Bug built by Pete Bowyer. Note the cambered wings.*

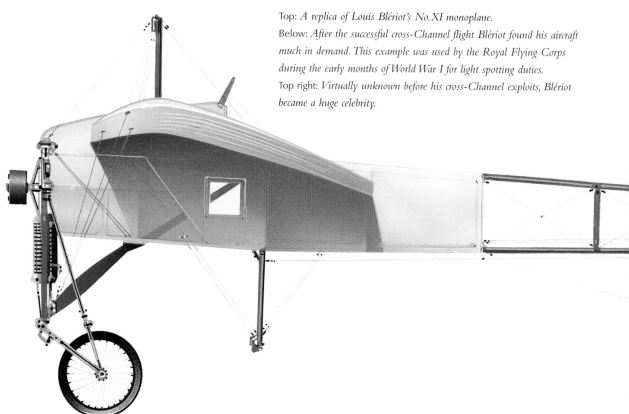

Top: *A replica of Louis Blériot's No. XI monoplane.*
Below: *After the successful cross-Channel flight Blériot found his aircraft much in demand. This example was used by the Royal Flying Corps during the early months of World War I for light spotting duties.*
Top right: *Virtually unknown before his cross-Channel exploits, Blériot became a huge celebrity.*

"Over There": Louis Blériot's Channel Crossing

One of the most famous pilots of the era before World War I was Louis Blériot, who achieved the first airplane flight across the English Channel in 1909. The challenge originated a year earlier when the proprietor of the London *Daily Mail,* Lord Northcliffe, heightened the public interest by offering £10,000 for the first man to make the Channel crossing. Blériot was already a great designer and pilot and decided to take up the challenge.

As in all good tales of overcoming the odds, the Frenchman had a rival: the half-French, half-English Hubert Latham. It was Latham who made the first attempt at crossing the Channel when he took off in his monoplane, *Antoinette IV,* from Sangatte near Calais on July 19, 1909. However, his sparkplugs failed about six miles off the French coast and he had to ease the aircraft into the water. The landing was a credit to Latham's piloting abilities—he stepped off a wing and onto an escorting French destroyer without getting a drop of water on him. Another airplane, sent to Sangatte for him to attempt the crossing again, arrived on July 22. It was at this point that two other contenders entered the arena. Firstly, and not taken too seriously, was the Comte de Lambert, who prepared a Wright biplane at Wissant, near Boulogne. More importantly, Louis Blériot prepared his "No.XI" monoplane at Baraques, also near Calais, and not too far from Latham. Both intended to take off on the 24th and then race the other to Dover, but bad weather scuppered their flights. Blériot knew the poor spell would not last long and so rose very early on the morning of the 25th to gauge the conditions. As Latham's team wondered at the commotion in the early hours, they could only stand in amazement as the "No.XI" took to the air at 4:41 a.m.

Before taking off, Blériot famously asked "Where is Dover?" to which one of his engineers replied, with a wave of his arm, "over there." This was aerial navigation at its simplest—Blériot had no compass with him. For this attempt the French destroyer, *Escopette,* was prepared to pick up the splashing Blériot when, rather than if, he crashed, as long as he was up to about 10 miles (16km) from the coast. Any further out and he was on his own. Around 20 minutes and 15 miles (25km) into the expected 40-minute flight the engine began to overheat. Fortunately for Blériot, early morning drizzle did just

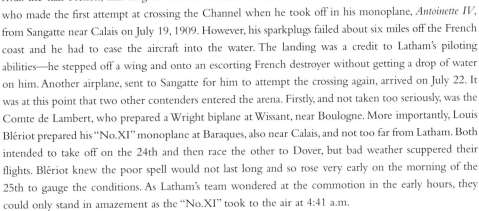

enough to cool it as the English coast came into sight out of the mist. Realizing himself to be too far north, he turned in order to spot a tricolor a French journalist was supposed to lay out as a landing zone. A strengthening wind ended any such sentimentalities and Blériot brought the "No.XI" down in North Fall Meadow near Dover Castle. Not quite in keeping with the momentous occasion, his welcoming party consisted of only the journalist and a rather confused local policeman.

Top: *A photograph reproduced from a contemporary newspaper source shows Curtiss's first successful flying boat at Hammondsport, New York, in 1912.*

service all around the world for many decades. The last US Navy Curtiss aircraft was the SB2C Helldiver, which entered service in 1943.

William E. Boeing

The Boeing aircraft company was formed by William E. Boeing in 1916. Boeing was the son of a timber merchant and dropped out of Yale University in 1903 to follow in his father's footsteps. From 1908, Boeing traveled to a number of air shows and airplane demonstrations all along the West Coast and tried to find a pilot that would take him as a passenger—he was hooked. When he finally got his flight in 1914 he became obsessed

with flight and together with his friend George Conrad Westervelt began to take flying lessons and consider airplane design. After building the B&W (standing for Boeing and Westervelt) seaplane, Boeing established Pacific Aero Products in 1916, which was renamed Boeing Airplane Company the following year.

The early years were profitable for Boeing. The US Navy bought 50 of his Model C seaplanes for service in World War I. In the 1920s the order book stood empty for a time and Boeing paid the bills by building furniture. But this was not a long-term lull—in 1927 Boeing was granted the San Francisco to Chicago airmail route, for which

Boeing Air Transport (BAT) was created. In 1931 BAT joined with National Air Transport, Varney Air Lines and Pacific Air Transport to form the new United Air Lines. The new conglomerate was not looked upon kindly by the US Government, which saw it as a monopoly, and in 1934 William Boeing was ordered to break up his aeronautical interests into three separate entities—Boeing Airplane Company, United Aircraft Company, and United Air Lines. Later that year, William Boeing sold his interests in all three companies. Although he returned to Boeing as a consultant in World War II, from the mid-1930s he devoted himself to breeding thoroughbred horses instead.

Top: Glenn Curtiss (left) and Henry Ford beside Curtiss's Flying Boat at Hammondsport.

Donald Douglas

While William E. Boeing had a brilliant business head, Donald Wills Douglas had an outstanding technical mind. Douglas had been at the US Naval Academy for three years when he decided to change direction and study aeronautical engineering at the Massachusetts Institute of Technology (MIT). Having been gripped by a demonstration by Orville Wright in 1908, the enthusiastic student completed his course in half the usual time and graduated at the age of 20. For the next few years Douglas worked with a number of aircraft companies including Glenn Martin, another legendary US aircraft manufacturer. By 1920 he was ready to start work on his own and moved to Southern California, where the weather was good for test flights. There Douglas teamed up with a wealthy and ambitious young man called David R. Davis. Davis wanted to fly and Douglas wanted to build, and with Davis's money both dreams were realized in the $40,000 *Cloudster*, which although failing to complete an intended transcontinental flight, gained fame and drew orders. As was commonly the case with fledgling aircraft, Douglas's first buyer was the US military, and the new company supplied torpedo bombers to the US Navy. Douglas remained at the helm as his company competed with Boeing in the commercial air market, and he saw the introduction of jet aircraft before he retired in 1967. He stayed on as honorary chairman until his death in 1981. In addition to his technical knowledge, Douglas is remembered for his wit and realism and is quoted as saying that "when the weight of the paperwork equals the weight of the plane, the plane will fly."

Lockheed

The third company which would compete in the jet airliner competition with Boeing and Douglas in later years was Lockheed, formed in 1926. Allan Haines Loughead (changed to Lockheed in 1934) was the youngest of four children and was inspired by his older half-brother's book, *Vehicles of the Air*, published in 1909. Allan went into business with another brother, Malcolm, in 1912,

Right: *William E. Boeing
(1881–1956) pictured in
November 1938.*
Below: *Donald Wills Douglas
(1892–1981).*

building a seaplane as a flying taxi service around
San Francisco Bay. At $10 a trip, this was not
successful and it was not until they established the
Loughead Aircraft Manufacturing Company four
years later that real progress was achieved. It was
at this time that they employed a young John K.
"Jack" Northrop (who later formed part of what
is now Northrop-Grumman), a great statistician
and designer.

World War I was over too quickly for
Loughead. Although the Navy were initially
interested in his F-1 seaplane, the Army were not
won over by the land variant, designated F-1A. As
the US military sold off its post-war surplus
aircraft very cheaply ($300 compared to $2500 for
new airplanes) companies like Loughead suffered
the repercussions. Loughead and Northrop
persevered and in 1926 designed a high speed
passenger-carrying monoplane. To put this into
production they needed financial backing, and a
local businessman, Fred S. Keeler, provided this by
investing $22,500 of the required $25,000 to
establish Lockheed Aircraft Corporation in
December 1926. The Lockheed "Vega" was the

company's first production aircraft. It came at a time when Charles Lindbergh had crossed the Atlantic from New York to Paris and the whole world had taken a renewed interest in aviation. The Vega was the aircraft of choice for many pioneering pilots, including Amelia Earhart and Wiley Post.

Through the 1930s, Allan Lockheed (as he was now known) founded a number of other aircraft manufacturers in California. After World War II, Lockheed remained a consultant to various companies and maintained only an informal link with the Lockheed Aircraft Corporation until his death in 1969.

Ferdinand von Zeppelin and the development of the airship

As with many aircraft, the airship was first developed for use as a weapon. Although experiments were made with airship development all over the world, the greatest achievements were made in Germany with the chief architect being Count Ferdinand von Zeppelin. An engineer in the German Army, the young lieutenant became interested in airships around 1874 after reading a lecture titled "World Mail and Airship Transport" by the German Postmaster General. With the flight of Renard and Krebs in France, airship development took on a new urgency in the mind of von Zeppelin as he recognized the use of lighter-than-air craft in war, having seen balloons used in the American Civil War and Franco-Prussian War. After leaving the army in 1890, he turned his full attention to airship design. His first model came three years later and was considered by the German War Ministry, but its two 11hp (8.2kW) Daimler engines were not powerful enough to provide adequate propulsion and so the

Below: The Loughead F-1 Flying Boat could carry 10 passengers with a maximum speed of 84mph (135km/h).

Right: An illustration of Renard and Krebs's airship in flight at the 1889 Universal Exhibition in Paris.

government did not invest in the project. However, one of the Ministry's men, Professor Müller-Breslau, suggested a cigar-shape design that was the foundation of all subsequent airships—soon to become known as Zeppelins.

Von Zeppelin's next two airships, *LZ.1* and *LZ.2*, failed because of engine trouble and instability, but "*Luftschiff Zeppelin No.3*" (*LZ.3*) finally secured government funding. In 1907 a 60 mile (97km) flight and an eight-hour airborne endurance record convinced the Airship Commission to grant von Zeppelin half a million marks (approximately $122,000 at the time) to build a Zeppelin capable of flying 435 miles (700km) non-stop and remaining airborne for 24 hours. *LZ.4* was the largest airship yet, but suffered similar engine trouble to the first two and burst into flames after crashing during a test flight in 1908. The persistence of von Zeppelin inspired the German public to raise six million marks ($1,460,000) for him to continue his work, but although two more airships were built for the German Army, they had lost interest.

Instead von Zeppelin decided to try the commercial market. The safety record was not promising—more than half of von Zeppelin's

Below: *Zeppelin LZ.127 Graf Zeppelin pictured over Tempelhof airport in Berlin.*

airships had crashed—but the public was excited by the prospect and towns across Germany began building hangars in anticipation of passenger flights. Swayed by the great enthusiasm of the German public, the *Deutsche Luftschifffahrts-Aktiengesellschaft* or DELAG (German Airship Transport Company Limited) was established in November 1909, and the airship *Deutschland* was built for its first service flight on June 22, 1910. The first regular airship service started from Friedrichshafen in 1910 and carried 34,000 passengers in the four years before the outbreak of war, whereupon in 1912 the German army, finally convinced by the airship, began to plan around a nearly all-Zeppelin air arm.

Count von Zeppelin died during World War I.

His company continued after him, but when the war ended the Inter-Allied Commission of Control seized the Zeppelin Company's airships and demanded compensation for those destroyed by their crews at the end of the war. Zeppelin looked set to go bankrupt, but a brilliant solution was conceived—instead of paying the United States its $800,000 share, Zeppelin, now run by Hugo Eckener, would build them an airship. The *LZ.126* (later renamed ZR-3 *Los Angeles*) had a 2,542,320 cu. ft (71,990m³) hydrogen capacity and was powered by five 251kW (350hp) Maybach engines. After landing *LZ.126* at Lakehurst, New Jersey, on October 15, 1924, and handing it over to the US military, Zeppelin began work on a larger version—the *LZ.127 Graf Zeppelin*.

Above: *The Graf Zeppelin lands at Friedrichshafen on Lake Constance after a journey to the United States.*

The R.101 Disaster: The Day the Dream Died

Britain had watched Germany's development of the airship and in 1924 began a three-year £1,350,000 research program to produce two large airships of its own. The two aircraft carried the designations R.100, to be built by Airship Guarantee Company (a part of Vickers), and R.101, which was to be constructed by the Air Ministry at Cardington. The government's R.101 was completed first and made its maiden flight in October 1929, but had terrible engine problems—in none of its tests did all five engines run properly at the same time. Another problem for the R.101 team was the recurrence of tears to the airship's skin and a lack of time to properly repair them. Without the public scrutiny, the private R.100 team, which included Dr Barnes Wallis (later of "Dambusters" fame), was under less pressure and built a superior aircraft. With the Great Depression hitting the United States, rumors abounded that only one airship would be kept. The R.100 was better, but the R.101 seemed to be favored. This was highlighted when Lord Thomson, the Air Minister and potential future Viceroy of India, told the R.101 team that he intended them to fly him to India at the end of September 1930. Sir Sefton Brancker and Wing Commander Colmore, the Director of Civil Aviation and Director of Airship Development respectively, warned Thomson that the R.101 was not airworthy, but the Air Minister was adamant.

On October 4, the R.101 began its flight to India later than originally planned with 54 crew and passengers and a temporary Airworthiness Certificate. At 2:05 a.m. on October 5, 1930, the R.101 went into a steep dive that was quickly corrected by the release of ballast. Just three minutes later, a shallower dive saw the R.101 scrape the side of a hill near Beauvais in France, causing the hydrogen to explode. All but six of those on board were killed, including Lord Thomson and Sir Sefton Brancker.

The R.101 crash brought an abrupt end to the British rigid airship program. Seven years later, the *Hindenburg* explosion in New Jersey threatened to ground all airships, but Zeppelin continued to experiment with helium up to the outbreak of World War II.

Above: *The spacious and luxurious interior of the R.100—airship passengers expected to travel in comfort and style. On the stairs is novelist and R.100 engineer Nevil Shute.*

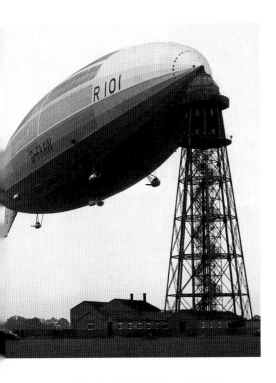

Above: *The British Air Ministry's R.101 was favored by the government, but was rushed into service. The haste proved fatal.*

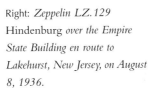

Right: *Zeppelin LZ.129* Hindenburg *over the Empire State Building en route to Lakehurst, New Jersey, on August 8, 1936.*

Above: *The debris of the R.101 after its crash at Beauvais on October 5, 1930.*

The *Graf Zeppelin* and *Hindenburg*

The *Graf Zeppelin* was the pride of Hermann Goering's *Deutsche Zeppelin Reederei* (German Zeppelin Airline), established in March 1935. However, it just wasn't fast enough to compete with airplanes making the same transatlantic flight. The *Graf Zeppelin* made just 72mph (116km/h) cruising with its five 530hp (395kW) engines. Zeppelin needed to improve on speed—and also safety. For the latter, helium gas was preferred to hydrogen because it was less flammable, but it also made the airship less buoyant, meaning that a helium-filled airship of similar dimensions as the *Graf Zeppelin* would have its payload reduced by several tons. Work began on this huge aircraft nonetheless. The United States was expected to provide the necessary helium. Unfortunately, the helium gas was not forthcoming, and the 800ft (243m) long *LZ.129 Hindenburg* was completed and filled with

Above: *The* Hindenburg *at one of its landing towers in North America during 1936.*
Left: *One of the most famous photographs in twentieth century history. The* Hindenburg *bursts into flames at Lakehurst, New Jersey, on May 6, 1937.*

hydrogen. As a publicity flight in March 1936, both the *Graf Zeppelin* and *Hindenburg* flew over Berlin. With these two mammoth airships, the German and US governments created the German-American Zeppelin Transport Corporation, intenting that two American airships would later join the fleet.

On May 4, 1937, the *Hindenburg* left its mooring at Frankfurt-am-Main on its usual flight across the Atlantic. Two days later it descended near Lakehurst, New Jersey as photographers and journalists tried to stir up some enthusiasm for yet

another airship arrival. All was not well as the ground crew took hold of the *Hindenburg*. There was a flash at the stern as static electricity sparked leaking gas, causing the hydrogen to explode and burn through the airship. The stern smashed into the ground and the nose slowly followed. As a radio broadcaster relayed the horrific news to the nation, survivors clambered out of the wreckage nearing the ground. Astonishingly, 62 of the 97 crew and passengers survived the disaster. After a joint German-American inquiry revealed the cause of the accident, the United States began selling the less flammable helium to Germany until Hitler's "union" with Austria in March the following year.

Although heavier-than-air craft have gone on to become one of the safest forms of transport, lighter-than-air balloons and airships had to wait over half a century before making a reappearance for passenger flights.

the golden age of aerial adventure

the innovators and the aces

The pioneers and entrepreneurs had proved that airplanes and airships could fly and make money, but it was the innovators and flying aces of the first half of the twentieth century who pushed aircraft to their limits—in both war and peace—and demonstrated what they could do.

Left: *An icon for a generation. In May 1932 Amelia Earhart became the first woman to fly solo across the Atlantic in her Lockheed Vega. Top: The 106mph (170km/h) Albatros C.VII was an excellent reconnaissance platform. Other Albatros aircraft served Germany's fighter pioneers well through 1916 and 1917.*

At the outbreak of World War I in 1914 many thought the conflict would be "over by Christmas." Many also believed Europe's Great Powers would decide the war by glorious cavalry charges. In this picture of the art of war, aircraft (and later tanks) were an unnecessary complication. The early development of aircraft in World War I was almost accidental—airplanes were initially used only for reconnaissance and locating targets for the artillery.

Fighters were developed to knock down enemy reconnaissance aircraft and prevent them from returning with valuable information, and bombers came into being to destroy the bases of the reconnaissance and fighter airplanes. These developments came about largely as a process of reaction and counter-reaction, but although the process was unplanned and haphazard, and despite the fact that few of those involved had any real vision of where the process was leading, the improvements yielded by the process were real and important.

Aerial scouts were invaluable in the opening exchanges of the war as the German armies swept into France. Reconnaissance aircraft provided both sides with

Above: *Roland Garros piloting a Morane-Saulnier monoplane fighter with metal deflectors on its propeller blades to protect them from the bullets of the machine gun.*

information and photographic evidence of the enemy's positions for artillery bombardment. The difficult part of the task was getting the information quickly to headquarters. This was done initially by simply dropping a written message over one's own positions. Later radio communications made the job easier.

The machine gun problem

The early fighters were basic reconnaissance or scout airplanes in which the pilot carried a rifle or revolver to take random shots at the enemy. The problem was how to fit machine guns, which had proved deadly in the trenches. Ideally, the guns had to be mounted along the centerline of the aircraft

for the pilot to aim straight and pull the trigger, so there were three choices: a "pusher" configuration, which soon proved to give inadequate performance; a machine gun mounted on the upper wing of a biplane; or on the fuselage, over the engine cowling. There were obvious difficulties inherent in both of the latter alternatives. With the first, the pilot had to stand up to fire, losing control of the aircraft as he did so (two-seater fighters which allowed the pilot to remain at his controls as the navigator fired did not have this problem, but were bound to be heavier and less manoeuvrable). The machine gun position over the engine, though more convenient for the pilot, had a more serious drawback—the bullets

Top: *Aircraft like the Bristol F.2B used a Huck's Starter, like the Model T Ford.*

Above: *The Fokker E.II was the second of Anthony Fokker's fighters to incorporate interrupter gear for the forward-facing machine gun.*

shattered the propeller as it spun in the line of fire. French and German engineers approached this problem differently, the former redesigning the propeller and the latter redesigning the gun. Morane-Saulnier attached steel plates to the propeller blades to deflect the bullets that hit it. Anthony Fokker, on the other hand, built an interrupter gear that timed the firing of the gun to that of the engine, so that the bullets were not

ejected when the propeller passed in front of the barrel. The Fokker E monoplane ("E" for "Eindecker") was the first to include this synchronized machine-gun system late in 1915.

British and French fighters could in theory outperform the Fokker E types, but the interrupter gear gave the German aircraft a significant tactical advantage. Developments in engine and airframe design were moving rapidly too. The Swiss, Marc

Sir Thomas Sopwith: From the Tabloid to the Snipe

Thomas Sopwith was to the Royal Navy as Glenn Curtiss was to the United States Navy. Thomas Octave Murdoch Sopwith first became involved in flying in 1910 and in the following four years established a test pilot school and flight school, through which many of Britain's best aviators passed. Upon the outbreak of war, there was no aircraft industry to mass-produce airplanes for the Allied effort. Into this breach stepped Thomas Sopwith and the Sopwith Aviation Company, based at Kingston-upon-Thames in Surrey.

Over the four years of World War I Sopwith built 16 types of aircraft totalling some 18,000 in all. The first was the Tabloid, built in 1913 and used as a scout for the British Expeditionary Force in France and Belgium. Only 40 Tabloids were built, but they led to the Sopwith Schneider, which won the 1914 Schneider Trophy reaching 92mph (148km/h). The Schneider in turn inspired the Sopwith Baby, which was produced from November 1914. The Baby was a floatplane which saw service with the Royal Naval Air Service (RNAS) combating German zeppelins with hand-thrown Ranken incendiary darts.

The famous Sopwith Pup, the first British fighter to incorporate a single machine-gun with interrupter gear, joined the war in September 1916. With a 80hp (60kW) engine it was a simple airplane to fly and was ordered by the RNAS for use in the development of aircraft carriers. Remaining in service until late 1917, it performed well against its main adversary, the Halberstadt D.II, because of its superior maneuverability. Next, Sopwith experimented with a triplane design to give the airplane greater lift. The short-winged Triplane was highly maneuverable and inspired Fokker to produce the similar Dr.I almost immediately. The successor to the Triplane was possibly the most famous British fighter of the war, the Camel, so-called because of the hump shape over its two synchronized machine-guns built into the engine cowling. The Camel began combat flights in July 1917 and the 5140 built were responsible for shooting down over 1200 enemy aircraft

The airplane considered to be the Allies' best on the Western front was also a Sopwith design, the Sopwith Snipe. A direct improvement on the experience of the Camel, the Snipe had a slightly more powerful 230hp (172kW) Bentley rotary engine which gave it a greater speed and altitude than its forerunner. Approximately 500 were built during the war, with a further 1000 joining the RAF before the aircraft was retired in 1927.

Thomas Sopwith received his knighthood in 1953.

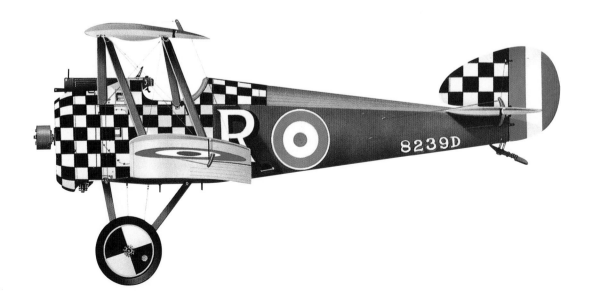

Above: *A Sopwith Camel takes off from the deck of the seaplane tender HMS* Pegasus *on November 1, 1919.*
Below: *The first of Thomas Sopwith's impressive aircraft—a Tabloid pictured in Monaco in 1914.*

Above: *Five hundred Sopwith Snipes saw action in World War I and were widely regarded as the best fighters on the Western Front.*
Left: *The Sopwith Camel F.1 was one of the most famous fighters of World War I and an equal match to any of its contemporaries.*

Above: *The success of the Sopwith Triplane, of which this is a replica, forced Fokker to build his Dr.I "Dreidecker" triplane.*

Birkigt, sought to improve on previous powerplants by positioning his engine's eight cylinders in a "V" shape. A circular frontal air-intake provided cooling for the engine. The best fighter to use this powerplant was the SPAD S.VII, which could reach 138mph (222km/h). Further changes to the engine included the starting mechanism. At the start of the war, the 100–130hp (75–97kW) engine of the Avro 504K was typical in that the propeller had to be swung by hand for ignition. As engines improved to 200–300hp (149–224kW), a manual swing was not powerful enough to start the engine and devices such as the Huck's Starter (as used with the Model T Ford car) were introduced for aircraft like the F.2A/B Bristol Fighter. In terms of airframe development, it was soon realized that the best fighters would be those with a short wingspan to aid maneuverability. The problem with short wings is that they produce proportionately less lift. The British solution was the Sopwith Triplane, whose third set of wings provided extra lift. It was followed almost

immediately by the more famous Fokker Dr.I "Dreidecker" (triplane).

World War I aircraft reached their technological peak with the British Sopwith Snipe, of which approximately 500 were built in the latter stages of the war, and the German Fokker D.VII, used by the Red Baron's *Jagdgeschwader I* ("Fighter Wing 1") after his death. These two aircraft incorporated all that had been learnt from engine and aerodynamic design and were worthy adversaries over the battlefields of France in 1918.

The aces

The term "Fighter Ace" was coined in France for any pilot who achieved five or more kills—it was devised as a publicity stunt to enthuse the public for the war in the air as the ground campaigns stagnated. The United States also used the phrase, but at first the British did not, believing that the elevation of any one pilot above his peers could damage team spirit. The first ace of the war was German Lieutenant Max Immelman, the "Eagle of

Lille" who flew the Fokker E.I monoplane, in which he made 15 kills before his aircraft was hit and broke up in a steep dive in June 1916. Germany's most famous ace, Manfred von Richthofen, was ruthless, but the first British ace was also extremely aggressive. Captain Albert Ball VC was famed for his head-on charges at the enemy, which required some skill and much blind courage. Ball flew the French Nieuport 17, a scout aircraft with a Lewis gun mounted on the upper wing. On May 6, 1917, his body was found unmarked beside his wrecked Nieuport near Lens after he had dived into cloud after a German airplane. Not yet 21 years old, he had achieved 47 kills. The highest-scoring Allied national aces of the war were Captain René Paul Fonck, Major Edward "Mick" Mannock VC and Captain Edward Vernon Rickenbacker. The Frenchman Fonck was second only to the Red Baron, scoring 75 kills (he went on to challenge Charles Lindbergh for the New York to Paris flight in 1927). Mannock was credited with 73 kills, but is known to have attributed a number to younger pilots in his squadrons to boost their morale. He was

Left: *British ace Captain Albert Ball achieved 47 kills before he was found dead aged just 20.*
Below: *Eddie Rickenbacker pictured in the cockpit of his SPAD. Rickenbacker recorded 26 kills in less than a year.*

Manfred von Richthofen – The Red Baron

Above above all other aces stood one man, known as *der rote Kampfflieger* (The Red Battle-flyer), *le petit rouge* (The Little Red), or The Red Baron—Rittmeister Manfred von Richthofen. Born on May 2, 1892, the son of Major Albrecht von Richthofen, the young Manfred was always destined for a career in the military. A fine athlete, he received his commission in April 1911 and joined the 1st Regiment of Uhlans as a cavalry officer.

The sodden ground of the western front battlefields did not permit glorious cavalry charges and Richthofen had to cast around for other opportunities. The air service appeared a fresh challenge and after meeting his hero, Oswald Boelcke, he joined the *Fliegertruppe* in 1915. Boelcke was the father of combat formation flying and left his legacy for his protégés in his *Dicta Boelcke,* which gave instructions on how and when to attack enemy aircraft and how to protect fellow pilots in combat. Although he crashed his plane on his first solo flight in October 1915, Richthofen went on to become a superb pilot and aerial marksman. He made his first kills in the summer of 1916, but these did not count towards his score because the victims crashed behind the Allies' lines and could not be confirmed. The first credited kill came shortly afterwards in September 1916, a month before Boelcke was killed in a mid-air collision. Germany had a new hero.

In January 1917, with 16 confirmed kills, Richthofen was awarded

Above: *Manfred von Richthofen, the most famous ace in history.*

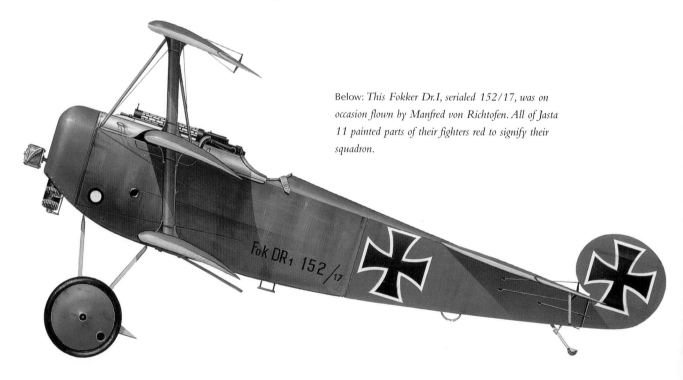

Below: *This Fokker Dr.I, serialed 152/17, was on occasion flown by Manfred von Richtofen. All of Jasta 11 painted parts of their fighters red to signify their squadron.*

the Pour le Mérite (nicknamed the Blue Max—the most prestigious Imperial German military medal) as the best living German flying ace. Given command of Jasta 2, Richthofen painted parts of his Albatros D.III red, gaining him the name the "Red Baron." The reason for this is still debated—was it for recognition by German troops on the ground, so they would not fire at him by mistake, was it for the blood of his victims, or was it because it was the color of his old cavalry regiment? In response, some British pilots painted their airplanes' noses red to signify that they were seeking out the Red Baron.

In 1917 Richthofen switched to the famous Fokker Dr.I Triplane. Although he flew a number of aircraft in the course of the war, Richthofen is best remembered for his Dr.I because it was the only one he painted completely red.

The end of this flying ace came on April 21, 1918, as he pursued Lieutenant Wilfred May's Sopwith Camel over Allied territory. Ignoring his own instructions, the Red Baron flew deeper into the French countryside, and Canadian Captain

Above: *The Red Baron in his cockpit. Richtofen was killed on April 21, 1918 as he battled with a Sopwith Camel behind enemy lines.*

Arthur "Roy" Brown in turn managed to get on his tail. The hunter became the hunted. As Richthofen turned to throw off his pursuer he was shot through the chest and his airplane slowly descended to land in a field below. It is still uncertain who fired the fatal shot. Was it an Australian anti-aircraft battery on the ground, as is mostly supposed, or was it a long-range burst from Captain Brown? As this last question remained unresolved, the Red Baron was buried by his enemies with full military honors, a mark of respect for the greatest flying ace of World War I with a total of 80 kills to his name.

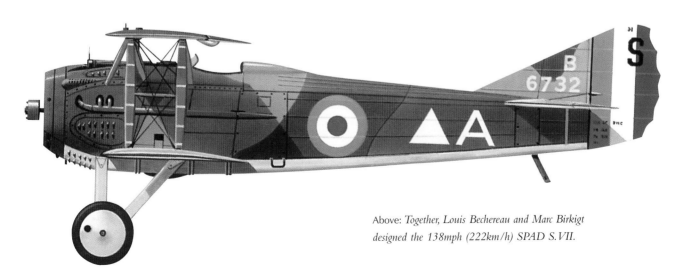

Above: *Together, Louis Bechereau and Marc Birkigt designed the 138mph (222km/h) SPAD S.VII.*

Above: A Sikorsky Ilya Murometz bomber pictured in 1914. Note the power and stability of the aircraft, which allows the two men to stand on its fuselage.

undoubtedly the best Allied patrol leader, planning flights to the tiniest detail, and was not ambushed once. His airplane caught fire in the air in July 1918 and his body was never found. Although the United States did not join the war until 1917, Rickenbacker scored 26 kills in less than a year thereafter. He was originally a racing driver, but became an engineer at the outbreak of war. He did not join the 94th Aero Squadron until March 1918 and so actually achieved his kills in just 8 months. He later became involved with Eastern Air Lines before flying on combat missions in World War II as an observer/consultant.

Early bombers

As military planners adjusted to the significance of aircraft in warfare in 1914 and 1915, they realized the only sure way to stop the flights of the enemy's reconnaissance and fighter aircraft was to destroy their bases. Early on in the war, pilots had realized that they should take small arms with them on flights to defend themselves from attack in the air, or if they were shot down. This then moved on a step as pilots began to take small bombs with them (although French pilots had experimented with light bombs before the war). These small bombs

were really only token gestures, but an important step in aircraft development had been made.

The first purpose-built bomber, the Bolshoi Baltisky B, was produced in Russia just before the war, but was too slow at 53mph (85km/h) to be used during the conflict and so only half a dozen were built. An improvement on this was the 78mph (125km/h) four-engined Ilya Murometz V, which could carry a 1120lb (508kg) payload. British and French bombers were either too small or too inefficient, but the Italians excelled with Gianni Caproni's airplanes. Caproni made the war's best bombers and his Ca.46 was the epitome of years of development. This three-engined biplane carried two rotating machine-guns and up to 1102lb (500kg) of bombs at speeds of up to 93mph (150km/h). It was so successful that licences were granted for versions to be built in Britain, France and the United States, in addition to the 225 that were built for the Italian war effort.

Initially Germany used airships as bombers. The German High Command decided to launch attacks on London with these huge, silent aircraft in 1916, beginning in the summer. British fighters and ground batteries failed to shoot down any airships until explosive and phosphorous bullets

Top: *The A.E.G. G.V/18 bomber.*
Above: *The Gotha G.V had a 1102lb (500kg) payload
and a range of 520 miles (835km).*

Right: *The great aviators appeared on advertising everywhere: here Amelia Earhart and Wiley Post are depicted on Carreras cigarette cards.*
Below: *Captain John Alcock and Lieutenant Arthur Whitten-Brown were treated to a heroes' welcome after crossing the Atlantic in 1919.*

were introduced to pierce the balloons and set fire to the hydrogen. In late September and early October 1916, German airships made the last concerted air raids on London as the advances in defence cost the German High Seas Fleet three of its new L.30 class of zeppelins. Although sporadic raids occurred until the end of the war, the serious offensive use of airships was ended.

Instead, German efforts switched to airplanes. In the ground support role for the German Army, A.E.G. introduced the G.IV, which flew day and night harassing the Allied frontline. For long-range raids on London there were three main manufacturers—Friedrichshafen, Zeppelin, and Gothaer Waggonfabrik AG. The Zeppelin Staaken R.VI was an attempt to reclaim the bombing role after the withdrawal of the airships. The huge R.VI carried seven machine-guns and up to 4400lb (1996kg) of bombs. The most famous bombers of the war were the Gotha bombers produced by Gothaer. The first of the G class, the Gotha Ursinus GI, first flew in 1915 and the first Gotha raid on London was made on June 13, 1917. Although these bombers were harder to shoot down than the earlier zeppelins, raids over London were stopped in May 1918, because many aircraft had been lost in ill-advised tactical support missions over the western front.

The innovators

In the century since the Wright brothers first flew the airplane has changed almost beyond recognition. This evolution has been made possible by pilots and designers continuously pushing the boundaries of air travel, as the chasing of "world firsts" has developed aviation. The pursuit of records and "firsts" accelerated the rate of technological development, and the record breakers—including Amelia Earhart, Alcock and Brown, and Charles Lindbergh—became familiar names. It is thanks to the innovators as well as the pragmatists that aircraft have made the world smaller.

Before and after World War I, the world watched as men and women took to the skies in search of

Below: *Alcock and Brown crossed the Atlantic in a Vickers Vimy in 1919. Alcock and Brown's aircraft is now preserved in the Science Museum, London.*

Harriet Quimby—Overshadowed Heroine

At a time when women's rights were at the forefront of the political agenda, Harriet Quimby became the first woman to obtain her pilot's licence. She was born in Michigan in 1875 and eventually settled in New York working as a photojournalist at *Leslie's Illustrated Weekly*. In October 1910, Quimby met John and Matilde Moisant at the Belmont Park International Aviation Tournament, where John won the race around the Statue of Liberty for the American team, making him a national hero. As the Wright brothers would not enroll female students at their flight school, Harriet and Matilde joined John and his brother Alfred's Moisant School of Aviation. Although other women flew at air shows and meetings, none managed to obtain a pilot's licence, and when Quimby passed her Aviator's Test on August 1, 1911, she was the first woman to do so.

After flying demonstrations at air shows, Quimby decided to attempt to emulate Louis Blériot's Channel crossing, but in reverse. She traveled to Britain secretly so as not to encourage a female rival to do the same, and then borrowed one of Blériot's own No.XIs for the flight. At 5:30 a.m. on April 16, 1912, Harriet Quimby took to the air. Taking 20 minutes longer than Blériot's crossing, she landed at 6:29 a.m., 30 miles (48km) from Calais, near the coastal town of Hardelot. Unfortunately her achievement was overshadowed by the loss of the Titanic a day earlier. Quimby's celebrations were limited to a champagne toast by locals in Hardelot as the Atlantic tragedy filled the world's front pages.

When she got back to the United States, Harriet Quimby was earning up to $100,000 for each appearance and demonstration flight at an air show. On July 1, 1912, she arrived at the Third Annual Boston Aviation Meet in Massachusetts in a two-seater monoplane and allowed a passenger on her stunt flight over Dorchester Bay. The ecstatic event manager, William Willard, won the toss over his son. As the crowd looked on, the airplane pitched forward and Willard was tossed from his seat, falling to his death. Without the balancing weight of a passenger, Quimby could only momentarily gain control of the aircraft before she too was thrown to the ground. Theories abounded as to what had caused the plane to lurch in such a way—did steering cables become tangled, did the excitable and ample-framed Willard lean forward to talk to Quimby and disrupt the balance? Some even blamed the lack of seat belts. What is certain is that in just 11 months in the air, Harriet Quimby had paved the way for other female pilots, licensed or not.

Top: *Harriet Quimby hand-starts the engine of her aircraft.*
Left: *Harriet Quimby (1875–1912) was the first licensed female pilot and the first woman to fly solo across the English Channel.*

fame and financial reward for achieving world firsts. Would these aviators reach their destinations in their sometimes unreliable craft?

The *Daily Mail* newspaper offered grand sums of money for aviators to accomplish various distance feats:

Cross-Channel = £1,000
London to Manchester = £10,000
Round-Britain air race = £10,000
Trans-Atlantic crossing = £10,000

On June 14, 1919, Captain John Alcock and Lieutenant Arthur Whitten-Brown took off from Newfoundland in a bid for the Trans-Atlantic prize. Carrying 860 gallons (3910 liters) of fuel, their Vickers Vimy bomber took 16 hours and 27 minutes to make the 1980 mile (3186km) crossing to County Galway, Ireland, landing on June 15.

Later that year, on November 12, Captain Ross Smith and his brother Lieutenant Keith Smith left Britain on an 11,294-mile (18,175km) flight to Australia. Landing on December 10, 1919, they claimed £10,000. Soon almost every crossing and race imaginable had been challenged, attempted, and achieved. Every one of these flights gained world headlines. But one challenge still remained, one that would prove that air travel was safe—the solo Atlantic flight.

Charles Lindbergh and the *Spirit of St. Louis*

Charles Augustus Lindbergh was born in 1902 and from a young age was interested in everything technical. He attended engineering college, but did not find it exciting enough, so in 1922 he went to Nebraska to learn to fly. In 1923 he bought a Curtiss Jenny and embarked on a short barnstorming career, during which his tricks included wing walking and parachuting. But the following year he joined the US Army Air Corps flying school at San Antonio, Texas, graduating first in his class in 1925. Although he stayed in the US Army Air Corp Reserve, Lindbergh began to fly air mail between Chicago and St. Louis.

Restlessly, Lindbergh's attention turned to the aviation prizes. In 1919 hotelier Raymond Orteig had offered $25,000 to the first person to fly non-stop from New York to Paris. What had become a national obsession also took hold of Lindbergh. René Fonck, the French wartime fighter pilot, had already made some unsuccessful attempts in 1926. Lindbergh set about finding financial support.

With backing of a group of St. Louis businessmen, Lindbergh made a deal with Charles Levine for the use of his Wright Bellanca. But the contract was never completed because a dispute opened up over who would pilot the Bellanca. Lindbergh had to look elsewhere.

Below: A test flight of the Spirit of St. Louis *over San Diego in May 1927.*

Left: *The first solo transatlantic crossing. Charles Lindbergh with the* Spirit of St. Louis.
Above: *Lindbergh and the* Spirit of St. Louis *were met by hundreds of excited well-wishers when the aircraft landed at Le Bourget.*
Below: *Byrd's Fokker F.VII* America. *Byrd never did reach Paris—his June 1927 attempt ended when he had to ditch his aircraft near Ver-sur-Mer in dense fog.*

In 1927 the $25,000 prize beckoned more challengers. Charles Levine and Clarence Chamberlain would fly their *Columbia*, Fonck prepared a Sikorsky biplane, Richard Byrd readied a Fokker tri-motor called *America*, and Noel Davis and Stanton Wooster also entered. Lindbergh set off for San Diego to discuss a design with the Ryan Aeronautical Company. For $6,000 plus the engine costs, Ryan built Lindbergh the *N-X-211 RYAN NYP*—more usually known as the *Spirit of St. Louis*. In two months, and at the final cost of $10,580, Lindbergh was ready to cross the Atlantic.

Before Lindbergh got airborne, the other competitors had tried and tested their machines. Levine and Chamberlain's *Columbia* broke its landing gear, Byrd's *America* suffered structural failure and injured three of his crew, and Davis and

Wooster died in tests. Flying the course in reverse, two Frenchmen, Charles Nungesser and François Coli, took off from Paris in May 1927 in *L'Oiseau Blanc* (White Bird) but never arrived in New York.

As the *Spirit of St. Louis* was a single-seater aircraft, Lindbergh would have to be his own engineer while still flying the aircraft, and struggle to keep alert for the whole duration of the flight, with no co-pilot to relieve him. But the prospects looked good when his 21 hour and 20 minute flight from San Diego to New York set a new transcontinental speed record.

On May 20, 1927, with 451 gallons (2050 liters) of fuel and five sandwiches, a tired Charles Lindbergh took off from Roosevelt Field, New York. He had not slept properly over the previous nights. Heavily laden, he just cleared the telephone

Right: *Upon returning to the United States, Lindbergh was given victory parades and celebrations wherever he went. Here he is pictured in Omaha.*

Far right: *Amelia Earhart in front of the Pratt and Whitney engine of her Lockheed 10.*

Overleaf: *Lockheed Vega* Winnie Mae *displays the legs of its first circumnavigation flight on its fuselage.* Winnie Mae *is now on permanent display in the Smithsonian.*

wires at the end of the runway and flew some of the crossing at just 10ft (3m) above the waves. But 33 hours and 30 minutes later he was an international hero as he touched down at Le Bourget, Paris. A European tour began almost immediately and sponsorship requests followed.

Returning to the United States aboard the USS *Memphis*, in New York Lindbergh was treated to the largest ticker tape parade ever. He was awarded the Congressional Medal of Honor, he was promoted to Colonel of the Air Corps Reserve and a Distinguished Flying Cross followed. But he turned down many offers of commercial endorsements, saying he was a flyer and not an advertiser. Instead he set about writing his story, which became an instant bestseller. He then embarked upon a goodwill tour of North and South America in the *Spirit of St. Louis*, meeting his future wife, Anne Morrow, in Mexico.

Charles Lindbergh had proved the airplane to be a safe form of transport and his tours in the *Spirit of St. Louis* proved its reliability. Stocks in the aircraft industry rose quickly and public interest in flight burgeoned. From 1927 Lindbergh became technical advisor to Pan American World Airways and helped establish Trans-continental and Western Airlines (TWA).

Amelia Earhart

Amelia Earhart was another legendary innovator, and following Lindbergh's solo flight from New York to Paris she became the first female passenger to cross the Atlantic (in Commander Wilmer Stultz's Fokker seaplane, *Friendship*, in 1928). Earhart was not satisfied with just being a passenger, and wanted to make the flight solo. On the evening of May 20, 1932, Earhart climbed aboard her scarlet Lockheed Vega at Harbor Grace, Newfoundland. The Vega was the airplane of choice for many of those attempting distance records, but on this occasion it gave her a good deal of anxiety. About four hours out, a section of the exhaust manifold cracked and began to leak hot gases, with flames lapping at the engine cowling. Although these subsided, Earhart noticed a petrol leak, and then her altimeter failed. As she ascended further into the cloud to avoid crashing into the sea, the manifold got worse again and a section broke off, but the Vega still rattled on towards Ireland. Seeing land below, Earhart descended to take a closer look at Donegal (although she was unsure of where she was exactly), before heading north over Londonderry. After thirteen and a half hours in the air, Amelia Earhart landed, the third person to cross the

NR105W

THE
WINNIE MAE
OF OKLAHOMA

LOS ANGELES TO CHICAGO · 9 HRS. 9 MIN. 4 SEC. · AUG. 27, 1930
AROUND THE WORLD · 8 DAYS, 15 HRS. 51 MIN. · JUNE 23 TO JULY 1, 1931
AROUND THE WORLD · 7 DAYS, 18 HRS. 49 MIN. · JULY 15 TO JULY 22, 1933

Below: *Amelia Earhart and her aircraft in*
Londonderry, Northern Ireland, on May 21, 1932.
Bottom: *Earhart's distinctive bright red Lockheed Vega.*

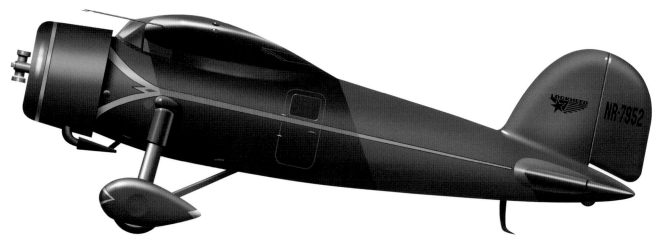

Atlantic by air, the first woman to do so, and also the fastest of the three.

In this pioneering age merely crossing the Atlantic was not enough for Earhart, and she set her sights on Ruth Nicholls's United States cross-continent record. Again making the flight in a Lockheed Vega, Earhart took off from Los Angeles, California, on August 24, 1932 and traveled 2500 miles (4023km) to land in Newark, New Jersey, just 19 hours later. Earhart's hunger for success was insatiable. She completed the hazardous 2408-mile (3875km) flight from Honolulu, Hawaii, to Oakland, California, in 18 hours and 16 minutes on January 11 and 12, 1935.

There was, however, one journey that proved just too far for Earhart. In June 1937 she took off with Captain Fred Noonan on a flight to circumnavigate the globe. After covering around 22,000 miles, two thirds of their route, their airplane was lost in the Pacific Ocean somewhere between British New Guinea and Howland Island on July 2. Amelia Earhart had taken the baton from Harriet Quimby and taken it a great distance.

Circumnavigating the globe

The first team to circumnavigate the globe successfully were Wiley Post and his navigator Harold Gatty in 1931, also in a Lockheed Vega. Post was born in Texas, but traveled around with his family before settling in Oklahoma. Interested in mechanics, he worked on the oilfields, until an accident cost him his left eye. With the $1,800 compensation he bought his first airplane and soon went on to become the personal pilot to F.C. Hall, a wealthy oilman. Hall bought a Vega and named it *Winnie Mae* after his daughter, and Post won the Los Angeles to Chicago National Air Race Derby in 9 hours, 9 minutes and 4 seconds on August 27, 1930 in this machine—his first success.

Wiley Post intended greater things the following year. He and his navigator Harold Gatty posed for photographers at Roosevelt Field, New York, on June 23, and at 4:55 p.m. the pair took off in an attempt to circle the globe with stops in Canada, Britain, Germany, the Soviet Union, Alaska, and Canada before returning to New York. Poor weather over the Atlantic necessitated the use of Post's blind flying equipment, which included an artificial horizon and a bank-and-turn indicator. After stop-offs in

Britain and Germany, the passage was again blighted by bad weather conditions as heavy rain impeded the flight over East Prussia to Moscow. The welcome in the Soviet capital was more than cordial as the *Ossoaviakhim* (Society for Aviation and Chemical Defence) plied the flyers with drink, regaled them with numerous stories and allowed them only three hours' sleep. The problems did not end there, as the *Winnie Mae* was refuelled in imperial gallons and not the smaller US gallons, making the Vega too heavy. More time was wasted as the surplus was removed. The flight did not get any better at the next airstrip, at Blagovestchensk, where the aviators and their airplane began to sink in the swampy ground. Over the Sea of Okhotsk, gale force winds forced Post to fly just 75ft (23m) above the waves. Alaska also proved difficult as the *Winnie Mae* was again sucked into sodden ground; and as Post revved the engine to get airborne the propeller struck the ground and bent its tip. Repaired again, it crashed down on Gatty's head as he attempted to restart the engine. Battered but alive, Gatty got back on board, and Post took off from a local highway—a firmer runway than the boggy airstrip. When the intrepid explorers finally returned to New York they were greeted by an escort of numerous airplanes as they came into land 8 days, 15 hours and 51 minutes after they had left. Predictably, the book that followed was titled *Around the World in Eight Days*, a play on Jules Verne's *Around the World in Eighty Days*. Post went on to repeat the feat solo two years later, making the flight in just 7 days, 18 hours and 49 minutes.

As was the case with many of the great early aviators, Wiley Post was killed in an air accident. Post and the humorist Will Rogers were surveying an air route between the West Coast and the Soviet Union when their engine failed as they took off from a river near Point Barrow in Alaska on August 15, 1935. Before her death, Post's widow agreed to sell the *Winnie Mae* to the Smithsonian National Air and Space Museum in Washington, DC.

The innovators and aces had done much to build the enthusiasm of the public for air travel and had risked their lives to improve performance. These men and women were the heroes of aviation, and have been an inspiration to the generations that came after them.

the development of commercial aviation

planes for profit

No sooner had man left the ground than he sought to traverse the world and open a new market in air travel. The pioneers of the 1920s had excited the world with feats of aviation, but creating a safe and reliable passenger service was another challenge altogether.

Left: *Passenger airliners opened up the world to all who could afford the fare. This image of TWA stewardesses beside their Boeing 307 perfectly sums up the glamour of the period.*

Top: *Business or pleasure? Airlines allowed people to experience new cultures or simply take their hobbies abroad. Here a passenger's golf clubs are being loaded aboard a British Airways Lockheed Electra.*

The first scheduled airline service appeared in January 1914, when the St. Petersburg–Tampa Bay Airboat Service began regular flights over the 20 miles (32km) between the two Florida towns. Instead of the two-hour drive around the bay, the Benoist flying boats made the journey in just 20 minutes. But the little Benoists could only carry the pilot and one passenger. Although the Airboat Service went bankrupt after just four months, the experiment showed the potential benefits of air travel, even if they were not to be realized immediately.

The true birth of the commercial airline came after World War I, as wartime engine development provided airplanes with three times the previously available power. Post-war aircraft could now boast up to 300hp (224kW) compared to the 100hp (75kW) maximum of prewar airplanes.

Europe saw a huge increase in the number of companies offering passenger services, focusing particularly on crossing the English Channel. George Holt Thomas registered Britain's first airline, Aircraft Transport and Travel Ltd, in October 1916, and introduced its first passenger service in August 1919. Thomas's London to Paris flights

Above: *The St. Petersburg–Tampa Bay Airboat Service was the first scheduled airline service, flying the little two-seater Benoist flying boat over the 20 mile (32km) route.*

Right: *The workhorse of Pan Am's early Central American routes was the Sikorsky S-38. Nicknamed the "Flying Duck," the S-38 made a steady 125mph (200km/h).*

of that year were the first post-war scheduled commercial service. The aircraft was a converted military de Havilland D.H.4A, flying out of Hounslow aerodrome.

Others soon followed suit. In Britain, Handley Page Transport and S. Instone and Co. emerged—in France, Compagnie des Messageries Aériennes and Compagnie des Grands Express Aériens. Europe quickly reached the stage where airline companies almost outnumbered prospective passengers, and inevitably some fell by the wayside. Many merged to form the first great European airlines: Imperial Airways of Britain, Air France, Deutsche Lufthansa, KLM of the Netherlands and Sabena of Belgium.

The Pan-Am Clippers

For many years one of the world's largest airlines, Pan American had a very modest start in the air travel business. Pan American World Airways made the first flight of its airmail service on October 19, 1927, making the 90-mile (145km) trip from Key West, Florida, to Havana, Cuba. The success of this short service encouraged Pan Am to reach out into Central America, starting in 1929.

The legendary Charles Lindbergh surveyed the potential routes and, although he preferred landplanes, amphibious aircraft were clearly more suitable for these new destinations. The workhorse for these new markets would be the Sikorsky S-38, and in total Pan Am operated 38 of these twin-engined eight-seat flying boats on its Central American routes.

Pan Am's real triumph came in opening up the Pacific. On April 16, 1935, a test flight for a trans-Pacific service flew from Alameda, California, to Honolulu in 18 hours and 37 minutes. On October 21, 1936, Pan Am opened its San Francisco–Manila service.

This was the age of the Clippers, named after the speedy sailing ships built in Virginia and Maryland in the nineteenth century. Pan Am operated three models of flying boats in the Pacific, the Martin M-130, Sikorsky S-42, and Boeing 314. The M-130 *China Clipper* opened the Central Pacific mail service between San Francisco and Manila and the S-42 *Samoa Clipper* inaugurated the Honolulu to Auckland mail and freight service in December 1937. Tragically, the *Samoa Clipper* crashed in

Left: *The age of the Clipper. The Martin M-130 flying boat* China Clipper *flew the San Francisco–Manila mail routes through the late 1930s and into the 1940s.*

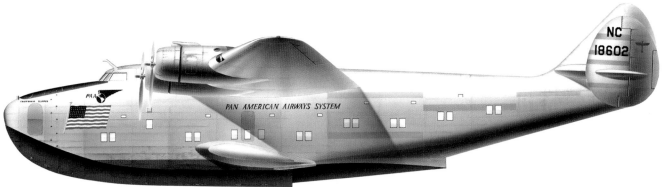

January 1938 killing all seven of its crew.

The final challenge for airlines worldwide was the North Atlantic service. With the delivery of the first new Boeing 314 to Pan Am in Baltimore on February 24, 1939, a new era had begun. On March 3 Eleanor Roosevelt named her the *Yankee Clipper*.

The *Yankee Clipper* was originally built for delivering mail, carrying 11 crew and with space for just 10 passengers. In March and April 1939 she flew from Baltimore to the Azores, Lisbon, Bordeaux, Marseilles, and Southampton before returning via Lisbon and the Azores. Her first mail flight to Europe took place on May 20, 1939; Captain A. E. LaPorte flew from Baltimore to Lisbon in 26 hours and 54 minutes before returning to Port Washington. The Port Washington–Marseilles mail service was

Above: *After the Boeing 314 Yankee Clipper had opened the transatlantic mail route, the* Dixie Clipper *began the first transatlantic passenger service. It is pictured here after its first successful passenger crossing.*

Left top: *The Pan Am clippers led the way for all subsequent transatlantic and transpacific flights until the mid-1940s.*

Left bottom: *The clean lines of the Boeing 314 are shown beautifully here. The* California Clipper *was the second Boeing 314 to enter service and was one of the last to be retired.*

inaugurated on June 28, 1939, and just two days later the *Dixie Clipper* made the first North Atlantic passenger flight from New York to Southampton.

The Boeing Clippers' passenger services were comfortable compared to those offered 20 years earlier. The passenger-carrying Model 314 variants could accommodate 74 daytime passengers or 40 on reclining seats for night flights. The cost of these flights was $375 one-way or $675 return, which, by today's prices, would equal approximately $4000 and $7500. But after little more than three months the transatlantic service was withdrawn due to the onset of war in Europe. Five of the Boeing Clippers later went into war service with the United States Air Force and Navy.

Europe flies south

As the American airline companies established transatlantic and Pacific routes, the Europeans looked to the southern hemisphere. British-built aircraft were designed for long flights to link up the countries of its former empire, such as South Africa and India. In the interwar period the British Air Ministry issued a requirement for a new four-engined long-range flying boat. In response, Short Brothers produced the S.23 or Empire class craft, which could carry two tons of mail or 17 passengers over an 500 mile (800km) route. When Imperial Airways were awarded the Empire Air Mail Scheme they bought 42 of the new Empire class (with Qantas operating the British–Australian routes) and in August 1938 a Short S.23 made the first scheduled mail flight from Southampton to Sydney.

France also looked south as it united its territories by air. René Couzinet built his most well-known airplane for the task. Although his Couzinet 71 tri-motor was difficult to fly, it crossed the Atlantic in 1933 and on May 28, 1934, the flying boat made the first flight of a scheduled South Atlantic mail service from Toulouse to Natal via Senegal. The Couzinet 71 was retired from service in 1937 and did not operate the route's post-war passenger flights.

Germany turned to lighter-than-air aviation to reach foreign shores. Forbidden to build an air force by the 1919 Versailles Treaty, between-the-wars experiments with passenger airships took on greater importance. The Zeppelin Company built the world's two most famous airships: the *Graf Zeppelin* and the *Hindenburg*. It was with these airships that Germany launched its commercial flights to South America. On May 18, 1930, the *Graf Zeppelin* left Friedrichshafen on a test flight to Rio de Janeiro. This became a regular service from March 1932 with one return trip per month to Recife, Brazil, until 1936. At the same time as the mighty airships traversed the Atlantic, Dornier flying boats were in operation in other regions. Landplanes would fly passengers down to seaplane jetties in Africa, then the flying boats would complete the journey to South America. It wasn't until the arrival of the Dornier Do 26 mailplane that the transatlantic flight could be made by a single aircraft. The Do 26 incorporated four engines, with two facing forward and two facing aft. Other beneficial characteristics included the ability to be catapulted from a ship and refuelled in flight. The advent of World War II ended the Dornier's South Atlantic service after just 18 mail runs. The Do 26s were taken over by the Luftwaffe and operated as a coastal patrol aircraft.

Of course, European attempts were made at crossing the North Atlantic with passengers. The first came directly after World War I, when the Italian Gianni Caproni unveiled his Caproni Model 60 in 1919. Caproni boasted that this huge eight-engined triplane flying boat could carry 100 passengers across the Atlantic. Two test flights were made: the first saw a successful "hop" across a lake and the second reached a height of 60 ft (18m) before an unknown fault caused the nose to dip, breaking the center wings and causing the prototype to crash into the lake. Plans were made to rebuild the Ca 60, but a shed fire ended Caproni's dream of reaching the United States.

Germany used various aircraft for the North Atlantic crossing and built them in larger numbers than the big aircraft manufacturers of Britain and France, though the big production runs came about primarily because of the clandestine needs of the future Luftwaffe. The Dornier Do X was a giant development of the successful *Wal* (Whale) class flying boats. The 12-engined Do X was designed in 1927 and launched two years later. Intended to carry 100 passengers on the transatlantic route, it first flew on July 12, 1929. A public demonstration flight over Lake Constance was made shortly afterwards, carrying 150 passengers and 10 crew (plus a number of stowaways). A good performance on this scenic flight augured well for the future. But despite a successful passage to South America and goodwill tour up to New York, Dornier could not find a buyer because of the Do X's high fuel consumption. Although only two more were built, it set a standard for the German flying boats that followed.

The Dornier Do 18 was built to replace the *Wal*-class aircraft. In total, 152 of these long-range mailplanes were built, with most seeing service in

Below: *Despite its power, range and performance, the Do X was rejected by airline companies because of its high fuel consumption.*
Right: *This picture shows perfectly the innovative push-pull propeller system used in the Dornier Do 26. The aircraft was used by the Luftwaffe in World War II.*
Bottom right: *Gianni Caproni built the massive Ca 60 to carry 100 passengers across the Atlantic, but the second test flight saw the center set of triplane wings break away, ending his dream of reaching America.*

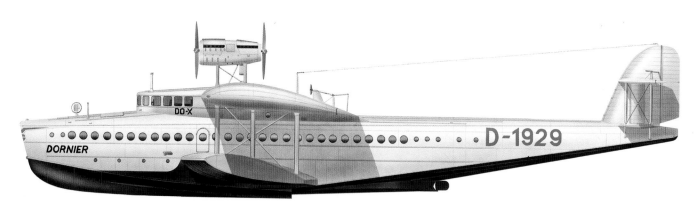

Right: *The original. Dornier's Wal class (pictured) spawned the Do 18 and laid the ground for all of Germany's other successful seaplanes.*

World War II as search-and-rescue and reconnaissance aircraft.

By far the most elegant and recognizable prewar German airliner was the Focke Wulf Fw 200 Condor, which first flew in 1937. With a 4072-mile (6558km) range, the 25-seat Condor was the only airliner capable of flying non-stop from Berlin to New York. A highly successful design, Adolf Hitler even had one as his personal aircraft. During World War II Condors were utilized as maritime patrol and reconnaissance aircraft, spotting targets for the U-Boat wolfpacks with deadly results.

In January 1935, the French six-engined Latécoère 521 flying boat made its first flight. The sole aircraft suffered a terrible setback the following year when it was was wrecked at its moorings by a storm. When rebuilt it went on to set a number of payload-to-height records. As well as its transport use, it was also able to accommodate up to 30 passengers at a time in its huge frame.

Imperial Airways also flew their Empire class flying boats on the transatlantic passage from Britain to Newfoundland via Ireland. With a range of only 810 miles (1300km), the Empires had to be refuelled in-flight by converted Handley Page Harrow bombers. A Southampton to New York service was introduced in August 1939 but was suspended the following month due to the outbreak of war.

Flight destinations demonstrated Europe's air travel priorities during the inter-war period, as the European empires looked to reach their dominions in Africa, South America and Asia more easily. The challenge of crossing the North Atlantic only fully gripped the European airlines from the mid-1930s. By the onset of war in 1939, technological improvements had made the world a smaller and more accessible place.

Above: *The Latécoère 521 offered comfortable travel for 30 passengers on two decks and with a forward-facing panoramic view.*

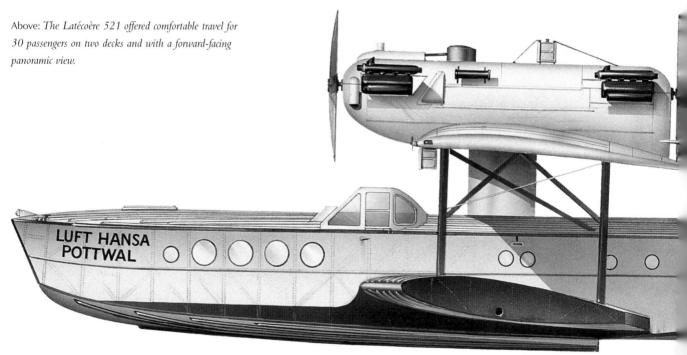

Above: *The prototype Focke Wulf Fw 200 Condor is pictured at Floyd-Bennett Field in New York after its 24 hour and 57 minute non-stop flight from Berlin on August 10 and 11, 1938.*
Below: *Dornier was Germany's finest builder of seaplanes during the inter-war period. Aircraft like the Superwal (pictured) proved very influential for the Luftwaffe during the early years of World War II.*

Inter-war aircraft development

With engine power vastly increased in the inter-war period, engineers looked at design and construction to further improve their aircraft. Throughout the 1920s mainland European manufacturers tested monoplanes, while Britain faithfully retained the biplane. At first there was very little difference between the two in performance terms. The British four-engined Handley Page HP.42 biplane traveled at up to 100mph (161km/h), while the largest European monoplane of the time, the German Junkers G-38, could reach 115mph (185km/h) despite producing 1000hp (746kW) more than the biplane.

The permanent shift away from biplanes began in the late 1920s and early 1930s as many designers

Above: *Old habits die hard. The four-engined British Handley Page HP.42 performed well against the early monoplane airliners beginning to emerge in mainland Europe, but this parity was not to last long.*

and engineers used the Schneider Trophy to demonstrate their innovative aircraft. Of the machines entering this annual air-racing contest, most were monoplanes. In 1927, racing at 281mph (452km/h), 70 percent faster than most of the world's fighters, the Supermarine S.5 proved that monoplanes were the future. In 1931 a Supermarine S.6 won the Schneider Trophy permanently for Great Britain, and provided technological knowledge which helped the company to develop its most famous design, the Spitfire.

A second innovation was the development of the all-metal airliner. The high-wing Ford Tri-Motor monoplane, nicknamed the "Tin Goose," was the first, with its corrugated fuselage and wings made of Duralumin, a metal as light as aluminum but twice as strong. The nickname was given because it was said to waddle down the runway as its three engines honked like geese. Between 1925 and 1933, Ford produced 197 Tri-motors for the commercial market, which were used as mail and freight carriers or 17-seater passenger aircraft. The "Tin Goose" offered the familiar and reliable Ford marque, and in 1930 was one of the first aircraft to employ stewardesses to provide in-flight food and beverages. Although production ceased in 1933, the life of the Ford Tri-motors continued and a "Tin Goose" is still operated to this day by the Kalamazoo Air Zoo museum for pleasure flights over Michigan.

In-flight service

The first airline to employ stewardesses was Boeing Air Transport, the predecessor of United Airlines.

Below: *The eight-seat Ford 4-AT was the first Ford-built Tri-motor. A military variant, the C-4, was built for troop transport during World War II. In total, 80 4-ATs and its variants were built.*

These early stewardesses had to be qualified nurses so they could deal with medical emergencies on board. In 1930 Boeing hired eight registered nurses to work on their Model 80As, one per airplane. This trial arrangement went on to establish a whole new profession as other airlines followed their lead in recruiting "air hostesses." Aside from serving food and drinks to passengers, other duties included ticket checking, carrying baggage, and maintaining the cleanliness of the cabin.

There were strict restrictions for those wanting to become stewardesses. As well as being registered nurses, applicants had to be single, aged 20 to 26, no more than 5ft 4in (1.63m) tall and weigh no more than 118lb (53.5kg).

Right: *In competition with United Air Lines' Boeing 247s, Douglas built a new series of airliners for TWA. The DC-2 (pictured) was the precursor of the famous DC-3 and began an industry rivalry that would last half a century.*
Below: *The cabin of a Boeing 247 displays the emergence of facilities we now take for granted. The 247 offered the height of air travel comfort for its day.*

The first modern airliners

The short and varied life of the "Tin Goose" was a result of the fast-moving and ever-growing aircraft production market. Just four years after Ford's Tri-Motor was introduced, the first aircraft recognizable to today's reader as a modern passenger airliner appeared in 1933 in the form of the Boeing 247.

The twin-engine Model 247 has been credited with making the Tri-Motor obsolescent, as these new airliners were technologically a world apart from the tri-motors and biplanes still in service worldwide. The all-metal alloy, low-wing Boeing 247 had an autopilot, retractable landing gear, the world's first wing flaps, de-icing equipment, variable pitch propellers, and two 550hp (410kW) Pratt and Whitney Wasp radial engines that allowed

it to climb with a full load on just one of those engines. For the ten passengers it offered a stewardess service, a soundproof cabin, a toilet (though not with running water), individual air ventilation, and thermostatically-controlled heating and cooling. Presented at the World's Fair in Chicago, an estimated 61 million people came to see it. The true airliner had been born.

TWA could not compete with the Boeing 247s of United Airlines with their current stock of aircraft and so approached Douglas for a worthy rival. Their first twin-engined airliner, the DC-1, flew in July 1933 and the second, the DC-2, shortly after that. The true competition to the Boeing 247 came in December 1935 with the maiden flight of the Douglas Sleeper Transport, or DC-3. The DC-3 could seat 21 passengers in

Below: *A Douglas DC-3 in service with PCA (Pennsylvania-Central Airlines) in the late 1940s.*

comfort (11 more than the Boeing 247) and was wider and faster than its competitor. It had space for 14 passengers in "sleeper" configuration. The DC-3 was a huge success, going on to dominate commercial air services and become the world's most famous airliner. By 1938 DC-3s made up 95 percent of American domestic schedules, and in 1939 the type was used by 30 airlines worldwide, delivering 90 percent of the world's airline traffic. At the outbreak of World War II approximately 450 had been sold to civil operators, but the war did not curtail the aircraft's career.

Douglas was approached to provide the United States and Britain with military versions for troop and equipment transport. In the guise of the C-47 Skytrain, C-53 Skytrooper and RAF Dakota, the DC-3 gained battle honors in North Africa, Normandy, Burma, the Himalayas and Arnhem. After the war, variants flew during the Berlin Airlift and the Vietnam War (as the AC-47 "Spooky" gunship).

In total, 803 DC-3s were built for the civilian market, over 10,123 for military use and a further 2700 under Soviet licence as the Lisunov Li-2. Even a Japanese version, the Showa L2D "Tabby," was produced. The number of these majestic airliners built is testament to their durability and adaptability. In the mid-1990s, approximately 400 DC-3s and C-47s still flew with 44 nations worldwide.

Above the weather

Boeing responded to the DC-3 with another world first. TWA pilot Tommy Tomlinson carried out research which concluded that an airliner could cruise smoothly "above the weather," at over 14,000ft (4000m). This would improve passenger comfort and cut down on fuel consumption. Tomlinson is estimated to have spent more time above 30,000ft (9140m) than all other pilots of the time combined, and so his suggestion was well heeded. One of the main problems with high

Above: *In response to the DC-3, Boeing introduced a world first. The Model 307 Stratocruiser was the first airliner with a pressurized cabin to allow it to fly "above the weather."*

altitude flying was the decrease in air pressure. At Mount Everest's peak (29,028ft/8824m), the pressure is less than a third of that at sea level. As air pressure decreases so does the amount of oxygen. Too great an altitude would result in a fatal lack of oxygen to the human brain. This, coupled with the extremely low temperatures encountered at high altitude, meant that high-flying airliners would need to maintain an artificial pressure and temperature inside the cabin. The result of Tomlinson's recommendation was the Boeing Model 307 Stratoliner. This was the first commercial airliner with a pressurized cabin, allowing it to fly higher than any other airliner then in service.

The Stratoliner first flew on December 31, 1938, and began its transcontinental service with TWA in July 1940. Timed at 13 hours and 40 minutes, the Stratoliner made the flight from Los Angeles to Newark, New Jersey, two hours faster than the DC-3. Pan Am bought three Stratoliners for its South American traffic, TWA bought a total of five and Howard Hughes bought one.

Navigation keeps up

The early short flights that were measured in minutes rather than miles hardly required maps, navigational experience, or technical aids. As the continental and intercontinental air routes opened up and more airplanes filled the skies, navigation systems of various kinds became necessary.

Daytime flight was not difficult, as visible landmarks could be used and pilots would often follow roads and railways to their destination. But with this as the only method of navigation, some questioned whether the airplane would ever challenge the dominance of the railway for passenger travel.

Night navigation by light beacons was introduced in the United States in the 1920s. In 1923 the US Army Air Corps set up a 80 mile-long (129 km) row of rotating light beacons between Columbus and Dayton, Ohio, for pilots to follow. This system was taken over by the Post Office in 1924 and a similar lighted route was established between Chicago and Cheyenne, Wyoming, as part of the $550,000 transcontinental line. This section was built first so that pilots could start their flight from one coast in daylight, fly the nighttime section over the lighted airway and then

Above: *Hughes's Lockheed 14-N2 in which he circumnavigated the globe at an average speed of 206mph (332km/h) in 1938.*

Above: *The Spruce Goose's only flight. The flight lasted only one minute but the aircraft passed into aviation history.*

Howard Hughes: Eccentric Pioneer

Howard Hughes Jr was born the son of a colorful oilman in Houston, Texas. His father's invention of a 166-edge rotary drill bit meant that at his parents' deaths in 1923, Howard Jr inherited approximately $900,000—a great deal of money at the time. This money was ploughed into California's two favorite pastimes—film making and flying.

After making his name with spectacular but commercially unsuccessful films such as *Hell's Angels,* Hughes turned to air racing, in which he set several records. In 1935 he co-built a specialized racing aircraft, the H-1, with Dick Palmer, and set a new landplane speed record of 352mph (567km/h). The H-1 then set a transcontinental speed record when Hughes flew from Los Angeles to Newark, New Jersey, in just 7 hours and 28 minutes in 1937. Hughes then turned his sights to the ultimate record—the round-the-world title. Over 3 days, 19 hours and 17 minutes in 1938 he circumnavigated the globe in a Lockheed 14, halving Wiley Post's time and also halving Charles Lindbergh's New York to Paris time en route. Because of these amazing feats, it is no surprise that Hughes came to be known as the second Lindbergh.

World War II changed Hughes's fortunes. As other Californian aircraft manufacturers produced countless aircraft for the war effort, Hughes only contributed the XF-11 high-speed reconnaissance aircraft (in which he suffered a near-fatal crash in 1946) and the *Spruce Goose,* neither of which actually flew until after the war.

The Hercules HK-1, or *Spruce Goose,* flew only once. The largest aircraft ever built, it got its nickname from being made entirely of wood because of the wartime metal shortages, although the wood was birch rather than spruce. On November 2, 1947, Hughes flew the *Spruce Goose* one mile across Long Beach Harbor at 80mph (130km/h), 70ft (20m) over the water before landing one minute later. The HK-1 was then returned to its hangar, never to be seen again in Hughes's lifetime.

Howard Hughes's life then took a downward spiral. Most of his ventures lost money, and usually a lot of it. Suffering from an addiction to painkillers, Hughes had a mental breakdown in 1958, which left him a recluse in his hotel rooms in Beverley Hills and Las Vegas.

When inducted into the Aviation Hall of Fame in 1973, he did not attend the ceremony and was instead represented by one of the crew from his 1938 circumnavigation.

Hughes died as he lived, in the air—in an ambulance flying from his home in Acapulco to Houston on April 5, 1976.

Below: *Based on the design of the P-38 Lightning and the earlier D-2, the XF-11 high-speed reconnaissance aircraft could reach 450mph (724km/h).*

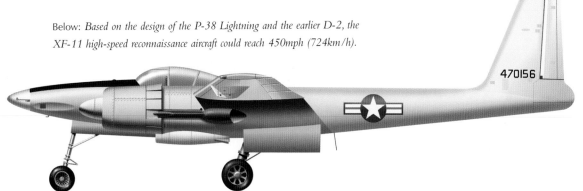

Above: *Early flight required no more than the solo pilot following lighted airways, but with distance records and intercontinental airline travel the navigator/radio operator became an important member of the crew.*
Right: *Radio-assisted navigation is far more reliable than manual calculation, but requires a more experienced navigator to master. Here a Boeing 314 navigator plots his course by the stars.*

land in daylight on the other coast. The beacons consisted of a 51ft (15.5m) steel tower and a generator shed. The tower housed a rotating one million candlepower beacon, visible for 40 miles (64km), and two course beacons, pointing to and from the destination. The generator shed had its own markings, visible in daylight. By mid-1925 the transcontinental lighted airway stretched from Rock Springs, Wyoming, to New York City.

On May 20, 1926, the United States Congress passed the Air Commerce Act. This gave responsibility of air travel development and safety to the US Government. The Aeronautics Branch of the Department of Commerce was established under William P. MacCracken Jr in August of the same year. The Post Office Department had previously run the air routes and the airfields because they were primarily used for airmail, but now they came under federal jurisdiction. From July 1927, MacCracken's branch took on the completion of the transcontinental lighted airway, which at the time included a system of lighted

beacons, 95 emergency airfields and 17 radio stations. The last beacon was lit in Miriam, Nevada, in January 1929.

Radio beacons were the next innovation to aid long-range navigation. In the 1920s the US Government introduced the Four-Course Radio Range. This simple but ingenious system consisted of a transmitter with two loop antennae at right angles to one another. One antenna emitted "A" in Morse code (dot-dash) and the other "N" (dash-dot). When the pilot was on course, flying directly between the antennae, he would hear a continuous tone. When to one side he would hear either a dot-dash or dash-dot, indicating where he was and where he should reposition his aircraft to regain his course. By the end of World War II, there were around 200 of these transmitters in operation in the United States. Other similar radio systems were also introduced from the 1920s, but were of limited use as they were subject to interference in bad weather.

The Four-Course Radio Range was superseded by a number of other radio navigational aids from the late 1940s. The direct replacement was the VHF Omnidirectional Range, or VOR, which emitted stronger signals and gave more precise information to an aircraft's onboard navigation system. VOR stations transmit different signals depending on their type, corresponding to the altitude of the aircraft they are designed to aid: terminal VORs cover a 25 nautical mile range, low-altitude VORs cover 40 nautical miles below 18,000ft (5482m), and high-altitude VORs have a 200 nautical mile range for airplanes flying between 18,000 and 60,000 feet (5482 and 18,276 meters).

Navigational aids like these could scarcely have been dreamed of when Alcock and Brown crossed the Atlantic in 1919 using just a compass and sextant. Compared to the cockpits of the aircraft of the 1920s and 1930s, the Vickers Vimy was a very simple machine. By the outbreak of World War II, blind flying instruments were the norm in aircraft. These new aids included a bank-and-turn indicator, air-speed indicator, a sensitive altimeter, rate-of-climb sink indicator, directional gyro, and artificial horizon. Blind flying schools were also established, a leader in the field being Imperial Airways, which had colleges in Croydon and Southampton.

Left: *Aircrew attending radio navigation training.*
Right: *Compared to that of the Vickers Vimy (top), the cockpits of the Boeing 247 (middle) and Lockheed Super Electra (bottom) are highly complex, giving the pilot the ability to fly in zero visibility with the aid of improved instrumentation.*

Airfields to airports

As early aircraft were so light, only a stretch of flat grass was needed for take-off and landing. The first airstrips were often racetracks or golf courses and the aircraft sometimes drew the same size crowds as the sports themselves. The first dedicated airports were established in Germany from 1910 for airship services. By 1912 the US had around 20 airports converted from fields and country clubs. In just seven years, however, there were municipal grass-strip airports built at Atlantic City in New Jersey, Tucson in Arizona, and Albany in New York.

The first hard-surface runways were built in the US in 1928, although it is disputed which came first, the one at Newark, New Jersey, or Henry Ford's at Dearborn, Michigan. At any rate, 1313- to 2955-foot (400- to 900-meter) concrete runways became widespread in the 1930s as air travel boomed.

Early airports took on the appearance of train stations to give a familiar setting and allay the fears of anxious flyers. Some airlines built their own airports in convenient locations, for example Pan Am's "Pan American Field" in Florida, the first land-based international airport.

The first great European airport, and the model for others worldwide, was the Tempelhof Airport in Berlin. Built in 1938, it was one of the largest buildings in the world, boasting a 330 by 160-foot (101 by 49-meter) waiting room and a mile-long hangar. Tempelhof had 300,000 passengers per year and a further 100,000 paid to watch the aircraft take off and land. The public's fear and uncertainty over air travel had been dispelled and more and more took to the skies.

Air Traffic Control

In the United States, as air travel increased, the Aeronautics Branch was renamed the Bureau of Air Commerce in 1934 to indicate its greater importance. The Bureau oversaw the creation of the first three Air Traffic Control (ATC) centers

before taking over ATC responsibilities fully in 1936. Initially, landing at an airfield involved following the flag and light signals of those on the ground. In time though, radio communications aided the pilots down onto the landing strip. The first radio-equipped control tower was built in Cleveland, Ohio, in 1930. The Instrument Landing System (ILS)—a ground-based system that guided the aircraft down a 3° descent to the runway using radio—was introduced in the 1950s. Depending on visibility, if necessary, such a system can guide the pilot in to land "blind."

In 1938, civil aviation was removed from the remit of the Department of Commerce as the independent Civil Aeronautics Authority was established. Two years later, back under the auspices of the Department of Commerce, the Authority was divided into the Civil Aeronautics Administration (CAA), dealing with safety, ATC and airway development, and the Civil Aeronautics Board (CAB), which covered accident investigation and financial regulation of the airlines.

The age of the airline had truly begun and, although World War II caused the cancellation of many passenger routes temporarily, the aircraft technology, navigational aids, and innovative minds were in place to herald a golden age of commercial flight.

Right: With the introduction of the Lockheed Constellation (pictured here in New York in 1956), the world began to feel a much smaller place.
Below: A United Air Lines Boeing 247. The large airline companies and manufacturers began to open up the world with even greater ease after World War II.
Bottom: Berlin Tempelhof airport (pictured here in 1928) was the model for other airports to follow.

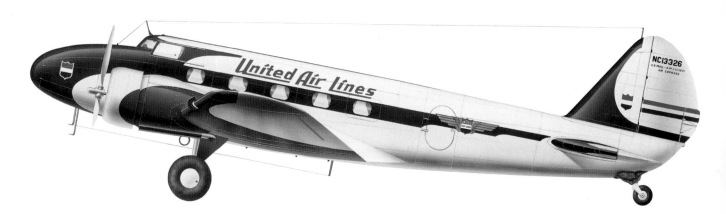

air power in a global war
raining destruction

On April 26, 1937, during the Spanish Civil War, the world saw the new horrors that air power was capable of when more than 40 Luftwaffe bombers devastated the town of Guernica, killing a third of the population and destroying seventy per cent of the town. It was a chilling prelude to the most destructive conflict in human history.

Left: *An RAF Short Stirling bomber is prepared for a mission. Introduced in 1941, but later overshadowed by the Avro Lancaster, the Stirling gave a good account of itself in service.*
Above: *Cities across Europe were devastated by the new heavy bombers developed since the end of World War I.*

Two years later it was Poland's turn to face the ferocity of *Blitzkrieg*—"lightning war." On September 1, 1939, 366 Luftwaffe aircraft, including Junkers Ju 87 "Stuka" dive bombers and three groups of 100 Heinkel He 111 heavy bombers, rained destruction on Poland's factories, airfields, towns and troop concentrations in preparation for attacks by ground forces. The Polish air force offered brave but futile resistance—its antiquated fighters were no match for state-of-the-art German air power.

When Britain declared war on Germany on September 3, the Royal Air Force (RAF) had a bomber fleet which included ten squadrons of Vickers Wellingtons, ten squadrons of Handley Page Hampdens, and nine squadrons of Armstrong Whitworth Whitleys. The Wellington was the first RAF bomber to attack Germany. On December 18, 24 Wellingtons from Nos.9, 37 and 149 squadrons attacked German ships in their home ports. Half did not return.

Top right: *A formation of Bristol Beaufighters over the coast of England.*
Bottom right: *A striking picture of a Royal Air Force Handley Page Hampden. This four-seat bomber was also used as a torpedo bomber and a minelayer.*
Below: *Vickers Wellington bombers of the RAF's No 30 Operational Training Unit. This early World War II bomber was designed by the legendary aircraft designer Sir Barnes Wallis.*

Further north, Finland was about to be shaken by Soviet air power. On November 30, the Red Army attacked with over 1000 aircraft including Tupolev SB-2 high speed bombers, Ilyushin DB-3 medium bombers, Tupolev TB-3 heavy bombers, and Polikarpov I-16 fighters. The Finnish Air Force faced them with a mere 114 operational aircraft, which included antiquated Fokker D.XXI and Bristol Bulldog fighters, Blackburn Ripon seaplanes, and Junkers K.43 light bombers. The Finns fought back bravely, but by March 1940 the weight of the Red Army's offensive was overwhelming and an armistice was signed on March 13, 1940.

Three days later, in a minor action compared with what was to come, the Luftwaffe hit the Orkney Islands, killing one civilian. Four nights later British Whitleys and Hampdens attacked a German seaplane base at Hörnum on Sylt in retaliation. On the ground, Adolf Hitler continued his territorial aggrandisement, attacking Denmark and Norway on April 9. Denmark's small air force, which included Gloster Gauntlet, Hawker Nimrod, and Fokker D.XXI fighters, proved useless against the Luftwaffe. Across the Skagerrak, Norwegian Gloster Gladiator fighters were having an equally tough time.

The capture of airfields at Trondheim and Stavanger in Norway allowed the Luftwaffe to operate their long-range Focke Wulf Fw 200 Condor maritime bombers against British shipping in the Atlantic (supplemented later by operations from bases on the French coast). German anti-shipping efforts were reinforced by Heinkel He 177 four-engined bombers, which could deliver torpedoes, bombs or even the HS-293A anti-ship missile—first used on August 27, 1943, to sink the Royal Navy corvette HMS *Egret*.

Left: *A Focke Wulf Fw 200 Condor of the Luftwaffe. This aircraft was used for long-range maritime attack during the Battle of the Atlantic. It could also act as a reconnaissance platform, searching out targets for U-boat attack.*
Above: *One of the best fighter aircraft of World War II, the Messerschmitt Bf 109.*

Allies in retreat

With the conquest of Denmark and Norway complete, Hitler set his sights on France. He ordered a lightning advance through the Low Countries, outflanking the Maginot line—a series of fortifications built to defend France against Germany. On May 10, 1940, the Nazi hammer struck the Netherlands, and then Belgium. Over 4000 aircraft took part, including Stukas, Junkers Ju 88 light bombers, Dornier Do 17 and He 111 medium bombers, and Messerschmitt Bf 109 and Bf 110 fighters. The operation against the Low Countries would also see the first ever use of gliders for landing troops and equipment. In the face of this onslaught, the combined Dutch, Belgian and French air forces, along with the RAF squadrons based on the European continent, could field 2330 aircraft—two-thirds of which were obsolete. At the same time Britain intensified its bombing of Germany, attacking oil and steel installations in Germany's Ruhr valley.

Belgium fell on May 26, its air force smashed. The *Blitzkrieg* steamroller now turned on the 400,000 British and French troops who were surrounded with their backs to the English Channel at Dunkirk. Supermarine Spitfire, Hawker Hurricane, Boulton Paul Defiant, and Blenheim fighters tried to fight off the Luftwaffe aircraft strafing the soldiers on the beaches, while the troops were evacuated by an armada of Navy and privately-owned ships. By June 4, 336,000 troops were back in the UK, but most of their equipment had been left behind. No sooner had Dunkirk surrendered than Paris came under attack, falling on June 14.

The Battle of Britain

With most of Europe under the Nazi flag, Hitler turned his attentions to Britain: but he knew the planned invasion of the British Isles, code-named "Operation Sea Lion," would be difficult. Almost 3000 Luftwaffe aircraft were ranged against Britain, including 1300 He 111, Ju 88 and Do 17 bombers; 280 Ju 87 dive bombers, and 790 Bf 109 and Bf 110 fighters. The RAF had just 640 Hurricane and Spitfire fighters to defend Britain's shores, yet the new science of radar, which could give advanced warning of air attack, would tip the balance in favor of "the few." Heavy Luftwaffe bombing raids began on August 8. Soon Bf 109 pilots were complaining to Hermann Goering, the head of the Luftwaffe, that their role escorting the bombers was hindering their efforts to hit back at the RAF fighters. But it was the losses incurred by the bomber force as they attacked RAF airfields and military targets in England that led Goering to change tactics, ordering the Luftwaffe to bomb civilian targets instead. This was his great mistake. Although German bombers made a huge attack against London on September 7, the RAF's airfields were now relatively free from Luftwaffe raids, and the fighters could engage the enemy to full effect. The Germans took heavy losses, and Operation Sea Lion was indefinitely postponed. RAF Fighter Command, whose pilots included participants from Canada, the USA, Poland, and Czechoslovakia, had won the Battle of Britain.

Key targets

But the bombing of the UK was by no means over. From November 1940, the Luftwaffe

Left top: *A Heinkel He 111 rains bombs on Warsaw, Poland.*
Left bottom: *Exiled Poles formed fighter squadrons in Britain, taking on the hated Luftwaffe in Spitfires.*
Below: *Fleet Air Arm Fairey Swordfish torpedo bombers played a vital part in the sinking of the German battleship* Bismarck.

attacked urban and industrial centers across Britain at night. Using radio-direction technology, bombers were guided to cities like Coventry, which was hit on the night of November 14/15, killing and injuring over 1100 people. London, Southampton, Bristol, Plymouth, and Liverpool suffered similar treatment. By May 1941, 40,553 people had been killed by 18,000 tons (18,288 tonnes) of high explosives.

Yet, the Fleet Air Arm was already taking the war to the Axis. Italy, under the Fascist leader Benito Mussolini, had declared war on the UK on June 10, 1940. On the night of November 11/12, 21 Fairey Swordfish torpedo bombers hit the Italian fleet in Taranto harbor. The battleship *Littorio* was sent to the bottom (although later re-floated in the shallow water) along with the battleships *Conte di Cavour* and *Caio Duillo*.

Greece and the Balkans

With his plan to complete the conquest of Western Europe checked, Hitler turned south. On March 1, 1941, German troops entered Bulgaria. Five squadrons of RAF Hurricanes were hurriedly sent to Greece to oppose any German advance. Just 500 Greek, Yugoslav, and British aircraft faced 1200 Luftwaffe aircraft. By the end of April Greece had surrendered and most of the British forces had been evacuated to Crete. On May 20, however, Junkers Ju 52 transports dropped paratroops, while 650 bombers and fighters attacked Crete's airfields, leaving only seven RAF fighters able to defend the island on the night of the invasion.

Aircraft improvements

Victory in the Battle of Britain had given the RAF a massive boost in morale, and important improvements in armament began. In 1941, the upgraded Spitfire Mk VC fighter entered service, equipping 71 squadrons, and was joined by the Hurricane Mk IIC fighter-bomber which could carry 1000lb (454kg) of bombs. These aircraft were used to harass Luftwaffe aircraft and bases in France and the Low Countries. In the west, RAF Coastal Command had improved its abilities to frustrate the German navy's U-boat submarines which were attacking British merchant ship convoys. Whitleys fitted with Air-to-Surface Vessel (ASV) radars could see U-boats traveling on the

Below: *The Battle of Taranto. The Swordfish was also instrumental in the attack on this Italian harbor on November 11 and 12, 1940. A force of 21 Swordfishes sank three Italian battleships in the port.*

Left: *Russian aircraft such as this Polikarpov I-153 would be vastly outclassed by the Axis powers during the Nazi invasion of the Soviet Union in June 1941.*
Above: *Arguably the most famous fighter aircraft in World War II. Reginald J. Mitchell's outstanding Supermarine Spitfire began its war on October 16, 1939, when RAF Spitfires shot down two Junkers Ju 88 bombers attacking Rosyth Naval Base in Scotland.*

surface at night or in bad weather. Consolidated PBY Catalina flying boats purchased from the United States could carry the ASV radar and depth charges. With the Catalina's impressive range, large tracts of the Atlantic could now be watched by the RAF, although many parts of the ocean were still unreachable.

Operation Barbarossa

On June 22, 1941, Hitler invaded the Soviet Union. Three Army Groups drove 50 miles (80km) into the USSR as Operation Barbarossa began, supported by 200 Stukas, 500 Ju 88, He 111 and Do 17 bombers, and 600 Bf 109E/F fighters. Only small numbers of hopelessly outdated I-16 fighters took off to meet the German advance. On the first day, the Soviets admitted to losing 1200 aircraft. This massive air superiority enabled He 111 and Ju 88 bombers to attack Moscow with high-explosive bombs and incendiary weapons.

On December 6, Georgi Zhukov, commander of the Red Army's Central Front, pushed the German advance back from the Soviet capital. Recovering from the surprise invasion, the Red Army rushed new aircraft into service, including LaGG-3, MiG-3, and Yakovlev Yak-1 fighters, Ilyushin Il-2 "Sturmovik" ground attack aircraft and Il-4 bombers. But the Luftwaffe was also

Erich Hartmann, the Ace of Aces

Erich Hartmann is credited as being the most successful fighter pilot in history. By the end of the war, the Luftwaffe Bf 109 pilot had shot down 353 aircraft. Hartmann said that the secret of his success was to "get close (and shoot) when he fills the entire windscreen, then you can't possibly miss." When his aircraft was attacked from behind he would send his accompanying wingman to dive low in front of him while he got behind the enemy to attack. These tactics might not have worked but for his superb eyesight, quick reflexes, and calm combat temperament.

Hartmann's efforts won him the Third Reich's highest decoration, the Knight's Cross with Oak Leaves, Swords and Diamonds. As the war drew to a close, like many Luftwaffe pilots, he headed west to surrender to the British and American armies as the Soviets approached Berlin. The British duly handed him over to the Red Army. He was tried as a war criminal and spent ten years in a Soviet labor camp, being released in 1955 to return to Germany. He was soon back in the pilot's seat with the new West German air force, commanding its first all-jet fighter squadron. He died in 1995.

Right: *The most successful fighter pilot of World War II, Erich Hartmann is pictured here in discussion with Major Gerhard Barkhorn, another Luftwaffe ace who himself notched up 301 kills in 1104 missions.*

Left top: *One of the most famous aircraft of the Eastern Front was the Soviet Ilyushin Il-2 "Sturmovik." The Sturmovik would later make life singularly unpleasant for German tanks and vehicles, but was vulnerable to fighter attack.*

Above: *A Nakajima B5N "Kate" torpedo bomber races down the flight deck of a Japanese aircraft carrier early in the Pacific war.*

improving its fleet with upgraded versions of the Do 217, He 111, Ju 88 and Ju 52. A long and bitter war raged across the vast expanses of the Eastern Front. Thanks largely to Stalin's poor judgement, the Red Army had originally been taken by surprise at the invasion, but Hitler misjudged the tenacity of the Russian people.

War in the Pacific

Following Hitler's Blitzkrieg example, the Japanese made a dramatic attack on the US naval base at Pearl Harbor in Hawaii on December 7, 1941, taking Japan to war against the world's most powerful economy. The attack was begun at 0600 by Commander Mitsuo Fuchida, leading a wave of Aichi D3A1 dive-bombers, Nakajima B5N bombers, and Mitsubishi A6M2 Zero fighters. He

was followed by a second wave, led by Lieutenant Commander Shigekazu Shimazaki with D3A1, B5N2, and A6M2 aircraft, which struck at 0715. By the end of the day the battleships *Arizona* and *Oklahoma* were destroyed, and *Nevada, West Virginia, California, Tennessee, Maryland,* and *Pennsylvania* were damaged. A host of other vessels, six Catalina flying boats, and 42 United States Army Air Force (USAAF) aircraft were also destroyed. More than 3500 American servicemen were killed or injured. Shortly afterwards, Germany joined her Axis ally and declared war on the USA. Also on December 7, Japan attacked the British forces in Malaya (Malaysia), landing at Kota Bharu. The RAF's Blenheims, Lockheed Hudsons, and Vickers Vildebeest could make little impact on the landings. Three days later, aircraft

Left: *The Day of Infamy: Pearl Harbor, Hawaii, December 7, 1941. US warships are set ablaze while the Japanese Navy conducts one of the most audacious air attacks in history.*

Right: *Handley Page Halifax bombers from the RAF's 35 Squadron in flight. The aircraft was the first British four-engined bomber to attack Germany during a raid on Hamburg on March 12 and 13, 1941.*

from the Imperial Japanese Navy would attack British ships which were attempting to prevent any amphibious landing by the Japanese on Malaya. The battleship HMS *Prince of Wales* and the battlecruiser HMS *Repulse* were sunk by Japanese bombers. This ignominious defeat would spell the end of the heavy warship as the decisive weapon in naval combat. The Pacific war would be decided by aircraft and their aircraft carriers. The Japanese made steady progress across the Malay peninsula and by February 15, 1942, Singapore had surrendered.

Allies strengthened

RAF Bomber Command had its punch strengthened in 1941 with the introduction of the Avro Manchester, Short Stirling, and Handley Page Halifax bombers. The force received a further fillip on February 22, 1942, when Sir Arthur "Bomber" Harris assumed command. Harris urged forward the introduction of the new four-engined Avro Lancaster, a development of the twin-engined Manchester, along with new navigation and bombing equipment to improve accuracy.

The struggle against Hitler in the west was also boosted by the arrival in England of the first units of the USAAF. From May 1942, Boeing B-17 Flying Fortress and Consolidated B-24 Liberator bombers began to deploy on airfields around eastern England. USAAF bombing doctrine dictated daylight attacks with formations of heavily-armed bombers defending themselves with their own guns, bereft of fighter protection. The RAF opted instead for night raids, and on the night of March 10/11 the Avro Lancaster made its combat debut with No 44 squadron attacking the German industrial city of Essen.

U.S. naval setbacks

Keen to strike back after Pearl Harbor, the United States Pacific Fleet ordered the carrier USS *Langley* to sea against the Japanese Imperial navy. On February 28, 1942, the *Langley* was to land 32 Curtiss P-40E Warhawk fighters on the Indonesian island of Java, but the carrier's movements were detected by Japanese planes and she was sunk along with her aircraft. That day the Japanese invaded Java, landing on the north coast of the island. Extending their grip southwards, the Japanese attacked the

Bombing the Rising Sun: the Doolittle raids

To avenge themselves for the Japanese attack at Pearl Harbor, the US decided on an audacious long-range attack on the Japanese home islands on April 18, 1942. Masterminded by USAAF Lieutenant Colonel Jimmy Doolittle, North American B-25 Mitchell bombers were positioned on the deck of the USS *Hornet* ready to strike at Tokyo. No one had ever attempted a mission launching twin-engined bombers from a carrier before. Although the Mitchells could take off from the ship, they could not make carrier landings on their return and therefore had to fly on to land at friendly airfields in China.

At 0800 operations got underway. During the preparations, a Japanese fishing vessel was spotted by a US Navy patrol plane. Nervous that the boat might have spotted the plane, jeopardizing the element of surprise, it was sunk. On the deck of *Hornet*, the bomber crews heard the order "Army pilots, man your planes" sent by Vice Admiral William F. Halsey, the flag officer in charge of the operation. By 0920 the aircraft were underway. All of the bombers reached their targets around Tokyo, Yokohama, and Nagoya, dropping their bombs on oil tanks, factories, and military installations, although the damage inflicted was relatively light. The aircraft then flew to China—and Russia, where some landed accidentally.

The raids did little physical damage, but gave a morale boost to the American public. The Japanese lost their sense of invulnerability, and the Japanese generals felt obliged to keep back some of their warplanes for home defence. The Japanese never made significant attacks against the mainland United States—but not for want of trying. On November 3, 1944, over 9000 balloons with bombs attached were launched into the upper reaches of the atmosphere, the winds carrying them to the United States. One thousand reached their destination, landing in several states including Alaska, Washington, and Oregon. On September 9, 1942, an attempt by a Japanese seaplane launched from a surfaced submarine to attack the forests of Oregon in the hope of causing catastrophic fires was equally fruitless.

Left: *A North American B-25 Mitchell bomber gets aloft from the flight deck of the USS* Hornet.
Top: *Mitchells crowd the* Hornet's *flight deck. With a shout of "Army pilots, man your planes," the bombers flew towards their targets in Japan. The Japanese retaliated against the US mainland with balloon bombs and isolated seaplane attacks.*

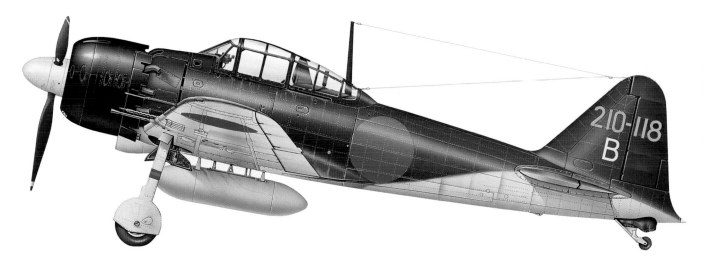

Above: *The most famous Japanese fighter of World War II, the Mitsubishi A6M3 "Zero". This aircraft was used from the attack on Pearl Harbor right up to the end of the Pacific War.*
Below: *Douglas SBD Dauntless dive-bombers lined up on the deck of USS* Yorktown.
Right: *An RAF Avro Lancaster bomber is prepared for a raid. Last-minute instructions are issued by the Flight Commander to his crew.*

Australian port of Darwin on February 19, 1942, with warplanes launched from the carriers *Akagi* and *Kaga*. They destroyed an Australian troopship, a freighter and an ammunition dump, a US destroyer, seaplane tender, several corvettes and tankers, and devastated the surrounding city.

Battle of the Coral Sea

The first major confrontation between the US and Japanese fleets took place between May 7 and 8, 1942, during the Battle of the Coral Sea, northeast of Australia—the first naval battle where the two fleets never saw each other. The Japanese carriers *Shokaku, Zuikaku,* and *Shoho* deployed 267 B5N,

D3A, and A6M aircraft, along with a clutch of land-based aircraft from Rabaul in Papua New Guinea. The US force comprised 103 aircraft including Douglas TBD Devastator torpedo bombers, Douglas SBD Dauntless dive-bombers, and Grumman Wildcat fighters from the carriers USS *Lexington* and USS *Yorktown*. These aircraft tore *Shoho* apart, but *Lexington* suffered serious damage from attacks by aircraft from *Shokaku* and *Zuikaku*. Disabled and floundering in the water, *Lexington* was sunk by the USS *Phelps* with several torpedoes after her crew had been taken off. *Yorktown* also suffered damage, leaving the USS *Enterprise* and USS *Hornet* as the only combat-

capable carriers in the Pacific theater. Yet some good had come of the battle. The US Navy had prevented a Japanese advance on Port Moresby in southern Papua New Guinea, which otherwise could have become a base for a Japanese invasion of Australia.

Back in Europe, strengthened with new aircraft, Harris mounted the first 1000-bomber raid on the night of May 30/31, 1942. Operation Millennium attacked Cologne in the Rhineland with 1,046 aircraft, 898 of which hit their targets at a cost of 40 planes.

Midway

As the RAF turned up the heat on the Third Reich, America got ready to embark on its decisive battle in the Pacific. The Japanese coveted the strategic island of Midway as an addition to their empire. It would form part of a defensive perimeter stretching across the Pacific from the Aleutian Islands in the north down to Wake Island and the Marshall and Gilbert islands in the south. It would also extend the Japanese early warning network and serve as a future base for operations against Hawaii.

But the Americans had intercepted Japanese signals and cracked their codes. As Admiral Isoroku Yamamoto, commander of the Japanese Combined Fleet, positioned the *Akagi*, *Kaga*, *Hiryu*, *Soryu,* and *Junyo* fleet carriers, along with numerous light carriers, battleships, destroyers, and escorts, the US Navy was preparing to attack. *Enterprise, Hornet,* and *Yorktown*—the latter having completed rapid repairs—were lying in wait with 203 torpedo bombers, dive bombers, and fighters as well as aircraft based on the island itself. Playing a game of hide-and-seek with the Japanese fleet, the American aircraft struck, sinking *Soryu* and

Kaga on 4 June. *Hiryu* and *Akagi* were both damaged and scuttled the next day.

Flushed with its gains, the United States pressed ahead with the invasion of Guadalcanal in the Solomon Islands on August 7, 1942, overwhelming the Japanese defences. Once on the island, US Marines worked hard to complete an airfield that would house US Marine Grumman F4F Wildcat fighters and Dauntlesses to fend off the persistent Japanese air attacks.

Fightback over Europe

By the summer of 1942 the bombing offensive against Nazi-occupied Europe gained momentum. On August 17, USAAF B-17E bombers attacked Rouen in France, the first US bombing mission flown from the UK. Two days later, 24 US aircraft supported the disastrous raid on Dieppe.

The Allies had planned to invade France at Dieppe using a force of largely Canadian troops. Spitfire Mk V fighters, Blenheims, and Douglas Boston light bombers attacked targets around Dieppe and provided support for the landing troops. Meanwhile B-17s attacked the Luftwaffe airfield at Abbeville. Initially only a small number of Bf 109 fighters and Focke Wulf Fw 190 fighter-bombers appeared to counter the Allied attack, but by the afternoon the Germans were sending large formations of Do 217 bombers to attack the troops, which were soon cut to pieces. The operation was abandoned. Air power failed at Dieppe because there was little communication between the landing forces and the aircraft. Moreover, there were too few ground attack aircraft to destroy battlefield targets.

North Africa

Two weeks earlier in North Africa, Erwin Rommel, commander of the Afrika Korps, had begun to advance east towards the Allied forces in Egypt. Commander-in-Chief of RAF Middle East Command, Air Chief Marshal Sir Arthur Tedder

ordered sorties to protect the British 8th Army as Rommel's forces advanced on Tobruk, west of El Alamein. On October 23, General Bernard Montgomery, commanding the British 8th Army, attacked the German and Italian positions at El Alamein, supported by six squadrons of Wellingtons. These were joined by RAF and South African Air Force (SAAF) Hurricane Mk IIC tank-busters which went hunting for enemy armor. By November 4, the Axis line had been broken and the Allies advanced to Mareth which was liberated in March 1943. The Axis armies were running out of supplies, because their ships bound for the ports of North Africa were subjected to constant air attacks. The last small pocket of Axis-held territory in Tunisia surrendered to the Allies on May 12, 1943.

Massive air power

The Pacific shook to another great conflagration a month later at the Battle of Santa Cruz Island, southeast of Guadalcanal. The *Zuiho* fleet carrier was hit by 16 Dauntlesses from the *Enterprise*, while the *Shokaku* was badly damaged. The US Navy lost 74 aircraft and *Hornet*. *Enterprise*, now the only American carrier in the Pacific, was also badly scarred.

Left: British troops wave to their airborne comrade. Allied air power was crucial to the successes in the deserts of North Africa. Fighter-bombers would operate in "cab ranks" where they would circle, waiting for targets to become available, providing a constant air power umbrella.

Below: Sharks' teeth such as those on these RAF Curtiss P-40s were popular decorations on combat aircraft during World War II.

On November 1, US Marines landed at Cape Torokina, on the central southern coast of Bougainville in the Solomons, accompanied by 21 B-24 bombers which hit the airfields at Kahili and Kara. Curtiss P-40 Kittyhawk, Bell P-39 Airacobra, and Lockheed P-38 Lightning fighters joined the battle and the US Navy brought in two new carriers, USS *Essex* and USS *Bunker Hill*, with another 200 aircraft. The invasion of Tarawa and Makin Atolls in the Gilbert Islands got underway on November 20, on the same day that the last pockets of resistance in Bougainville were crushed. It was the largest concentration of naval air power in history. The strategy of rolling back the Japanese Empire by taking only key islands, known as "island hopping," was now paying dividends.

German losses

As the Japanese lost ground in the Pacific, the Germans were having problems on the Eastern Front. In the fall of 1942 the German 6th Army was attacking Soviet forces in the city of Stalingrad, but the Soviets were resisting desperately. By November 23, the Soviets had counter-attacked, encircling the German forces laying siege to the city. The Germans tried to re-supply their beleaguered army by air, but the landing zones for their transports soon came under a ferocious Red Army artillery barrage. Soviet aircraft attacked the airfields, preventing take-off, and their fighters shot down many of the lumbering transports once they were in the air. Behind the German lines in Stalingrad, what was not destroyed by Soviet guns was destroyed by the Russian winter. At the beginning of February 1943 the German 6th Army was forced to surrender.

A few days before, the USAAF had carried out its biggest strike on Germany to date when 91 heavy bombers attacked Wilhelmshaven. A box formation had been adopted to give the bombers

Left: *A formation of USAAF Flying Fortresses. These aircraft, which were also operated by the RAF, could bring thirteen 0.5in (12.7mm) machine guns to the fight, and drop up to 7983kg (17,600lb) of bombs.*

Right: *A Lancaster with its revolutionary "bouncing bomb." Code-named "Upkeep," this weapon, designed by Barnes Wallis, would be the integral component to Operation Chastise, the destruction of the hydroelectric dams in Germany's Ruhr valley industrial heartland.*

Below: *Wing Commander Guy Gibson of the RAF's 617 Squadron surveys the damage done to the Möhne dam after he led the squadron in the "Dambusters" raid of May 16, 1943.*

the highest possible mutual protection from attack. Meanwhile, smaller aircraft were making a big difference. On April 13, 1943, USAAF Republic P-47 Thunderbolt fighter-bombers entered combat for the first time, hitting targets in St Omer, France. They were joined by aircraft from the 66th Fighter Wing of the USAAF VIII Fighter Command. By the end of the year the USAAF and the RAF had 2200 Spitfires, Hurricanes, Hawker Typhoon fighter-bombers, P-38s, and North American P-31 Mustang fighters on UK airfields.

Determined to obliterate Germany's industry, Bomber Harris pulled off one of his most dramatic raids on the night of May 16/17, 1943, when 19 Lancasters from RAF 617 squadron under Wing Commander Guy Gibson attacked the dams on the Möhne, Eder, Sorpe, and Schwelme rivers, where hydroelectric power stations supplied energy to factories in the Ruhr valley. Specially designed 9250lb (4196kg) bouncing bombs were used which breached the Möhne and Eder dams. Eight Lancasters were lost during the raid.

Over the Atlantic, an increased number of B-24 Very Long Range (VLR) Liberators was having an effect on the Battle of the Atlantic. The tally of merchant shipping destroyed by U-boats fell from 814,000 tons (827,024 tonnes) in the month of November 1942 to 130,000 tons (132,080 tonnes) in the last six months of 1943. The VLR aircraft, along with Catalinas, Sunderlands, and Wellingtons, were now based in Iceland to close the mid-Atlantic blind spot.

Kursk

Back in the Soviet Union the Axis forces were being pushed westwards. On July 5, 1943, in Operation Zitadelle, German Panzer divisions attacked the Kursk salient—a "bulge" in the Red Army front line. Stuka dive-bombers and powerful Henschel Hs 129 anti-tank aircraft supported the offensive effectively, but the Soviets ground down the German assault with deep field defences, and then counter-attacked with massive tank armies. The Red Army brought over 3000 tanks into battle, making it the biggest tank battle in history—and they were supported by 20,000 artillery pieces. The German commander asked for permission to withdraw his forces in the face of the Soviet counter-attack, but he was overruled by Hitler. The Soviets advanced northwards out of the

Left: *An RAF Consolidated B-24 Liberator helps to protect an Atlantic convoy in 1944.*
Above: *The Armstrong Whitworth Albemarle was initially designed as a bomber, but spent most of its service life as a glider tug and special transport aircraft.*
Below: *An RAF Lancaster unleashes bombs from its weapons bay. This aircraft could drop up to 14,000lb (6350kg) of ordnance.*

salient towards Orel. In the air, the once total air superiority of the Luftwaffe on the Eastern Front disappeared, and the Germans lost 900 aircraft in the week-long battle.

Tightening the knot

Although the Dieppe raid had been a disaster, the Allies were finally able to take European territory from the Axis on July 10, 1943, when they invaded Sicily. Tedder had 104 squadrons of Spitfires, Bristol Beaufighters, Hurricanes, Mosquitoes, P-38s, P-39s, and P-51s at his

disposal, along with 95 bomber squadrons, which included Bostons, Martin A-30 Baltimores, Mitchells, Martin B-26 Marauders, Blenheims and Halifaxes, B-17s, and B-24s. Halifax, Armstrong Whitworth Albemarle, and Douglas DC-3 Dakota transports also proved vital.

The defeats at Kursk and Sicily, and the increasing weight of the bombing campaign against Germany, prompted much soul-searching in the Luftwaffe. Many fighter units were redeployed from Italy or the Eastern Front for the defence of the Reich. Ground attack units that had

Right: *Soviet pilots disembark from their Yakovlev Yak-9D fighters.*
Below: *The Junkers Ju 88 was one of the most versatile warplanes in history, and by the middle of World War II had become the Luftwaffe's most important tactical bomber.*
Far right: *A formation of US Navy Grumman F4F Wildcats. This aircraft participated in all of the major battles in the Pacific theater and also saw service in North Africa.*

previously flown Stukas were upgraded to fly Bf 109F/Gs, and night operations increased as the Germans began a largely ineffectual campaign against the Soviet rail network.

By September 3, the British Eighth Army, which had tasted success in North Africa, was conducting landings from Sicily across the Straits of Messina, with heavy air support from RAF and USAAF bombers. On September 9, US troops landed at Salerno. The Italian government had surrendered to the Allies on the previous day, but a substantial German army remained in the country.

Further north, on the night of November 18/19, Harris sent more than 400 bombers to attack Berlin. A similarly heavy raid was undertaken against Mannheim—the first occasion

on which two heavy raids on the Reich were performed simultaneously. The RAF was especially keen to destroy Germany's oil supplies. With its bid to capture the oil fields in the southern USSR thwarted, the Reich was running on a finite fuel tank, and the lack of aviation fuel would eventually ground the Luftwaffe.

The Allied hands on the Reich's throat were tightening. The Allies now had a foothold in Italy while the Soviets moved slowly but surely towards Hitler's front door. On January 15, 1944, 1200 aircraft from the Red Banner Baltic Fleet and the Soviet Shock Army liberated Russia's second city, Leningrad. Soviet aircraft such as Yakovlev Yak-9 fighter-bombers and Lavochkin La-5FN fighters routed the depleted Luftwaffe,

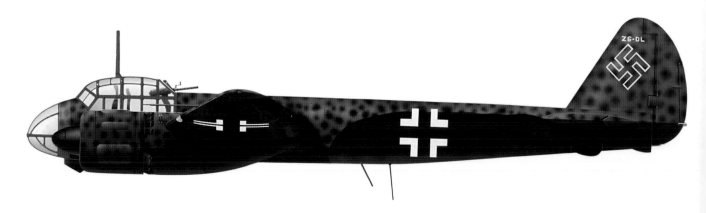

killing experienced pilots like Heinz Schmidt and Max Stolz, who had downed 173 and 198 enemy aircraft respectively.

In the Mediterranean the relative ease with which the Allies established themselves received a setback at Anzio, south of Rome. The landing at Anzio was intended to hit the right flank of the German Army which stretched from the River Garigliano in the southwest, northwards to Ortona on the Adriatic coast. Prior to the landings at Anzio on January 22 the Allies had attacked airfields in central Italy, preventing the Luftwaffe from carrying out a single reconnaissance mission. This allowed 30,000 American and British troops to land largely unopposed from the air. But a delay in the advance allowed the Germans to move armour forward to prevent the Allies from moving off the beaches. Meanwhile the Luftwaffe moved Do 217 and Ju 88 bombers to attack the Allied forces on the ground. On March 15, the Allies attempted to force the German line, bombing the monastery at Monte Cassino in one of the bitterest battles of World War II. The German defensive line stood firm until May when the Allies finally broke through. The Anzio pocket was duly freed and on June 4 Rome was liberated.

Operation Flintlock

In the Pacific, the United States undertook Operation Flintlock on January 31, 1944, invading Kwajalein and Namur in the Marshall Islands. Air support was provided from six fleet and six light carriers, with Wildcats and Grumman F6F Hellcat naval fighters. In the six days it took to capture the Marshall Islands, 150 Japanese aircraft were destroyed at a cost of 49 aircraft. The next target was the Caroline Islands. Truk atoll received the first American air strikes, in which US Navy pilots destroyed 125 Japanese aircraft parked nose-to-tail on an airstrip. Another 30 merchant vessels, a cruiser and three destroyers were also hit. Although the Japanese were receiving new aircraft including the Mitsubishi A6M5 "Zeke" fighter-bomber, the Yokosuka D4Y3 "Judy" dive bomber, and the Nakajima B6N1 "Jill" torpedo/attack bomber, they were being flown by inexperienced crews because so many veteran pilots had been killed.

On June 1, 1944, the massive Boeing B-29 Superfortress, arguably the most advanced aircraft of World War II, entered service with the 58th Very Heavy Bombardment Wing. Four 2200hp (1641kW) engines propelled this aircraft to speeds of 358mph (576km/h) at altitudes of 20,000ft (7620m). A remarkable 3970 aircraft were

Left: *A Boeing B-29 on a Pacific island airfield.*
Below: *A Spitfire of the RAF's 453 Squadron in invasion markings on June 6, 1944—D-Day.*

produced by Boeing, Bell, and Martin. Because of its range, this aircraft was reserved for the vast Pacific theater, and before long the bomber was raining destruction on the Japanese home islands.

D-Day

Four days later, on the other side of the world, the largest invasion force that the world had ever seen prepared to land on Europe's doorstep. Operation Overlord landed 145,000 Allied troops on the beaches of Normandy on "D-Day," June 6, 1944. To confuse the Germans, a huge deception operation had been planned. On the night of June 5/6, Lancasters from 617 squadron dropped thousands of strips of silver foil, codenamed "Window," to confuse German radar. "Window" formed massive slow moving clouds which drifted across the channel mimicking the radar signature of an invasion fleet. Halifaxes and Stirlings performed similar missions off

Boulogne, which confused the Germans about where the invasion was coming from, and therefore where best to deploy their defences.

As the assault got underway, USAAF transports including Douglas DC-3s of the USAAF 11th Troop Carrier Command dropped paratroops behind the beachheads. Meanwhile Stirlings, Halifaxes, Albemarles, and RAF Dakotas dropped 4310 paratroops and towed 100 gliders to their targets. Allied fighters provided cover, although the German air defence had already been weakened. Only 500 serviceable aircraft of all types were available to the Luftwaffe for the air defence of the Normandy area. Prior to the invasion, the Allies had spent much time softening up the Luftwaffe, which was already on its knees. Between January and June 1944, 25 percent of the Luftwaffe fighter force was destroyed either in the ground or in the air. At the same time, the German aircraft industry was battered to a pulp.

Left: *Allied troops in high spirits as Operation Overlord gets under way, displaying their thoughts on their mission on the side of a glider.*
Right: *A USAAF Martin B-26 Marauder in invasion stripes.*
Below: *A Japanese aircraft blazes seawards in a clouded sky after attempting to attack the USS Kitkun Bay.*

The Development of the Jet Engine

As war raged, the work of a few specialists, working in deepest secrecy on opposing sides, was to mould the shape of warplanes to come.

Frank Whittle was born in Coventry in 1907. While studying at the RAF Staff College at Cranwell, Whittle was introduced to the thorny dilemma of the time: airplanes flew faster and more efficiently at high altitudes, but contemporary piston engines could not perform efficiently at that height because the air was too thin. In 1929, aged just 21, Whittle presented a thesis on the jet engine. Whittle's engine drew air through a compressor and into a combustion chamber where it was mixed with fuel and ignited. As the hot gases exited the rear of the engine, the aircraft was propelled forward. As the gases escaped they turned a turbine, which drove a shaft that in turn operated the compressor. This concept was patented in 1930, but the Air Ministry were not impressed. From late 1935, Whittle began to make detailed designs for his experimental engine, which he named the Whittle Unit (WU). The following year he established Power Jets Ltd to advance the building of the engine. Fortunately the Air Ministry finally took an interest just as Power Jets Ltd ran out of money. But the work did not go smoothly. In the WU's first test in April 1937 the engine ran out of control, as the combustion was too intense. A redesign using ten separate combustion chambers went some way to alleviate this problem, but the problem recurred on the WU's second test run a year later.

The British Air Ministry's hesitancy meant that Germany became the first country to fly a jet aircraft. Hans von Ohain was a PhD student at the Aerodynamic Research Institute of the University of Göttingen, where he developed a design for a simple jet turbine. In 1933 Max Hahn, the owner of an automobile repair company, built an engine to von Ohain's design which, when first tested in 1934, worked more like a flamethrower. Unperturbed, von Ohain approached Ernst Heinkel and together with

Below: *The Gloster E.28/39, the first British jet aircraft to fly, takes to the air at Farnborough in 1945.*

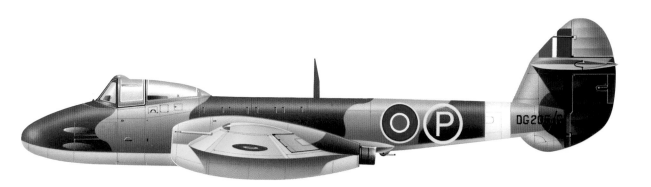

Hahn the three worked on the Heinkel Sonderentwicklung (Special Development) No.1, or HeS1 engine. In 1937 and 1938 they tested the engine with hydrogen fuel and vaporized fuel, and in 1939 the HeS3 became the first turbojet engine to operate in flight when it was attached to the underside of a Heinkel He 118 bomber. Later that year, on August 27, the Heinkel He 178 became the first aircraft to use a turbojet as its sole propulsion system.

The British jet engine was still two years behind, but Whittle had solved many of the early problems by late 1939. Approval was granted for a single-engine experimental airplane and the Gloster E.28/39, also known as the Pioneer, took off from Cranwell on May 15, 1941. On this first 17-minute flight, Flight Lieutenant Gerry Sayer took the aircraft up to 339mph (545km/h), and a later test flight reached 450mph (724km/h). The Air Ministry ordered a twin-engine interceptor and gave the contract to other companies, nationalizing Power Jets Ltd and relegating it to a research and development role. Whittle stepped down from his own company, later suffering a breakdown, and the RAF ordered him to retire on the grounds of poor health. As small compensation, Whittle received the £10,000 "Inventor Award" in 1946 for his work.

Allied wartime jet research culminated in the Gloster Meteor, which first became airborne in 1943, and the American Bell XP-59A Airacomet, which first flew in 1942.

A selfless man, Whittle distributed the award money among his colleagues at Power Jets. Although knighted in 1948, he found more appreciation in the United States and became a research professor at the US Naval Academy in Annapolis, Maryland. Sir Frank Whittle died in Baltimore in 1996.

Above: *One of the first twelve prototype Gloster Meteors.*
Below: *The Gloster Meteor was originally to have been named the "Thunderbolt," although this was changed in order to avoid confusion with the American Republic P-47.*

Prior to the landings, much effort was expended to destroy bridges in order to hamper any German reinforcement efforts once the landings got under way. Three weeks before the assault, German airfields 130 miles (209km) from the landing beaches came under attack. Once the assault began, the aerial firepower fielded by the combined air forces was immense: 15 squadrons covered the landing ships; 54 covered the beaches; 33 fighter squadrons escorted heavier bombers and glider formations; another 33 hit targets inland from the landing area while 36 provided direct air support to the invading troops. While many historians have stressed the importance of ground and naval forces during Operation Overlord, the air effort is often overlooked. In truth, the Allies' crushing air power was a key factor in the successful invasion of Normandy.

The Axis crumbles

Five days later, the decisive Battle of the Philippine Sea got under way in the Pacific. The Japanese-held islands of Saipan, Tinian, and Guam came under attack from over 200 Hellcats and Avengers, destroying 36 enemy aircraft on the ground. The next day the defending Japanese ships were attacked and US Marines were able to land on Saipan four days later. The Japanese were crumbling. The carrier *Hiyo* was hit on June 20, eventually sinking, along with *Shokaku* and *Taiho*. The carrier *Junyo* was hit by two bombs, whilst *Zuikaku* was struck along with the light carrier *Chiyoda*.

By August 1944, organized resistance was collapsing as the Allies swept through northern France. Paris was liberated on August 25; Brussels and Antwerp would follow on September 3 and 4 respectively. Allied ground efforts were reinforced with an increase in bombing raids against Germany. Although the new Messerschmitt Me 262 jet fighter and Me 163 rocket interceptor had begun to attack the bomber formations, long-range fighters were dispatched to Germany's airfields to prevent the Luftwaffe from getting airborne, while the Germans were running out of fuel and trained pilots. Hitler's Reich was being

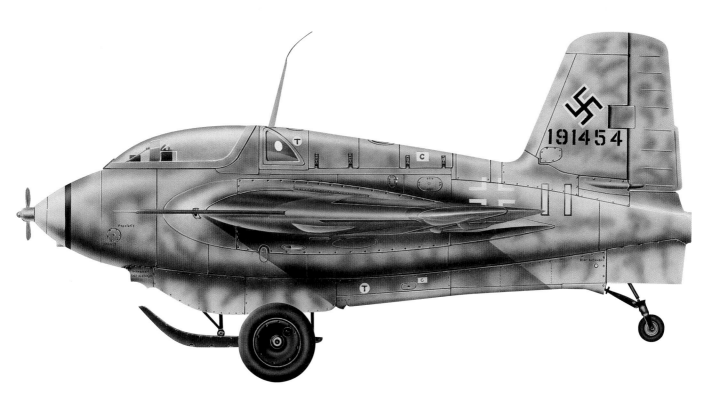

Above: *A brainchild of Dr Alexander Lippisch's "Project X" programme, the Messerschmitt Me 163 Komet was a rocket-powered defensive fighter.*
Left: *The test pilot of the first Messerschmitt Me 262, Fritz Wendel, waits on repairs to its BMW 003 turbojets.*

turned into rubble from above, and by April 1945 the Allies were running out of targets.

Firestorm

However, the lack of targets did not prevent the German city of Dresden being reduced to ashes in one of the bitterest Allied bombing raids of the war. On the eve of St Valentine's Day, 1945, a force of around 550 RAF Lancasters dropped incendiary bombs on the city, unleashing a devastating firestorm. The heat was so intense that road asphalt caught fire. The Lancaster's work was finished off at midday on February 14, when 450 USAAF Flying Fortresses bombed what was left of the city. Estimates of the dead range between 130,000 and 200,000. Exact figures are unknown as many of the victims were literally cremated alive. Dresden was a city of no strategic or military significance and before the raid it had been noted for its architectural beauty and antiquity. A similar treatment had been visited on the German industrial and port city of Hamburg on July 24, 1943. During this attack, the firestorm reached 1000°F (537°C), killing 40,000 of the city's inhabitants, most of whom were women and children. The attack was nicknamed Operation Gomorrah by the bomber crews.

The final push

On the Eastern Front, German resolve stiffened the closer the Soviets got to Berlin. To this end, the Red Army launched an offensive south towards Romania by two Soviet army groups and over 1700 aircraft from the Soviet 5th and 17th Air Armies. Romania fell three days after the offensive began on August 23. Bulgaria followed on September 8. The Luftwaffe forces in the Balkans put up a stiff fight, but were overwhelmed.

The winter of 1944/45 saw the Soviets begin their final push on Germany. On January 13, the Soviets drove towards East Prussia, meeting stiff resistance at Königsberg. Warsaw fell four days later. Further west the US 1st Army crossed the Rhine, and Cologne fell to the Allies on March 7. The Red Army captured Vienna on April 13. Three days later, the final battle of the European theatre began with the Soviet advance on Berlin. In the process their armies linked up with the Americans at Torgau. The Axis was doomed. Mussolini was assassinated by partisans on April 28. Adolf Hitler committed suicide in his Berlin bunker two days later, and by May 2 the city had fallen to the Red Army. The unconditional surrender of the German armed forces was signed by Admiral Karl Dönitz and General Alfred Jodl on

Above: *Bombs fall from a B-29 during a raid on the Japanese city of Kobe on June 5, 1945.*
Left: *The ruins of Berlin, pictured in May 1945 after the city was taken by Soviet forces.*

May 7 outside Rheims in France. The war in Europe was over.

Endgame in the Pacific

Yet the war in the Pacific was still raging. US forces attacked the Philippines on January 9, landing 67,000 troops under the command of General Douglas MacArthur on Luzon. But the 262,000 Japanese troops on the island provided stiff resistance, and a new weapon appeared on the Japanese side. The escort carrier USS *Ommaney Bay* sank after being hit by a Japanese suicide "kamikaze" attack. The USS *Kitkun Bay* and USS *Kadashan Bay* were both damaged in similar attacks, causing their retirement from the battle. It was not until March 4 that Manila was captured, by which time more than 40,000 GIs lay dead on the island, and 360 aircraft had been lost.

The efforts to persuade the Japanese high

command that defeat was inevitable received a boost on January 20, 1945, when Major General Curtis E. LeMay was appointed head of USAAF Bomber Command. Inheriting a force of Superfortresses, LeMay revised the US heavy bombing tactics, building on his experience in the European theatre. B-29s from airfields on Guam and Tinian would drop incendiary bombs on cities on the Japanese mainland to create firestorms. The defensive payload of the bombers was reduced to increase the bomb load.

LeMay's theory was put to the test on the night of March 9/10, 1945, when a raid by 334 B-29s devastated Tokyo, setting the city ablaze. Over 10 square miles (25km²) was reduced to ashes by incendiary bombs. Estimates of the dead (mainly civilians) range from 80,000 to 200,000. Similar raids were unleashed on Nagoya, Osaka, and Kobe, destroying 29 square miles (75km²) of Japan's industrial centers. The biggest bombing raid of the war so far was made on the night of May 25/26,

when B-29s eradicated over 35 square miles (90km²) of Tokyo in an incendiary raid. The destruction visited on the Japanese capital by B-29s had left half of the city flattened.

By March 14, 1945, US armed forces were ready for an assault on the tactically important island of Iwo Jima. After a fierce and bloody battle, the US 10th Army and 16 carriers took the island, which was then used as a stepping stone to Okinawa. The assault on Okinawa began on March 23 with air bombardments by over 1000 aircraft from the 13 fast carriers, six light carriers, and 19 escort carriers. The invasion, the biggest of its kind in the Pacific, began on April 1, 1945.

Final blows

On April 6, the giant Japanese battleship *Yamato* set sail from Japan. She was ordered towards the US invasion fleet at Okinawa in a desperate maritime suicide attack, in an effort to destroy as much of it as possible before being overwhelmed by US ships

Below: Japanese bomber crews relax at an airfield in Japan in 1945. Behind them stands a Mitsubishi G4M "Betty" bomber.

Above: *The Soviet La-7 was a lightweight fighter with a top speed of 422mph (680km/h).*

Below: *The mushroom cloud stretches 20,000ft (6000m) above the Japanese city of Hiroshima.*

Lucky Kokura—Unlucky Nagasaki

B-29 No. 44-27297 had cost around $639,000 at World War II prices. It entered USAAF service with the 393rd Bomb Squadron on April 19, 1945, and was later transferred to the 509th Composite Group. Named *Bock's Car* after its pilot Frederick C. Bock, it would conduct several training flights dropping a bright orange projectile called "Pumpkin."

On August 9, Pumpkin was swapped for "Fat Man"—a plutonium atomic bomb which would create the world's third nuclear explosion. Taking off from Tinian, the aircraft began to burn fuel at a higher rate than anticipated after a fuel selector switch had broken. This meant 600 lb (272 kg) of fuel in a tank as a useless dead weight, and a chronic fuel shortage.

Once airborne, the bomb was armed by connecting the firing circuits to the fuse. The aircraft was intended to bomb the city of Kokura. *Bock's Car* was supposed to rendezvous with an accompanying aircraft which carried photographic equipment. The B-29's crew circled for 40 minutes looking for the other aircraft, which they eventually spotted flying above them.

Back at Tinian the wait for *Bock's Car* was excruciating. General Thomas Farrell, who was in charge of the mission, at one point walked outside of his office to vomit. Although Kokura was the primary target, when *Bock's Car* arrived the city was obscured by cloud. Instead, the bomber flew to its second target, the port city of Nagasaki. Captain Kermit Beahan, the bomb aimer, who had turned 27 that day, got a fix on his target and the 10,000lb (4536kg) bomb was released. At 1102, the bomb exploded 1640ft (500m) above the city with a force of 21kT, killing 40,000 instantly, and injuring 60,000.

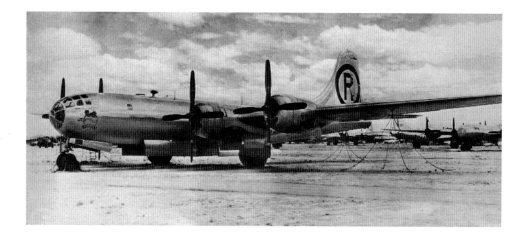

Above: Bock's Car, *the aircraft that dropped the atomic bomb on Nagasaki.*
Left: Bock's Car *would carry "Fat Man" to its target. The device weighed 10,000lb (4536kg) and had a 5ft (1.5m) diameter.*

and aircraft. But the *Yamato*'s departure was spotted by Martin PBM Mariner reconnaissance aircraft, which followed her. She was attacked by 280 carrier aircraft, including 98 Avenger torpedo bombers. Ten torpedoes, five bombs and 24 hours later, she sank taking 2498 of her crew to the bottom.

In Southeast Asia, Rangoon was finally liberated on May 2, after an amphibious landing by the 26th Indian Division. There were still a large number of Japanese troops trapped in the hinterland of Burma. Sick and malnourished but stubborn, the force was determined to break out across the Sittang River in East Burma. This was prevented by the RAF, which spent ten days battering the Japanese with over 3000 sorties, dropping 1,500,000lb (680,000kg) of bombs. The Japanese army in Burma was finally defeated by the end of July.

By mid-July the final blow of the war in the Pacific was being tested at Alamogordo in New Mexico. On July 16, a plutonium bomb code-named "Gadget" was exploded on the desert test site with a force of 20,000 tons (20,320 tonnes) of TNT. This was the culmination of the top-secret Manhattan Project (so-called because the head office of the project was in Manhattan).

Less than one month later, "Little Boy"—a different type of bomb using uranium—was exploded at 0815 on August 6 over the Japanese city of Hiroshima. It was dropped by a specially modified B-29 named *Enola Gay* after the mother of the bomber's commander, Colonel Paul Tibbets. The bomb exploded 1,900ft (580m) over the Aioi Bridge with a yield of 15 kilotons, equivalent to 15,000 tons of TNT. The blast killed 75,000 instantly—many thousands more died later from the after effects of the bomb.

Japan finally surrendered on August 14. The most costly conflict in human history ended as it began, with a dramatic and decisive air attack. The atomic explosions had closed a dramatic chapter in human history, but at a stroke had opened another. If the airplane had been important during World War II, it would be vital in the Cold War.

Below: The aftermath of the atomic bombing of Hiroshima, which killed approximately 300,000 people.

the evolution of the modern airliner

leaving on a jet plane

After World War II, the airline industry went through some big changes as jet technology made airliners more efficient and halved flight times. The era began with the 310mph (500km/h) Constellation and culminated in the 1200mph (2000km/h) Concorde.

Left: *With more than 4000 in service, the Boeing 737 is one of the most popular airliners ever and operates worldwide.*

Top: *The Boeing Stratocruiser was based on the wartime B-29 bomber and incorporated many of its design innovations.*

World War II changed perceptions of aviation, removing anxieties and uncertainties as thousands learned to fly in air forces, and millions became used to seeing airplanes overhead. The smoothest application of military technology to civil aircraft came in the United States, where the relevant technology had developed furthest. The knowledge and technical experience of producing long-range bombers like the Boeing B-29, with its pressurized cabin and powerful engines, helped manufacturers slide straight back into commercial production immediately after the war. In 1946 TWA took delivery of its first Lockheed Constellations and Boeing began to roll out its Model 377 Stratocruisers, which were effectively enlarged B-29s.

The immediate post-war era was the heyday of the piston-engined airliner. Pan Am and TWA both began transatlantic services with Constellations in February 1946. In Britain, the British Overseas Airways Corporation (BOAC) still operated seaplanes for its Commonwealth routes and quickly found itself lagging behind the American carriers. While British-built piston-engine landplanes like the Bristol Type 170 Freighter were maintained for short commercial flights such as the cross-Channel "hop," the larger companies "bought American," with BOAC ordering Constellations and Stratocruisers. But although the later developments of the Constellation and the

Above: *The Douglas DC-7 was one of the best, but also one of the last, piston-engined airliners.*

new Douglas DC-7 were superb aircraft, they paradoxically represented the beginning of the end for the piston-engine airliners, because although manufacturers and passengers demanded more from their aircraft, the performance of these airliners could not be bettered with the existing technology.

The problem with existing airliners was that they had reached their optimum performance levels. The piston engine requires a good supply of air for combustion, and at high altitudes where the air is thinner the amount of thrust is substantially reduced. Through the 1920s and 1930s designers developed the supercharged piston engine, which compressed air and enabled aircraft to fly higher at full power. Even with the supercharger, however, the effectiveness of the piston engine declines at

around 40,000ft (12,000m). The power of the best piston engines peaked at around 3,000hp (2240kW), restricting speeds to about 500mph (800km/h). A new engine was needed, and in Europe an answer was already being developed.

The dawn of the jet age

Toward the end of World War II the German Heinkel He 178, the Messerschmitt Me 262 and the British Gloster Meteor had demonstrated the advantages of jet engine technology. It was not long before the jet engine was taken up by the commercial airline industry. De Havilland gave British aircraft manufacturing a boost when it flew the jet-engined Comet prototype on July 27, 1949. The de Havilland plan for a jet airliner began in February 1945 and the final four-engined, 36-

Top: *Piston-engined aircraft such as Silver City's Type
170 Freighter continued to fly short-haul flights.*
Above: *A Lockheed Super Constellation of KLM.*

passenger configuration for the Mk 1 Comet was agreed in August the following year, with two prototypes being ordered in January 1947. BOAC ordered eight and British South American Airways bought six of the £250,000 Comet Mk 1s. On May 2, 1952, BOAC introduced its Comet service between London and Johannesburg. So successful was the Comet on this route that the 450mph (725km/h) Mk 1 halved flight times and a clear profit was made in the first year of operation. With the later Mk 1A and Mk 2, Britain became the world leader in commercial jet aircraft production. But disaster struck in 1954, when three Comets crashed mysteriously. All orders for Mk 2s were canceled and all Mk 1s and 1As were withdrawn from service, with the exception of 1As in the Royal Canadian Air Force (RCAF).

An inquiry was held to investigate the cause of the Comet crashes. The board found that the accidents were due to metal fatigue disintegrating the pressurized cabin. This knowledge was used to improve Comet design for the later Mk 4, developed from the Mk 3 prototype. Just one month after the inquiry published its conclusions, BOAC ordered 19 144-passenger Comet Mk 4s. The first BOAC Mk 4 London to New York service began on October 4, 1958.

Although orders came in from far and wide, the reputation of the Comet never fully recovered from the 1954 accidents. De Havilland appeared to have achieved a great coup for British manufacturing when Capitol Airlines placed an order for four Mk 4s and ten Mk 4As, but this sale was too good to be true. Capitol found itself in financial difficulty and was bought by United Airlines in 1961, who canceled the order. The Mk 4A was never built. A market for the improved 525mph (850km/h) Mk 4B and Mk 4C opened

Above: *Engineers work on the pressurization units and engines of a de Havilland Comet Mk 1 at London (now Heathrow) Airport.*

Above: *De Havilland was the first manufacturer to introduce a jet airliner. This photograph emphasizes the clean, elegant lines of the Comet Mk 4C.*

الطيران الجوية السودانية

SUD

Left: *The pinnacle of de Havilland's achievements—the Comet Mk 4C. Only 74 of the Mk 4 variants were built, many seeing service with airlines in the Middle East, including Sudan Airways.*

up, but in total only 74 Mk 4s, Mk 4Bs, and Mk 4Cs were built. BOAC flew its last Comet service in 1965 and de Havilland went on to use the Comet as the basis of the RAF Nimrod maritime patrol and reconnaissance aircraft. Despite the less-than-smooth development of the Comet, de Havilland had shown that the jet-engine airliner was the future of passenger travel. The gauntlet had been thrown down to its American competitors.

The Boeing 707

On July 15, 1954, Boeing flew its Model 367-80 jet-engine tanker for the USAF. The aircraft went on to become a huge success as the KC-135, which is still in service today with a total of 732 produced. In 1956 the USAF gave permission for the 367-80 to be developed as the commercial Boeing 707 airliner.

The Boeing 707 was the first American jet airliner and was bought in very large numbers by carriers worldwide. The first production model flew on September 20, 1957, and was approved by the Federal Aviation Administration (FAA) a year later. Pan Am were the first buyers, ordering 20 707s (along with 20 DC-8s from Douglas at the same time), first using them on the New York to London route in October 1958. The 707 was a comfortable airliner with seats six-abreast, and came in short- and long-bodied versions for different roles. The first true long-range model was Boeing's 707-320 Intercontinental series, with which Pan Am began transatlantic services on August 26, 1959, carrying 189 passengers. Including military versions, 878 Model 707s and 154 Model 720s (a shorter and lighter 707 variant) were built.

The European turboprops

In the late 1940s Britain again introduced a world first: the Vickers Viscount, the first civil turboprop airliner. The turboprop works in a similar way to a jet engine, except that the turbine drives a propeller shaft. The advantage of the turboprop is that it is more efficient than a piston engine, and does not consume as much fuel as a jet at low speeds. The short- to medium-range Viscount was first flown on July 16, 1948, and made its inaugural service flight in July 1950 with British European Airways (BEA). The 47- to 60-seat Viscount 700 was the first British airliner built in large numbers for the American market, with Capitol Airlines taking 60. Other British manufacturers followed Vickers in exploiting the turboprop design. The two early market challengers were the 74-seat medium-range Bristol Britannia, which flew its first service in February 1957, and the smaller short-haul Handley Page Herald, the prototype of which followed in March 1958. To compete with the larger Britannia, Vickers came up with two solutions. A design specification by BEA and Trans-Canada Air Lines (now Air Canada) resulted in the 139-seat Vickers Vanguard, which entered service with BEA in 1961. Another new competitor was the 151-seat VC-10, which first carried passengers in 1964 and ultimately led to the 163-seater Super VC-10 the following year.

But the British turboprop airliners did not make a significant enough impression in the United States for American manufacturers to want to challenge Vickers and Bristol. Beech, Convair, and Fairchild made small short to medium-range passenger and freight turboprop aircraft, but nothing to make the profitable transatlantic

crossings. Instead the new turboprop designs came from Antonov in the Soviet Union and Fokker in the Netherlands; the former building the largest and the latter, one of the best-selling.

While their comrades Tupolev concentrated on rolling out a fleet of jet-engined passenger aircraft, introducing the Tu-104 in 1957, Antonov produced a series of successful turboprops including the An-22, unveiled in 1965. At 190 feet in length (57.9 meters), the An-22 is still the largest turboprop ever built. Primarily a freighter, it could accommodate up to 29 passengers and an 176,350lb (80,000kg) payload. A 724-seat airliner version was considered but never built. The An-22 began service with Aeroflot in 1967, and in October of that year set 14 payload-to-height records, reaching 25,748ft (7848m) with 220,500lb (100,018kg) of cargo. In total, 66 aircraft were built.

In the early 1950s, Fokker designed the Fo27 Friendship as a replacement for the veteran Douglas DC-3. A contract was also signed with the Fairchild Engine and Airplane Corporation (later Fairchild Hiller) in the United States to build the Friendship under licence as the F-27. The first Fokker F.27 prototype flew on November 24, 1955, and the first production model on 23 March the following year. Aer Lingus made the first scheduled F.27 flight on December 15, 1958. The F.27 and F-27 flew with a wide range of major airlines and niche operators across the world and more than 200 examples of the type remain in service today. Fokker built 579 F.27s and Fairchild 207 F-27s in all.

The golden age of the jet airliner

As development of the jet engine continued on both sides of the Atlantic, turbojets maintained their lead over turboprops, but SNCA Sud-Est of France brought in a truly innovative design feature. In October 1951, the Comité du Matériel Civil asked French manufacturers for a national jet

Below: With a 6800 mile (11,000km) range, the Antonov An-22 can deliver its massive cargo almost anywhere in the world. Here, an An-22 is pictured during an earthquake relief operation in Georgia.

Above: *An artist's impression of the Hurel-Dubois HD.45, one of three designs considered by the French Comité du Matériel Civil in 1952 for the first French national jet airliner.*

airliner, but the formal specification did not indicate the number or type of engines. In March 1952, the competing designs were reduced to three: the twin-engine Hurel-Dubois, Sud-Est's X-210 design with three engines clustered round the tail, and the four-engine S.0.60. When Rolls-Royce developed its Avon jet engine into the more powerful R.A.16, Sud-Est removed the third central engine, but retained a design with the two other engines on either side of the rear fuselage. Resubmitted in July 1952, the Sud-Est design for what would become the Caravelle was accepted in September of the same year.

Although an unusual configuration at the time, when wing-mounted engines were standard, there were many benefits to fuselage-mounted engines. Aerodynamically, engine-less wings were "cleaner," and the flow of air into the engine was easier as air follows the contours of the fuselage, making the engine more efficient. Take off and landing performance was also improved as the engine position offered better thrust on shorter runways. With the fuel tanks in the wings, rear-mounted engines also reduced the risk of fire. Passengers were made more comfortable because cabin noise was significantly lower.

Sud-Est's first prototype flew on May 27, 1955, and its success led to Air France ordering 12 planes in early 1956 with an option for a further 12. The Caravelle I went into production later that year. Sud-Est and SudOuest merged in March 1957 to form Sud-Aviation. Caravelle Is were delivered to Air France and Scandinavian Airlines Systems (SAS) throughout 1959 and production soon began on the improved IA, which was delivered to Finnair on February 1960. By the end of 1960, 105

Braniff International: The Texan Trendsetter (1928–1982)

At a time of immense growth in jet airlines, one company added that little bit of extra style. Brothers Paul Revere and Thomas E. Braniff inaugurated Paul R. Braniff Inc in June 1928 when they introduced an air service between Oklahoma City and Tulsa. Shortly afterwards the company was bought and merged, however, so the Braniff brothers decided to re-establish their independent airline as Braniff Airways Inc in Oklahoma City in 1930. As Braniff expanded in the early 1930s it was awarded airmail contracts from Chicago to Dallas ("From the Great Lakes to the Gulf"), and later from Texas into Mexico. Paul sold his share of the company to his brother in 1936 and in June 1942 Thomas moved the Braniff Airways Inc headquarters from Oklahoma City to Dallas, reflecting the shift of its main business.

Braniff branched out into the Central American and Caribbean air travel market throughout the 1940s. In 1943, Braniff obtained Aerovias Braniff for its Mexican service and three years later was granted routes in the Caribbean, and Central and South America. That same year, Braniff changed its name to Braniff International. The expansion continued as Mid-Continent Airlines was bought to increase the number of Braniff routes from 38 to 70.

Thomas Braniff died in an air accident in January 1954 and Charles Beard succeeded him as president of Braniff International. Beard oversaw a period of great change and excitement. In December 1959, Braniff began its "El Dorado" Boeing 707-227 service. A regular jet service between the United States and Latin America was introduced from April the following year.

In July 1964 Troy Post of the Greatamerica Corporation and three Braniff shareholders bought a controlling 57.5% share in the airline and set about making it reflect contemporary art and fashion. In March 1965 the first BAC One-Eleven was delivered to Braniff, and Jack Tinker and Partners, an advertising think-tank, were tasked to restyle Braniff's image. Part of this initiative was Emilio Pucci's couture collection for Braniff's stewardesses. Artist Alexander Calder was later commissioned to create an artwork titled Flying Colors of South America on a DC-8 in 1973. In October of that year, the plane was unveiled at Dallas-Fort Worth Airport. Calder also created Flying Colors of America on a Braniff 727-200 for the bicentennial celebrations.

By early 1966 Braniff shares had increased eight-fold to $200 each and the airline was still expanding. By early 1967 Braniff had bought and merged with Panagra, part of the powerful W.R. Grace and Pan Am alliance, at a cost of $30 million; and by 1969 Braniff was an all-jet airline, flying Boeing 707s, BAC One-Elevens and Douglas DC-8s. In 1971, 35 Boeing 727s were ordered to add to the fleet, along with a number of new 747s. Braniff's fiftieth anniversary heralded an

Above: *The Boeing 727, seen here in Braniff livery, was Boeing's first and only three-engined jet.*
Below: *All of Braniff International's Boeing 747s displayed the famous orange livery.*

even bigger and better service. The 1978 deregulation of US air travel saw the airline request 620 new routes from the Civil Aeronautics Board (CAB), as it was believed that large airlines would better survive the drawbacks of deregulation.

The end for Braniff International began in 1979 when, although a $700 million order was placed with Boeing for 727s and 747s in October, *Business Week* reported that there were financial problems. Braniff had expanded too much too soon, and 1979 was less than kind, as a national recession reduced passenger numbers and fuel prices increased. At the end of the year, Braniff announced losses of $44 million. European and Pacific services were reduced in 1980, before the latter were withdrawn altogether. The entire fleet had to be mortgaged and when a proposed merger with Eastern Airlines collapsed early the following year the outlook was very bleak. In February 1982, $128.5 million losses were announced (shortly afterwards First Class was removed from all Boeing 727s, replaced by the single cheerily titled "Texas Class"). On May 12, 1982, Braniff International became the first major US airline to file for bankruptcy, after 74 years' service.

Above: Braniff's fleet included a large number of Boeing 727s, as well as 707s and 747s.
Below: Alexander Calder's "Flying Colors of South America" Douglas DC-8.

Above: *Alitalia was the first airline to operate the Sud-Aviation Caravelle with the Lear Autoland system.*
Right: *Scandinavian Airlines Systems (SAS) was the first foreign customer of the Caravelle I, receiving its first aircraft in 1959.*

Caravelle Is, IAs, IIIs, and VIIs had been ordered, but the major and most popular Sud-Aviation Caravelle model was the series VI. The VI-N first flew on September 10, 1960, and United Air Lines ordered 20, the largest single order for a Caravelle.

A further innovation in the Caravelle design was the automatic landing system. The first automatic landing was performed by prototype 01 on September 29, 1962, as trials were carried out with the Lear 102 autopilot and the Smith Autoland. American Elmer Ambrose Sperry invented the autopilot and demonstrated it in Paris in 1914, but William Powell Lear Sr developed the technology to the point where it became indispensible. In the late-1940s Lear perfected the F-5 Autopilot which could lock onto signals and land in practically zero

visibility. For an automatic landing, the pilot selected the function 5 miles (8km) short of the runway and the autopilot then maintained the track and altitude of the aircraft precisely, all the way down to the ground. The first Caravelle to enter service with the Lear automatic landing system was an Alitalia aircraft in early 1966. These new Caravelles were very popular in Europe, but although Douglas signed a contract to market Caravelles in the United States, American carriers tended not to look abroad for their airliners.

Transatlantic competition

The big three American aircraft manufacturers, Boeing, Douglas and Lockheed, developed various configurations of twin and tri-engine jets through the late 1950s and early 1960s. Introduced by Delta Air Lines in 1959, the first Douglas jet airliner was neither, as it carried four engines. In all, Douglas produced 556 DC-8s in seven variants; the most widely ordered being the DC-8-60 series, which could make the transatlantic crossing with up to 260 passengers. Five years later, in 1964, Eastern Air Lines began services with Boeing's first tri-engine jet, the Model 727. The 727 was a 189-seat airliner with the same engine configuration as the original Caravelle design, with one engine over the central fuselage and two more either side of the rear fuselage. The success of the 727 led to the development of British and American rear-mounted twin-engine airliners through the 1960s. The 89-seat BAC One-Eleven flew its inaugural service with British United Airways (BUA) in April 1965. In December of the same year, Delta began flights with the 139-seater Douglas DC-9. Nine hundred and seventy-six of these twin-engine jets were delivered, compared to just 239 One-Elevens.

From Baby to Jumbo

Boeing then reverted to the wing-mounted engine layout of the late-1950s. Known as the "Baby Boeing," the short-range Model 737 first flew on April 9, 1967. The original version entered service with Lufthansa in February the following year, and a "stretched" 150-seat version appeared six months later. Due to its light weight and consequent low fuel consumption—just 0.034 liters per seat per kilometer—the 737 was a huge success. Its low weight also meant that the Baby Boeing paid lower airport fees for landing, taxiing, and parking. At between $41 and $68.5 million each, the 737 is excellent value for money and over 4000 have been sold worldwide.

Maintaining the conventional under-wing engine mounting, Boeing created the world's first wide-bodied, or "jumbo," jet, the Model 747. This aircraft was again the result of studies for a military transport design, but in April 1966 Pan Am made a $525 million order for 25 Boeing

Below: The cabin of a Douglas DC-8 in the late 1950s. Compared to the interior of the first airliners, the reclining seats and individual air vents and lights offer luxurious comfort.

Above: *Boeing sold more than 1800 727s, including 129-seat 727-100s (pictured). Most aircraft produced were stretched 189-seat 727-200s.*

747s, initiating the commercial project. Two years later, the first prototype rolled out and flew for the first time on February 9, 1969. The 747 was officially unveiled to the world at the Paris Air Show in June 1969, before beginning its passenger service with Pan Am on January 21, 1970. This passenger and freighter jet has also

been developed to more specialist tasks. Two 747s have been specially modified to transport NASA space shuttles, the first such flight taking place in February 1977.

Two 747-200s have been delivered as USAF "Air Force One" presidential transports. Others were active in Operation Desert Storm in 1991 as

Top: *The 737 has overtaken the 727 as Boeing's most successful production aircraft.*
Above: *The presidential Boeing 747 "Air Force One" flies over Mount Rushmore, monument to presidents of an earlier age.*

Above: *Carrying over 500 passengers, the Boeing 747 is operated by every major airline.*
Left: *The Boeing 747, displayed at the Paris Air Show in 1969, dwarfs its predecessor, the 707.*

troop transports, freighters, and tankers and in Operation Restore Hope in Somalia between December 1992 and January 1993 as freighters. By 2002, nearly 1300 Boeing 747s had been delivered, now costing between $185 million and $215 million each. Work is currently underway on a new model, the Boeing 747-400ER, for passenger, freight, and military use.

American tri-jets

To compete with the Boeing 747 Douglas and Lockheed began producing their first wide-body aircraft. The Douglas DC-10 and Lockheed L-1011 Tristar were developed from an American Airlines specification for a wide-bodied twin-engine airliner, but both companies convinced American Airlines to consider a three-engine jet with a larger capacity. The DC-10 first flew in August 1970, three months before the Tristar. The main American carriers were torn between the two, but the swiftness of the DC-10's time from program launch to first flight impressed many. The first American Airlines DC-10 service was launched in August 1971, but the aircraft suffered some early setbacks, including an incident in 1972 when a fault with the aft cargo door caused a DC-10 to lose all hydraulic and steering capability. Although this flight landed unharmed, the same fault in March 1974 caused a Turkish Airlines DC-10 to crash fatally in Paris. With the reliability of the DC-10 in question, the Tristar found new impetus, and later in the 1980s TWA promoted the

Below: American Airlines launched its first service with the Douglas DC-10 tri-jet in 1971.

Tristar as one of the safest airliners in the world. Despite this boast, Lockheed was more a military transport manufacturer than an airliner constructor and the Tristar project did not run smoothly. Although TWA, Eastern Airlines and Delta all made firm orders, production was slow. One of the Tristar's main hold-ups was with the RB.211 turbofan engines which were meant to be provided by Rolls-Royce, a company which had been having financial troubles. When Rolls-Royce filed for bankruptcy in 1970, the British Government wanted assurances that the Lockheed contract would be fulfilled as a condition for giving financial aid. A new company, Rolls-Royce Motors Ltd, was established in 1971, but as a result of this political and financial wrangling the first Tristar did not enter service with Eastern until April 1972, eight months after the DC-10. American Airlines never did fly Tristars. A combination of lateness and unfamiliarity meant that Douglas outsold Lockheed nearly two-to-one, delivering 446 DC-10 aircraft (including the military KC-10 tanker) to the Tristar's 250. Lockheed had needed to sell 500 planes to break even. Lockheed has not since produced a design for a commercial airliner, sticking instead to military transport.

Introducing the turbofan

With newer and better-performing aircraft came the need for an even more efficient powerplant. Modern airliners are powered by another variation

Above: *A modern turbofan, the Rolls-Royce Trent
700, currently used by 23 operators worldwide.*

of a jet engine: the turbofan. While the turbojet performs well at high speeds and the turboprop excels at low speeds, the turbofan fills the middle ground. The workings of a turbofan are very similar to a turbojet: a jet engine makes up the core, with a fan at the front and a turbine at the rear. As air is drawn into the intake, some air flows into the core for compression as in a normal turbojet, and some is directed around the core. Propulsion is partly produced by the thrust from the jet engine core and partly by the fan. With two forms of thrust for the same amount of fuel, a turbofan aircraft is more fuel-efficient than a turbojet, and can take an aircraft to speeds between 250 and 650mph (400-1045km/h).

757 to 777

In the late 1970s Boeing went from strength to strength, expanding its family of jet airliners, all of conventional under-wing engine configuration. United approached Boeing with an order in April 1978 that brought the next addition to the Boeing fleet, the Model 767. This 350-seat airliner made its first service flight with United on September 8, 1982. Six variants were made, totalling 851 aircraft.

The smaller 757 followed in 1983. This 289-seater medium-range jet has the lowest operating cost of any airliner in its class. Although over 1000 have been delivered, there have been no new orders placed for the 757 since 2001. Faced with a downturn in the American airline industry since the attacks of September 11, 2001, Boeing are reviewing their production plans.

Boeing's latest jet airliner is the long-range Model 777, intended to fill the gap between the 747 and the 767. The first 777 service was flown by United between London and Washington, DC on June 7, 1995, and 367 have been delivered so far.

Europe catches up

The main competitors for the Boeing 777 are the Airbus A330 and A340. Airbus is a conglomerate of European manufacturers that includes Aérospatiale, Deutsche Airbus, CASA of Spain and British Aerospace. The first Airbus model was the 361-seat A300, which made its maiden flight on October 28, 1972. Over the following three decades, Airbus has seized a large portion of the short to medium-range airliner market, selling over 2000 aircraft in this category worldwide. Technologically advanced, the Airbus A320 was the first commercial airliner to use the fly-by-wire system, in which there is no direct connection between the pilot's cockpit controls and the plane's rudder and flaps. Instead, the pilot's instructions are relayed to a control system, which converts the signal into an action. The fly-by-wire system can overrule a pilot's command if it deems it unsafe, but there is a debate as to

Above: *The Boeing 777 is intended as a replacement for the long-range 747 and to fill the gap between the 747 and the 767.*
Below: *An Air Seychelles Boeing 767-ER. This extended-range variant has extra fuel tanks in its wings, giving it a range of more than 6900 miles (11,000km).*

whether this removes too much control from the pilot, who may need to make snap decisions if faced with a mid-air collision, for example.

Having sold around 2500 aircraft up to 2002 (including orders for the A318 currently being built), mainly to domestic European airlines, the greatest achievement for Airbus has been to design aircraft which can compete with the best of those produced by American manufacturers. The A330 and A340 were launched simultaneously on June 5, 1987. The A340 made test flights through late 1991 and early 1992 before the A340-200 and A340-300 variants entered service with Lufthansa in January 1993. The A330 was tested with General Electric and Rolls-Royce Trent engines from November 1992 before Air Inter flew its inaugural A330 service in January 1994. At the start of the twenty-first century Airbus is forcing Boeing to reconsider its future design options.

Below: The Airbus A320 was the first airliner to incorporate the "fly-by-wire" electronic control system.

Breaking the Sound Barrier

Systematic experiments into supersonic flight began back in 1943, when the British Government issued specification E.24/43 for a "transonic aircraft" which could achieve speeds of one and a half times the speed of sound (Mach 1.5). At altitude this is around 660mph (1060km/h). Despite being almost complete, the aircraft that resulted from this specification, the Miles M.52, was canceled in February 1946. It was left to the United States, and Chuck Yeager's Bell X-1, to break the sound barrier in level flight, reaching Mach 1.06 on October 14, 1947. In February the following year, another US aircraft, the Douglas D-558-2 Skyrocket, achieved Mach 2. The first British supersonic flight came on September 6, 1948, when John Derry reached 700mph (1127 km/h) in a dive from 12,192 meters to 9144 meters in a swept-wing de Havilland D.H.108 Swallow.

The concept of supersonic passenger transport, or SST, has been around since the 1950s. Despite losing the supersonic lead to the Americans, Britain led the field in SST research, and in 1956 the Supersonic Transport Advisory Committee (STAC) was established. In designing an SST aircraft, one of the first decisions to be taken was over the shape of the wing, which had to provide aerodynamic efficiency at both high and low altitudes and speeds. For a target speed of Mach 2, the best wing design would be highly swept, but for low altitude control a straight trailing edge was required. The delta wing was the natural outcome of these requirements. The decision to use a delta wing was reached by SST researchers in France, the Soviet Union and the United States quite independently. Three of the main contributors to STAC—Bristol, English Electric, and Vickers—merged in 1960 to form the British Aircraft Corporation (BAC). All manufacturers were asked to submit designs for an SST aircraft. Ultimately,

BAC's 223 won out, but a condition of the BAC project was that consultation be allowed with foreign designers and manufacturers. America wanted to approach SST solo and Germany was not interested, but France already had an SST project underway. In early 1961 designs for the 125-seater BAC 223 and the 70- to 80-seater Sud-Aviation Super Caravelle were unveiled. The two SST designs were remarkably similar in all respects. In June 1961 BAC and Sud-Aviation met to discuss a collaborative design. This led to the historic formal agreement of November 29, 1962, that ultimately led to Concorde.

A race to the skies then began, with an unexpected competitor. At the Paris Air Show in 1965, the Soviet Union unveiled its own SST, the Tupolev Tu-144. In line with airliner development worldwide, Tupolev had produced rear-mounted twin-engine jets and tri-jets in the 1960s, and an SST project was a logical next step. Because of its similarity in appearance to the Anglo-French

Above: On September 6, 1948 the de Havilland D.H.108 Swallow became the first British aircraft to break the sound barrier, 11 months after Chuck Yeager's Bell X-1.

Left: *Everything about Concorde is specifically designed for supersonic flight. The long conical nose must be lowered when landing to offer the pilot an unobscured view of the runway.*

Right: *The need for a swept wing for high speed and a straight trailing edge for low altitude control resulted in Concorde's famous ogival delta wing.*

Below: *British Airways was one of only two operators of Concorde—world economics and environmental concerns put paid to dreams of huge foreign sales.*

design, the Tu-144 was later dubbed Konkordski or Concordski.

In the United States work got underway on an American-built SST. The FAA estimated that within 30 years the SST program would produce over 500 aircraft. Boeing and Lockheed duly came up with designs and presented models of the 733 and L-2000 respectively in December 1966. Although the L-2000 was easier to construct, it was slower and louder than the Boeing and so on May 1, 1967, Boeing received an order for two 733s, now named the 2707. The American solution to the wing question was a variable geometry design that offered a conventional wing form which could be swung back to produce a delta shape at high speed. However, problems with the ambitious Mach 3 target speed (such as softening of the aluminium surfaces) and opposition over sonic boom noise pollution forced the Senate to

cancel the project in 1971. From that point on Europe led SST development from the front.

The first Anglo-French SST prototype, Concorde 001, was unveiled at the Aérospatiale factory in Toulouse on December 11, 1967. After initial confusion over the name (BAC called it Concord and Aérospatiale called it Concorde), the official title was chosen with the French spelling, Concorde. The first flight was made just over a year later, on March 2, 1969, nine weeks after the Tu-144. Concorde reached Mach 1 on October 1, 1969, and Mach 2 on November 4, 1970. The maximum speed the Anglo-French aircraft achieved was Mach 2.05 (1354mph or 2179km/h) at 57,000 ft (17,373m).

Once again, the Tu-144 was first, taking to the skies as a fully operational aircraft in December 1975 delivering airmail and freight between Moscow and Alma Ata as a trial run for passenger

Above: *The $14.25 million Challenger 300 is one of Bombardier's new "super midsize" private jets capable of transcontinental flight.*
Right: *The comfortable commute—the "state room" of a Canadair Global Express.*

services. The 128-seat Concorde production model entered service with BA and Air France a month later on January 21, 1976. But the demand for SST aircraft had been hugely overestimated, in part due to environmental concerns that had not been dreamed of in the early 1960s. In total, only 14 Concordes were delivered, although these continued to serve BA and Air France successfully for nearly 30 years.

The Tu-144 was not so long-lived. After a serious crash at the 1973 Paris Air Show and the in-flight failure and crash of an upgraded Tu-144D in 1978, the Soviet aircraft was withdrawn from service in June 1978. Only 17 were built, including the prototype. In the 1990s NASA modified a Tu-144 as a testbed for a second-generation SST aircraft, under the title of the High Speed Commercial Research program, at a cost of $350

Ahead of his Time: Sir Freddie Laker, Father of the Discount Airline

Set up in 1966, Laker Airways was one of the first "no-frills" airlines at a time when air travel was booming. Freddie Laker introduced his Douglas DC-10 "Skytrains" in November 1972, with chartered flights to holiday destinations in the Mediterranean. Laker's "Skytrains" were not approved for US service until 1977, at which time the "Skytrain" London to New York service cost a mere $186 (£118) single, or $236 (£150) return. Business was booming.

So that American carriers didn't lose out to Laker, the Senate Commerce Committee passed a bill deregulating air routes and fares, allowing airlines greater freedom—but spelling the beginning of the end for Laker's success. Half-full airliners dropped their prices and saw their passengers return. Even Laker's introduction of a non-stop London to Los Angeles service in 1979 was not enough to keep his competitive edge. In 1980 Laker ordered a batch of Airbus A300s to turn his fortunes around, but it was not enough.

In support of Freddie Laker, members of the public offered donations to help Laker Airways out of their financial hardship and, in total, just over £1 million was raised. But on February 5, 1982, Laker Airways went bankrupt, owing £270 million. All of Laker's aircraft were ordered to return to Britain that night. One DC-10 was impounded at Gatwick for unpaid landing and parking costs. Six thousand Laker passengers were brought home by BA, Pan Am, British Caledonian, and Air Florida, happy to honor the Laker return tickets now the upstart airline was out of the running.

For just over a decade, Freddie Laker had done far more than provide cheap flights; he had inspired other entrepreneurs. Following in his footsteps came Richard Branson, who established Virgin Atlantic in 1984. Ryanair and easyJet also owe their existence in part to Freddie Laker's no-frills gamble. In recognition of his contribution to air travel, Freddie Laker received a knighthood in 1978.

1982 was not the end for Laker. In September 1995 Laker announced that he would be re-establishing Laker Airways. In 1996 Laker Airways Bahamas began a charter service with Boeing 727-200s out of Fort Lauderdale. A short-lived transatlantic service was attempted in 1997, but only the Caribbean service remains.

Top: *A BAC One-Eleven in service with Laker Airways in the early 1970s.*
Below: *Laker Airways was the first European operator of the Douglas DC-10 when it introduced its "Skytrain" service.*

million. The project was cancelled in 1999, however, and the Tupolev was sold.

After a devastating crash in France in July 2000, all Concordes were grounded while checks were made and new safety measures introduced. Services resumed in November 2001, but on April 10, 2003, the decision to cease all Concorde services in October 2003 was announced. Air France ceased its flights on May 31. The reason given was the increasing cost of keeping the aircraft in service. Despite attempts to keep at least one aircraft flying, all the remaining Concordes were retired to museums by November 2003.

Private Jets

Not all passenger flights are made by supersonic aircraft flying for multibillion-dollar airlines—small 8–10 seat private jets make up an important part of the aircraft market. After the terrorist attacks of September 11, 2001, sales of private jets rocketed as business passengers lost faith in airline security. Since then the demand has dropped dramatically, and 2003 saw the worst year for the main manufacturers Bombardier (which produces

Learjets, Challengers, and Globals), Cessna, and Gulfstream. However, industry experts expect an upturn in the market to begin in 2005.

At present, a modern private jet will cost between $19 million for a Cessna Citation X and $43 million for a Gulfstream V, but the current trend is for fractional ownership. This growing market involves a customer buying into a private jet, their share being called a "card." Cards cost between $100,000 and $300,000 for a 25-hour timeshare, depending on the aircraft involved. Fractional ownership schemes currently make up around 40 percent of manufacturers' order books.

The "No-Frills" Revolution

In 1971 Rollin King and Herb Kelleher began flights between Dallas, Houston, and San Antonio under the banner of Southwest Airlines—the first American low-cost airline. The business plan was simple: customers would be attracted by a cheap and reliable service. By 1973, Southwest was making a profit and four years later was listed on the New York Stock Exchange. By 1990 it was worth $1 billion and another ten years later was the fifth largest airline in the United States.

In Europe, the fortunes of Laker, King and Kelleher inspired a new wave of budget airlines. In 1985 Ryanair began a turboprop service between Waterford in the Republic of Ireland and London Gatwick. The following year, Ryanair bought London European Airways and began a Dublin to London service. The larger airlines began to take notice. At the time, BA and Aer Lingus charged $250 (£209) for the Dublin to London flight, but Ryanair was asking just $114 (£95). But Ryanair had tried too much too soon, operating too many types of airliner and running into serious debt by

Top: Southwest Airlines' fleet consists of only Boeing 737s. Pictured is one of its 737-300s in its traditional livery.
Below: Rebuilding Ryanair to operate just Boeing 737s, Michael O'Leary offered his aircraft as flying billboards.

Right: *One of easyJet's Baby Boeings. The orange tail of easyJet's Boeing 737s is now a common sight at airports throughout Europe.*

the end of the 1980s. In reaction to this, Ryanair relaunched as a definitive "no frills" airline like Southwest, and standardized its fleet to operate just Boeing 737s. Ryanair also offered their planes as flying advertising space, with Jaguar cars, Kilkenny beer and the *News of the World* newspaper taking advantage. So successful was this reorganization that in January 2002 chief executive Michael O'Leary placed an order for 100 Boeing 737-800s, the largest single order for the series. Leasing a number of these out to other airlines would provide a healthy return.

After September 11, 2001, many airlines froze—but instead Ryanair offered flights for as low as $22 (£15). This promotion, seen as the airline fighting back at the airborne terrorists, was warmly received by the public. In January 2003, Ryanair bought another low-cost airline, Buzz, and set about withdrawing its unprofitable routes. Although some complain of poor service and shabby planes, investors rate Ryanair second in Europe, behind Lufthansa.

Another airline to seize the "no frills" opportunity was easyJet. The introduction of such services owes a great deal to changes in European law as well as the entrepreneurs of the 1960s and 1970s. An "open skies" policy was initiated in 1987 as the European Union deregulated air travel. Previously, routes, fares, and capacity were decided by inter-governmental agreements. Since 1987, any airline with an Air Operators Certificate could use any route, set their own prices and carry as many passengers as they wished. EasyJet was an airline eager to take advantage of this deregulation.

The founder of easyJet, Stelios Haji-Ioannou, started with just two Boeing 737s and defined the company as a "virtual airline," bringing in pilots and other staff on contract from its first flights in 1995. The first aircraft the airline fully owned was not purchased until April 1996. The company also transfixed Britain with its fly-on-the-wall TV documentary *Airline*, profiling the easyJet staff and making some into household names. Around nine million viewers per episode watched the fifth series, aired in spring 2001.

But why have King, Kelleher, O'Leary, and Haji-Ioannou succeeded while Freddie Laker failed? One of the most important factors for the European "no frills" airlines was the 1987 deregulation of air travel. This literally opened the skies for all who had the money and drive to establish an airline. Secondly, and more globally, the Internet has revolutionized the way people prepare for travelling. The World Wide Web makes it so much easier for people to browse and compare airline prices before they book their tickets online, rather than relying on a travel agent earning commission. Southwest was the first of these airlines to introduce a website. These two factors have given the contemporary discount airlines a greater chance than Freddie Laker had in the 1970s and early 1980s.

Although September 11, 2001, stunted growth in the air industry, a combination of opportunity and entrepreneurship has at least offered to mitigate the aircraft manufacturers' diminishing order book problems. The passengers are reaping the rewards.

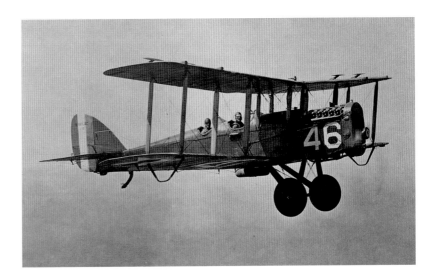

the development of air cargo
cinderella's wings

It may lack the dash and glamour of air combat or space travel, but for almost a century the development of air freight has had a major effect on aviation. Once the Wright brothers had performed their first successful flight at Kitty Hawk, North Carolina, it was inevitable that the potential of the airplane to carry things as well as people would be exploited.

Left: Not known for its beauty, the Blackburn Beverly entered service as a large freighter with the Royal Air Force in 1956. It gave stellar performances in Asia, Africa, and the Middle East.
Top: In 1918, the US Post Office Department reinforced its fleet of Curtiss JN-4s with an order for 100 de Havilland DH.4 biplanes purchased from the US Army.

While new passenger-carrying airplanes soared overhead, cargo aircraft were slower to get going. In 1910 a bolt of silk was flown from Dayton to Columbus in Ohio in what was perhaps the first demonstration of an air cargo flight. The development of air cargo did not truly start until the United States Post Office began using aircraft to carry mail. On May 15, 1918, the air carriage of mail from New York to Washington, DC began. Congress had given the go-ahead for the flights, appreciating that they would also allow student pilots in the Army Signals Corps to gain experience. One year later, the American Railway Express company experimented with a Handley Page bomber, carrying 1100lb (550kg) of freight from Washington, DC to Chicago. By the 1920s American businesses were beginning to realize that the speed with which aircraft could distribute goods allowed them to keep less stock in their warehouses, saving on space, rent, and labor costs—using what is today known as "just in time" logistics.

In the late 1920s air freight enjoyed rapid growth in America. By 1931, 1,303,302lb (581,177kg) of cargo had been carried by air, a sizeable increase from the 45,829lb (20,801kg) carried in 1927.

Luftwaffe workhorse

In 1932 the Junkers Ju 52/3m took to the skies, opening a new chapter in air freight. A boxy, three-piston-engined aircraft with a corrugated metal skin, the Ju 52 was used by the Nationalists during the Spanish Civil War, as well as by the Nazi Condor Legion, which also participated in the conflict. The aircraft would later become the workhorse of the Luftwaffe during World War II. Despite its ungainly appearance, "Tante Ju"—as the aircraft was nicknamed—would remain in use around the world for over forty years. One example flew in Ecuador until 1971, and the Spanish Air Force retained its aircraft until 1975.

Around the same time as the Ju 52 made its maiden flight, Douglas unveiled its DC-2. While this aircraft was ostensibly designed to carry passengers, the US Navy and Marine Corps ordered small numbers of the C-33 freighter version of the DC-2, which had larger tail surfaces.

Douglas followed the DC-2 with the legendary DC-3, known as the C-47 in US military service.

This versatile and rugged aircraft, which first flew on December 17, 1935, could be configured for both passenger and cargo flights, and was used by both civil and military customers throughout World War II and beyond. Many aircraft are still in use as freighters today.

Despite the advances of the 1930s, it was not until 1940 that the world's first scheduled air freight service got underway. On December 23, United Airlines used a Douglas DC-4, a design which had begun flying two years earlier, to deliver mail from New York to Chicago. However, United's foresight did not attract enough customers and the service was under-used, ending four months later.

Cargo in World War II

War had been raging in Europe since 1939. The USAAF was slow to realize the importance of cargo aircraft in military operations, but in 1940 it noticed that Germany had used Ju 52 aircraft to drop paratroopers when invading the Netherlands

Below: German airborne infantry prepare to board Junkers Ju 52 transport aircraft in preparation for the invasion of Crete in May 1941.

Above: *The US Navy also used the DC-3, designated the C-53B, in very cold climates. The aircraft were fitted with an extra fuel capacity and skids on their undercarriage.*

and realized that dedicated cargo aircraft could prove useful for the movement of troops and equipment in the Pacific. A retired US Navy aviator, Paul I. Gunn, was a key figure in developing cargo aircraft for military operations, known in military parlance as "airlift." Before the war, Gunn had operated his own cargo airline using a fleet of Beech 18 aircraft. The USAAF noticed his talents and persuaded him to rejoin the military. He was given command of a USAAF transport squadron to move troops and cargo around the Philippine islands. In 1942 he was transferred to Australia to command the 21st Troop Carrier Squadron (21st TCS), which with

the 22nd TCS saw action in Papua New Guinea, supporting Australian troops fighting on the island. Cargo was either unloaded on the ground or "airdropped" to the land below using parachutes.

In May 1942 the remarkable Messerschmitt Me 323 "Gigant" entered service with the Luftwaffe in Europe. This ugly, six-engined giant used many innovative features now standard on today's purpose-built cargo aircraft. Freight was loaded via a hinged "clamshell" nose. An undercarriage of ten flexible wheels could "squash down" to work like caterpillar tracks on rough airstrips. The aircraft could make an assisted

Below: A Douglas C-54 Skymaster on the taxiway at
Okinawa airfield. The aircraft is evacuating wounded
soldiers from this Pacific island in May 1945.

take-off, with rockets attached to the airframe giving add power on short runways—a technique used with the Lockheed C-130 Hercules over twenty years later. The Gigant's payload could include up to 130 troops, 60 stretchers or 8700 loaves of bread.

The USAAF employed two other notable aircraft for cargo hauling during World War II, the C-46 Commando, which entered service in 1942, and the Douglas C-54 Skymaster, a military version of the Douglas DC-4 airliner. With a payload of 28,000lb (12,700kg) and a strengthened floor, the C-54 was a useful long-range freighter in the Pacific. Some aircraft remain in service today as water bombers for fighting forest fires.

The war was accelerating the development of transport aircraft in the United Kingdom too. On July 5, 1942, the prototype Avro York, a transport development of the Avro Lancaster bomber, made its maiden flight. As well as giving a sterling wartime service to the RAF, the York saw passenger service with the BOAC and British South American Airways.

In the Pacific theatre the pioneering work undertaken by Paul Gunn received a boost with the appointment of Lieutenant George C. Kenney as Chief of Staff for General Douglas MacArthur's air operations in the Pacific. Kenney realized that airlift was essential in the war against Japan, because it would give added mobility to ground troops. His theories proved correct in October 1942 when an airlift moved an entire infantry division into Port Moresby, Papua New Guinea, an operation which would have taken several weeks by sea.

Away from the Pacific, airlift was vital the following November when troops from the US

Below: *The Messerschmitt Me 323 was a revolutionary aircraft. Dangerously slow in a wartime situation, it featured several innovative features now common on today's cargo aircraft, including a hinged cargo-door nose.*

Right: *A USAAF Curtiss C-46 transport disgorges paratroopers over a rugged landscape.*
Below: *Paratroopers check each other's equipment before boarding a Douglas C-47 during the campaign for Sicily in the Mediterranean in 1943.*

Army's 82nd Airborne Division, together with British paratroopers, were carried into battle during Operation Torch, the invasion of North Africa. Cargo aircraft also brought supplies to the front line as ground troops pushed inland. The success of the airlift for Operation Torch was repeated again on July 9, 1943, for Operation Husky, the invasion of Sicily. Not only were cargo aircraft essential, but towed gliders filled with troops and equipment landed behind enemy lines and played a vital role. This arrangement of gliders and freighters was also crucial for Operation Overlord, the Allied invasion of Normandy, which began on D-Day: June 6, 1944.

Freighters continued to prove their worth as the Allies pushed inland. During the Battle of the Bulge in December 1944, the US Army 101st Airborne Division was surrounded by German troops at Bastogne in Belgium. C-47 Skytrains were used to resupply the troops on the ground, helping to save the division. World War II was airlift's "coming of age." US General Dwight D. Eisenhower, Supreme Allied Commander in Europe, would later comment that the C-47 was one of the most important weapons of the war.

Post-war giants

Throughout the war the USAAF had no aircraft the size of the Me 323, but on September 5, 1945, the Douglas C-74 Globemaster made its first flight, and for a time would be the largest aircraft in the world. The Globemaster could carry 125 troops, 115 stretchers, or 50,000lb (24,948kg) of cargo. The aircraft even featured a self-contained elevator, located in the mid-fuselage, to speed up loading. The C-74 had a cameo role masquerading

Above: A Bristol 170 Freighter in use as an air survey aircraft by engineers prospecting for oil in Iran. Right: A 4.1in (105mm) howitzer is ejected from a Fairchild C-119 Flying Boxcar during the Korean War. Three 100sq ft (9m²) parachutes will slow the 5000lb (2268kg) piece during its descent, allowing it to land undamaged for use by UN troops. Below: A Douglas C-74 Globemaster in flight over mountainous terrain.

as a Chinese cargo aircraft in the 1969 film *The Italian Job.*

The end of 1945 also saw the first flight of the utilitarian Bristol 170 Freighter. A simple, boxy design, the aircraft featured clamshell doors for loading and unloading cargo. The first prototype flew on December 2, and the aircraft soon attracted the interest of civilian operators. The Mk. 32 Freighter was built with a combined passenger cabin and cargo area into which cars could be driven, allowing holidaymakers to take their vehicles on trips abroad—a feature shared with the Aviation Traders Carvair. One Bristol Freighter remained airworthy in Canada as late as 1999.

The Soviets relied heavily on the licence-built C-47, the Lisunov Li-2, throughout the war, but in 1946 the Ilyushin design bureau unveiled the Il-12 "Coach." Resembling a DC-3 with a nosewheel, the aircraft had a clumsy appearance and required a supporting strut when the aircraft was loaded from the rear to prevent it from toppling over. A total of 3300 were built, the majority of which were in Red Army service.

US innovations

The USAAF ended World War II with a collection of ageing freighters which needed urgent replacement. To this end, American aircraft companies began to design aircraft like the Fairchild C-119 Boxcar, a development of the C-82 Packet which first flew on September 10, 1944. A curious design, the Boxcar had two booms extending back from the wings to support the aircraft's tailplane, and a fuselage in the middle forming a central "pod." The entire rear of the fuselage could open to allow the loading and unloading of cargo. By the time production ended in 1955, over 1150 had been built.

The age of the USAAF freighter fleet in the late 1940s, combined with the onset of the Cold War and the recognition of the importance of cargo aircraft in World War II, encouraged the newly formed US Air Force (USAF) to pour new resources into freight aircraft of all shapes and sizes. This was necessary to move US troops and their equipment rapidly between military outposts across the world from Guam to Great Britain.

Having enjoyed success with its C-54, in 1946 the Douglas aircraft company had won a contract from the USAF to design and build a large, long-

Right: In service with the USAAF in a previous incarnation as the C-69 during World War II, the civilian Constellation re-entered US military service in 1948 as the C-121. Most were used for early warning patrols, although a few were operated as freighters.

range freighter. Douglas unveiled its C-118 Liftmaster based upon the company's DC-6 airliner.

Another cargo aircraft procured to re-equip the freighter fleet was the Lockheed C-121A. This aircraft was the result of a USAF competition to develop a multi-purpose aircraft that could be rapidly converted to carry light cargo, passengers, troops or casualties. The C-121A was the military cargo conversion of Lockheed's Constellation airliner, with a strengthened floor and rear cargo door. The Constellation had been in USAAF service during the war as the C-69, although the design lost out to the C-54 as the USAAF's preferred four-engined transport. The C-121A never quite cut it as a freighter and the majority of aircraft delivered to the USAF served as EC-121K Warning Star early-warning aircraft, which gave valuable service detecting enemy fighters during the Korean War.

The Berlin Airlift

Cargo aircraft were put to the test in June 1948 by the Berlin Airlift. After the partition of Berlin into zones of occupation by the victorious Allied powers, the western Allies (France, Britain, and the United States) fell out with the Soviet Union. The Soviets, who occupied their own segment of

Berlin on the eastern side of the city, were alarmed at the western Allies' proposals to establish what would become West Germany, a country which would initially be under the control of the western Allies and which might later challenge Soviet control of eastern Germany. Moscow was also unhappy about the so-called "Truman doctrine," which promised to "support free people who are resisting attempted subjugation by armed minorities or by outside pressure." The USSR believed that this was an attempt to prevent the spread of international communism. Soviet anger eventually boiled over, and all American military personnel were ordered out of Berlin on April 9, 1948. By June 24, road, river and canal access had been sealed off by the Soviets. The only way to supply the 2,008,943 Berliners in the western sectors of the city, which the Soviets had in effect besieged, was by air.

This was easier said than done. The Americans had 102 C-47 aircraft, each of which could carry 3.5 tons of cargo, although these were later supplemented by C-54 Skymasters. The British had a number of Dakotas, plus Avro Yorks and Handley Page Hastings, which were quickly pressed into service. West Berlin had two airports, Tempelhof and Gatow, which could handle large aircraft. The airlift operation—known as "Vittles" and "Plain Flare" by

Left: On a rainy day at Berlin's Tempelhof airfield, food and other essential goods are offloaded from a C-47 onto waiting trucks during the Berlin Airlift.
Above: Berlin children watch as Allied planes ferry in essential goods in a non-stop chain of freighters.

the Americans and British respectively—began on June 26. The entire operation was supervised by Major General William H. Tunner, who had organized the Allied airlift into China during the closing stages of World War II. A renowned transportation expert, it was said that the thing Tunner hated above all was to see aircraft lying idle on the apron when they could be flying supplies into Berlin.

For the next thirteen months, Tunner's aircraft flew in everything Berlin needed, including coal, food, oil, and medicines. Salt was even delivered using Short Sunderland flying boats, which landed on Lake Havel in the middle of Berlin. Aircraft were landing at the city's airports once every two minutes, 24 hours per day, in all weathers. The Soviets eventually lifted the blockade on May 12, 1949, after protracted negotiations. Meanwhile the airlift continued until September 30 to ensure that supplies in the British, American, and French sectors

were replenished. During the operation American aircraft had delivered 1,783,572 tons (1,812,109 tonnes) of supplies; the British delivered a further 541,936 tons (550,607 tonnes). Between them, C-47 and C-54 aircraft travelled 92 million miles (148 million km) at a cost of 101 lives. The airlift also brought about a new airport at Tegel in the French sector. Tegel was constructed in just three months to allow more aircraft to land in the city and is now Berlin's main airport.

Airlift in Korea

The success of the Berlin Airlift and the ever-escalating transport needs of the US armed forces spurred on initiatives to design new heavy-lift aircraft. One such aircraft was the Douglas C-124 Globemaster II, which made its first flight on November 27, 1949. An updated version of the C-74 with a deeper fuselage and more powerful engines, it used the same wings as its predecessor.

Above: *Short Sunderland flying boats were pressed into service to help relieve the Soviet blockade. This aircraft is in the process of transferring 140 cases of egg powder onto a waiting barge in July 1948.*

Nicknamed "Old Shaky" by its crews, the design included combustion heaters to warm the cabin, wing and tail de-icing equipment and a weather radar mounted in the nose. Although the C-124 was short on comfort, it had two cranes mounted in the fuselage which could each lift 16,000lb (7257kg) of cargo along the 77ft (23m) long fuselage. The aircraft could carry 74,000lb (33,566kg) of cargo loaded via the clamshell doors and ramps underneath the nose, and could be converted to carry 200 fully-equipped troops, or 123 stretchers and accompanying medical staff. During the Korean War the aircraft played a vital role in airlifting US Army vehicles into the theatre. Airlift was essential in Korea, as C-124s, C-47 Skytrains and C-119 Boxcars ferried supplies, dropped paratroops and evacuated the wounded. C-124s would later play an equally important role during the Vietnam War. Journeys in Old Shaky could be long, and a return trip from Travis Air Force Base (AFB) in California to

Tan Son Nhut AFB in South Vietnam could take 97 hours.

In 1950 the USAF took delivery of its first Convair C-131 Samaritan, a military transport variant of the CV-240 airliner. This aircraft was used primarily for MedEvac, and to supplement the flying ambulance role played by the Lockheed C-121. It could carry 27 stretchers or 37 seated casualties.

Although lacking the Globemaster II's capacity, the contemporary French Nord Noratlas was a versatile freighter which made its maiden flight on September 10, 1949. Resembling the C-118 Boxcar, its career stretched into the 1980s, despite the fact that production ended in October 1961. The type was exported to West Germany, Israel (where it served in the 1956 Suez Crisis, the 1967 Six Day War, and the 1973 Yom Kippur War), Niger, Nigeria, Chad, and Greece. In French service it saw combat during the war in Algeria and during the Suez Crisis. The freighter also found some limited civilian service with Air

Above: *Reflecting the Cold War political realities of a power balance between the superpowers based on nuclear deterrents, the Douglas C-133 Cargomaster was built to carry US nuclear missiles.*

Right: *Korean laborers take a momentary respite from their runway repairs to glance upwards at the C-119 above their heads, flying in to resupply UN troops during the Korean War.*

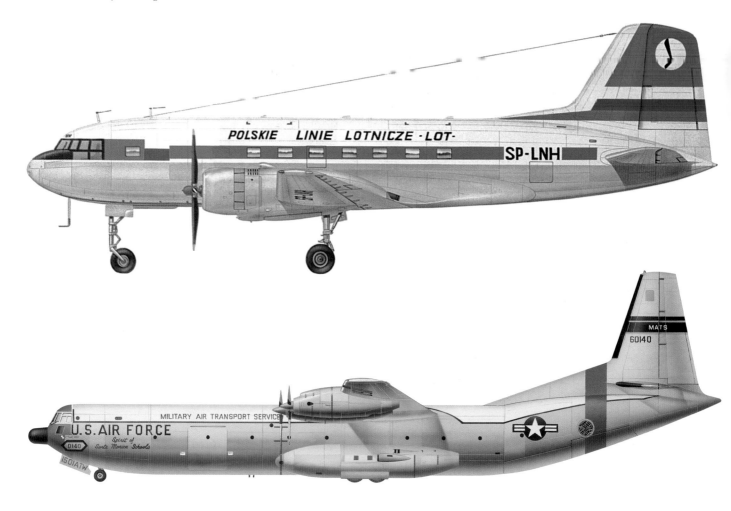

Algérie and the French airline Union des Transports Aériens (UTA).

As the war raged in Korea, the Soviets introduced the Ilyushin Il-14 "Crate." Based on the earlier Il-12 design, this aircraft had a safer airframe and better engines. The aircraft eventually entered service with the Soviet Air Force and later with Aeroflot in 1954.

One year after the Il-14's first flight, the Boeing C-97 Stratofreighter entered service with the USAF in 1951 to supplement its fleet of Globemaster II heavy, long range freighters. Based on the Boeing 377 Stratocruiser airliner, it performed a variety of roles ranging from transport to air-to-air refuelling, MedEvac and search and rescue.

Dedicated freighter

The Il-14, C-97 Stratofreighter and C-131 Samaritan were all derived from airliners from which the seats had been removed to make space for freight. But on April 23, 1956, the revolutionary Douglas C-133 Cargomaster flew for the first time. Conceived as a dedicated freighter, the aircraft shared a similar configuration to the C-130 Hercules. It was primarily designed to carry USAF Intercontinental Ballistic Missiles (ICBMs), and to fly supplies to isolated USAF ballistic missile warning radars near the Arctic circle, although the aircraft gave valuable service in Vietnam. Unlike most earlier freighters, the Cargomaster featured the high-wing design which would become a key design feature for later heavy lift aircraft.

The Cargomaster's main undercarriage was housed in two "blisters" on either side of the fuselage below each wing, to avoid taking up valuable space in the main hold. Large side-loading doors and a combined rear loading door and ramp were also included in the design. The 157ft 6in (47m) fuselage was pressurized and heated.

Top: *The Soviet-built Ilyushin Il-14 "Crate" operated as a short range transport and passenger aircraft. This aircraft is depicted as being in service with LOT, the Polish national carrier.*
Above: *The Douglas C-133 Cargomaster would provide the template for future military freighters, right up to the modern Boeing C-17 Globemaster. It could carry the equivalent of 22 loaded railway boxcars.*

Above: *The Boeing C-97 Stratofreighter had a "double bubble" fuselage, created by grafting an upper structure onto the airframe of the B-29 Superfortress.*

British designs

In 1955 the RAF had issued a requirement for a new freighter to replace its ageing Avro Yorks. The successful design was the turboprop-engined Armstrong Whitworth Argosy. A twin-tailboom aircraft similar to the Noratlas and Boxcar, the aircraft featured a "stepped" cockpit on top of the fuselage. The prototype flew on January 8, 1959, and as well as serving with the RAF, the aircraft flew commercially with British European Airways, Riddle Airlines in the United States, Safe Air in New Zealand and on parcel delivery flights for IPEC in Australia.

Another RAF freighter, the piston-engined Blackburn Beverley, had entered service in 1956. Described as one of the ugliest aircraft ever built, the fixed-undercarriage Beverley gave sterling service with several RAF Squadrons in Aden, Brunei, Kenya, Malaysia, and Tanzania. A stepped cockpit was mounted over the obese-looking fuselage, and the tail boom could accommodate 36 passengers. A prototype flew on June 20, 1950, and was so un-aerodynamic in appearance that Blackburn engineers reportedly placed bets on whether the aircraft would actually fly. Forty-seven Beverleys were produced, some of which coincidentally served with the RAF's 47 Squadron, which was formed in Beverley, Yorkshire, the aircraft's namesake town.

Canada keeps up

In 1956 De Havilland Canada began work on a rugged, hard working freighter known as the DHC-4 Caribou, which made its maiden flight on July 30, 1958. The DHC-4 was produced in response to a US Army request for a Short Take-Off and Landing (STOL) aircraft which could operate from unprepared airstrips as short as 1,000ft (300m) in length, which could be hastily prepared near the battlefield. The aircraft saw US

Army service until 1967, when it was transferred to the USAF and redesignated the C-7.

It is not unusual for a freighter to load its cargo through its nose, as with the Lockheed C-5 Galaxy, the Antonov An-124 Ruslan "Condor" and the Aero Spacelines Guppy series. Nor is it unusual to use clamshell doors or a rear ramp to load and unload cargo. But the so-called "swing-tail" design of the Canadair CL-44—in which the entire tail of the aircraft could swing sideways to allow the loading of cargo into the rear fuselage—was a genuinely novel idea.

The Canadair CL-44 was based on Canadair's earlier Yukon transporter, which in turn was derived from the Bristol Britannia four-turboprop airliner. The swing-tail design allowed cargo to be rapidly loaded and unloaded and was also adopted on some DC-4 and DC-6 freighters. Several airlines were enthusiastic about the CL-44, which first flew in 1959, although few eventually operated them. Flying Tiger Line and Seaboard World Airlines ordered 12 and seven of the aircraft respectively, but Japan Cargo Airlines and BOAC abandoned their planned purchases. The days of the civilian turboprop freighter were coming to an end. In a few years time the Boeing 707 airliner would be ferrying both passengers and air freight around the world.

Top: *The first prototype Series 100 Armstrong Whitworth Argosy took its maiden flight on January 8, 1959. Argosys operated in Singapore, Australia and the United States as freighters.*
Above: *A De Havilland Canada C-7A Caribou pictured on a training exercise in June 1975.*
Right: *A Canadair CL-44 freighter of the Flying Tiger Line.*

Above: *The Guppy series of outsized cargo freighters used a swing nose for loading and unloading. They were used by the Airbus consortium for many years to ferry airliner parts between Airbus production centres.*
Right: *The standard workhorse freighter of the Soviet Union and later Russia, the Antonov An-12 "Cub."*

Outsize guppies

The swing-tail design of the CL-44 formed the template for the Guppy series of transport aircraft, the first of which made its maiden flight on September 19, 1962. Some of the oddest aircraft in aviation history, Guppies were specifically designed for the transport of oversized cargo in their hugely expanded and heightened fuselages. One of the main roles of the Super Guppy, which was based on the Boeing Stratocruiser airframe, was to move components for the Saturn V rockets used by the Apollo space program to Cape Canaveral in Florida. Before that, the rockets were moved from their factory in California via a slow boat through the Panama Canal to the launch pad. Guppies would later be used by the Airbus consortium, moving large airliner components from factories across Europe to the Airbus assembly line in Toulouse, France.

Rugged and reliable

In 1962 the Antonov An-12 "Cub" entered service in the Soviet Union, one of the most rugged and successful freighters ever designed; over 900 examples were built until production finished in 1973, and aircraft were exported to Algeria, Bangladesh, Egypt, India, Iraq, Poland, Syria, Sudan, and Yugoslavia. Following the example of the C-133 Cargomaster and C-130 Hercules, the aircraft could be loaded via its rear fuselage, but the cargo area was not pressurized. A 5070lb (2300kg) gantry crane was also included for moving cargo around the aircraft. The An-12 was built under licence in China as the Shaanxi Y-8, and a purpose-built helicopter-carrying variant—the Y-8A—was also constructed. This version omitted the internal cranes to give the extra headroom needed for helicopters.

Vietnam

As the "Cub" began to be introduced by the Soviet Union and her allies, the United States was intensifying its involvement in Vietnam. President Lyndon Johnson had increased the presence of America's armed forces as they, alongside their South Vietnamese counterparts, tried to prevent Communist North Vietnam from overrunning the South and installing a Marxist regime. Transport aircraft played a key role in the conflict, moving troops and equipment around the country much as they had done in Korea. One freighter which came of age in Vietnam was the Fairchild C-123 Provider. Based upon the Chase YC-122 prototype, the design had two piston engines (later supplemented with two jets) on high-mounted wings and a rear loading ramp. Fairchild, which had acquired Chase in 1953, built over 300 examples of the Provider, and it was exported to Saudi Arabia and Venezuela. The last squadron of C-123 aircraft (which eventually ended up in USAF Reserve service) stood down in 1982.

Left: *Troops and equipment of the US 1st Air Cavalry Division are loaded on board C-123 and CV-2B transports. The soldiers and aircraft would participate in Operation Masher, one of the largest search and destroy missions of the Vietnam War.*

As good as the C-123 and C-7 Caribou proved in the early years of the war, the US Air Force cargo fleet was insufficient for the task in hand. The C-130 Hercules had entered service with the USAF in 1956 as a replacement for the Boxcar. Almost ten years later, in 1965, C-130s came into their own, as aircraft from the USAF 779th Troop Carrier Squadron began to fly personnel and supplies from Thailand into Vietnam. C-130s would be important throughout the conflict moving everything from mail to aircraft parts. C-130 flights to and from the theatre were known as the "Bangkok Shuttle." The aircraft went on to perform many other roles, as detailed elsewhere in this book, and remains in service with many air forces around the world today.

President John F. Kennedy's first official act upon his inauguration in 1961 was to order the development of a jet-engined military freighter to allow America's armed forces to move their troops and equipment around the world quickly and efficiently. The aircraft would need a range of at least 4027 miles (6482km) and the ability to carry a 60,000lb (27,216kg) payload. The result was the Lockheed C-141 Starlifter, which first flew on December 17, 1963—the 60th anniversary of the Wright brothers' first flight. In 1964 the first aircraft was delivered to Tinker Air Force Base, Oklahoma. Soon it would be ferrying troops and equipment to Southeast Asia and returning with casualties, as the cost of US involvement in Vietnam escalated. Shortly after the Starlifter entered service, it became clear that its fuselage—designed primarily to carry the LGM-30 Minuteman-II ICBM—was insufficient for other requirements. The solution was to stretch it by

23.3ft (7.16m) which increased the payload by 20,030lb (9086kg) to 90,880lb (41,222kg). The stretched aircraft was known as the C-141B. This version of the Starlifter was to remain in service for more than 30 years, and was notably used to airlift forces, equipment and supplies to Saudi Arabia during Operation Desert Shield, the prelude to Operation Desert Storm. During the military campaign to evict Saddam Hussein's forces from Kuwait following his invasion in August 1990, the USAF moved 482,000 personnel and 513,000 tons (521,208 tonnes) of cargo.

Flying car ferries

In the late 1940s, the Bristol 170 Freighter had shown that an aircraft could be used as a car ferry over short distances. This idea was again pursued in 1961 with the Aviation Traders Carvair. An adaptation of the DC-4, the Carvair had a stepped cockpit in a hump above the forward fuselage, giving the aircraft the appearance of a stunted, prop-powered Boeing 747. This design allowed the nose to be opened so that cars could be driven into the fuselage. Passengers were housed in the rear of the aircraft. Up to six family sedans could be loaded onto the aircraft along with 22 passengers. The Carvair entered service with British Air Ferries, Aer Lingus of Ireland, and Aviaco of Spain, as well as other airlines in Australia, France, and Luxembourg. However, it could not compete with the new low-cost ferries and the fast cross-Channel hovercraft, which began services from Ramsgate to Calais in the Carvair's last year of commercial flights. Ultimately, Carvairs served around the world, carrying all manner of outsized loads until their retirement in the 1980s.

Carrier Onboard Delivery

It is not just troops on the ground which need to be transported and supplied. The US Navy's nuclear-powered aircraft carriers, with their legions of aircraft and personnel, have a voracious appetite. For this purpose Grumman designed the C-2 Greyhound, which made its maiden flight on November 18, 1964. Powered by two turboprop engines, the aircraft could rapidly deliver 10,000lb (4536kg) of cargo or 26 passengers to an aircraft carrier. A rear ramp allowed matériel to be loaded and unloaded from the aircraft. The C-2 operated alongside Grumman's C-1 Trader, a similar aircraft used for Carrier Onboard Delivery (COD), which entered US Navy service in January 1955 and which could lift 3500lb (1587kg) of cargo or nine passengers.

Giants of the 1960s

The Short Belfast was one of the largest and most impressive British aircraft of the 1960s, although only ten were built. The Belfast was designed as a strategic freighter for the RAF, able to carry up to 150 fully-armed troops or two Chieftain Main Battle Tanks. It was said that the cargo hold was big enough to carry two single-decker buses. The Belfast had a 136ft (41m) fuselage and a 158ft (48m) wingspan. Each of the RAF's ten aircraft was appropriately named after a famous giant, *Goliath* and *Enceladus* being two examples. Following its service with the RAF, the freighter continued to fly with Heavy Lift Cargo Airlines Ltd, where it was often chartered to the US Air Force to carry oversized loads.

Below: *A US Air Force vehicle unloads cargo from a Lockheed C-141 Starlifter. Along with the C-130, this freighter also gave impressive service during the Vietnam War.*
Right: *A Grumman C-1 Trader performs a "Carrier Onboard Delivery." These aircraft were replaced by the Grumman C-2 Greyhound in 1965.*

In the 1960s the United States continued to forge ahead with huge, long range freighters designed to carry heavy military equipment such as tanks, mobile bridges, and helicopters. Building on the success of the Hercules and Starlifter, Lockheed won a contract in 1965 to produce a heavy freighter for the USAF. The result was the C-5 Galaxy, which at the time was was the largest aircraft in the world. The first Galaxy was delivered in June 1970, serving with the 437th Military Airlift Wing at Charleston AFB, South Carolina. With the capacity to carry 270,000lb (122,472kg) of freight loaded through the nose or via the cargo ramp at the rear, the C-5 was nicknamed "the box that the C-141 came in." An undercarriage of 28 wheels can "kneel" to bring the fuselage floor closer to the ground for loading and unloading. The undercarriage also allows the aircraft to land on roughly-prepared airstrips. There are 73 passenger seats in the rear fuselage, above the cargo hold. A crew of six fly the aircraft and there is space behind the cockpit for a relief crew.

While the United States was introducing jet propulsion for its long range freighters, the Soviet Union was still wedded to turboprop cargo aircraft. On February 27, 1965, Antonov's massive An-22 "Cock" flew for the first time. Designed to perform a similar role to the large American freighters and able to carry tanks and mobile missile launchers, 75 of the aircraft were built before construction ceased in 1974. The An-22 was delivered to both the Soviet Air Force and Aeroflot. Between 1967 and 1975 the aircraft set several records, including lifting 98.2 tons (100 tonnes) to 25,748ft (7848m). It also set a speed-with-payload record, carrying 110,250lb (50,000kg) over a 621 mile (1000km) fixed circuit at an average speed of 378mph (608.5km/h).

Soviet multi-tasker

Two years after the An-22 took its maiden flight, the Soviet Air Force made a request for an aircraft to replace the An-12 "Cub" in the heavy-lift role. The Ilyushin Il-76 "Candid" was the Soviets' first

purpose-built jet-powered transport aircraft. This swept-wing aircraft carried four engines beneath its wings and its voluptuous appearance delighted the Soviet Generals. The great Russian aviation designer Andrei Tupolev once said that "a good looking plane cannot fly badly," and the Il-76 did not disappoint.

This Soviet behemoth made its first flight on March 25, 1971. A highly successful aircraft, the Il-76 could convey 126 paratroopers and their equipment at speeds of up to 512mph (825km/h). The aircraft made an important contribution to the Soviet war in Afghanistan in the 1980s. It flew 14,700 missions during the conflict, transporting 90 percent of the Soviet troops who served in the war and 75 percent of their equipment. A strong

airframe allowed the aircraft to take considerable punishment when attacked by anti-Soviet Mujahideen guerrillas armed with heat-seeking missiles and anti-aircraft guns.

Several variants of the Il-76 have been produced, including some with stretched fuselages. They have served as zero-gravity research platforms, as fire engines carrying flame-retardant chemicals and water, and in a variety of other roles in addition to their everyday military and civilian cargo functions. They have played a vital role in delivering food and humanitarian supplies to war-torn states like Ethiopia and Bosnia. Because of their versatility and global reach, it is said that it is hard to find an airport where the Il-76 has not been.

Above: *A Short Belfast unloads the fuselage section of a Fokker F-28 aircraft in Holland. The fuselage has been returned to its manufacturer for repairs.*
Right top: *Two of the USAF's heaviest freighters: a C-141 (foreground) is overshadowed by a Lockheed C-5 Galaxy. The Galaxy is one of the largest aircraft ever to fly.*
Right bottom: *The Antonov An-22 "Cock" was designed to land on rough airstrips and to withstand the harsh Soviet winters.*

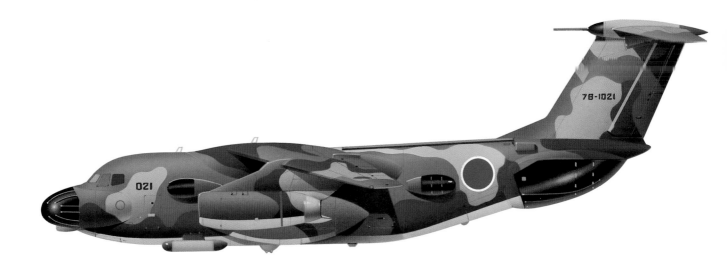

Air mail development

Aircraft like the Armstrong Whitworth Argosy had performed a valuable role as a flying postbag during the 1960s, and mail flights had been important in establishing the air carriage of cargo as a viable enterprise. The delivery of urgent mail by air was further revolutionized in 1973 when Federal Express was founded, initially operating a fleet of Dassault Falcons. The first few years of trading were difficult, but by 1976 the company was making money, helped by the use of cargo aircraft to move parcels speedily. By 1982 Federal Express had 39 Boeing 727s and four Douglas DC-10 airliners that had been converted into freighters. In 1989 the airline acquired Tigers International Inc, the owners of the famous cargo operator Flying Tiger Line. This allowed Federal Express to become the largest all-cargo airline in the world.

Freight moves forward

The freighter market was not just restricted to Soviet, European and American aircraft designs. In 1974, Japan unveiled its Kawasaki C-1, and the first

production aircraft made its maiden flight in December. Designed as a replacement for the Japanese Self Defence Force's C-46 Commando, the C-1 could carry 26,266lb (11,900kg) of freight. This payload was rather disappointing, and the aircraft attracted little interest outside Japan.

The growth of airfreight led Boeing to develop a new version of its highly successful 747 airliner. Entering service in 1975, six years after the 747's first flight, the 747 Combi was formed by partitioning the basic 747 fuselage into a passenger cabin and freight area, allowing the aircraft to be filled with both airfreight and passengers. An all-freighter version of the 747 was also produced, with a hinged nose for loading and unloading. Environmental control of the fuselage allowed everything from small boats to cut flowers and vegetables to be carried across the world.

Utility and STOL designs

At the other end of the cargo-carrying spectrum from the giant Short Belfast was the Shorts C-23B Sherpa, developed from the Shorts 330, which

Left: *Built to replace the ageing Curtiss C-46 in service with the Japanese Self Defence Force, the Kawasaki C-1 represented Japan's debut in tactical jet freighter design.*
Below left: *Although most familiar as a passenger aircraft, the Boeing 747 is also available as a capacious freighter variant. It can be loaded with cargo through its nose or through a side cargo door.*
Below: *A Short C-23 Sherpa in service with the US Army National Guard.*

The Shuttle Piggyback

As well as helping the world's vegetables to arrive fresh, the 747 was indispensable to NASA's Space Shuttle program. The Jumbo allowed the Space Shuttle to be carried from Edwards AFB in California—the original landing site for the Shuttle—back to the launch pad at Cape Canaveral, Florida. NASA owned two specially modified 747s for this purpose. Both aircraft have additional vertical surfaces on the tail which improved stability when the Shuttle is fixed atop of the 747's fuselage. A streamlined tail cone also covered the Orbiter's tail to minimize the drag caused by its engine nozzles. The converted 747s are less frequently used these days, now that the shuttle lands back at Cape Canaveral and the future of the Shuttle program is in question.

It took around $1 million, 200 people and a week of work to transfer the Shuttle from one site to another on the 747. During the flight, a "pathfinder"—usually a NASA C-141—flew ahead of the 747-Shuttle ensemble to spot bad weather so that the aircraft and its precious cargo could avoid it. The inside of NASA's 747s are completely empty, to save weight. One NASA official commented that "you could host a pretty good party in the cabin." The addition of the Shuttle to the 747 airframe caused a vibration to be heard throughout the airframe during the flight due to the turbulence caused by the Orbiter.

The two NASA 747s (which were acquired from American Airlines and Japan Air Lines) have not just been used to move the Shuttle. In the early days of the program they were used to airdrop the Orbiter. The Shuttle would "take off" from the Jumbo once airborne and would then glide back to earth to test its flight characteristics.

Above: *A specially configured 747 was used to launch the Space Shuttle during landing trials before it took to space.*
Below: *NASA's 747s are also invaluable for ferrying the Space Shuttle to and from its landing and launching site.*

Above: *The Antonov An-74, based on the earlier An-72, features high-mounted turbojet engines which give excellent short take-off performance.*

made its maiden flight on August 22, 1974. With a practical rectangular fuselage and high-set wing, the Sherpa is able to move troops and vehicles, perform airdrops and carry out MedEvac missions operating from rough airstrips. The C-23B entered service with the US Army in 1985 and could carry 7000lb (3175kg) of freight or 30 passengers. The USAF also used the Sherpa to move aircraft spare parts around Europe.

The Sherpa is a close relative of the equally odd looking Shorts Skyvan, although the latter aircraft had a fixed undercarriage and a payload of 4500lb (2041kg). It has been described as a "caravan with wings."

In 1977 Antonov unveiled the An-72 "Coaler" STOL freighter which made its first flight on December 22, 1979. Owing much to the earlier Boeing YC-14, the aircraft had two engines positioned in large pods atop the wings. This was to prevent them from sucking in debris like small

stones, which could wreck the engine when the plane was flying from unprepared airstrips. The engine exhausts blow out over the top of the wings, giving extra lift and reducing the required runway length during the take-off run.

Size matters

Until 1982 the Lockheed C-5 Galaxy had been the largest freighter in regular service. It lost that crown on December 26, 1982, when the massive An-124 Ruslan "Condor" first took to the skies. This long-range freighter entered service with the Soviet Air Force and Aeroflot from 1986. Like the Galaxy, the Ruslan can kneel to offload its cargo and can operate from unprepared surfaces thanks to its 24-wheel undercarriage. The aircraft has a maximum take-off weight of 892,872lb (405,000kg) and a range of 2795 miles (4500km) with its maximum payload. Flying empty with a maximum fuel load, this can be extended to an astonishing 10,250 miles

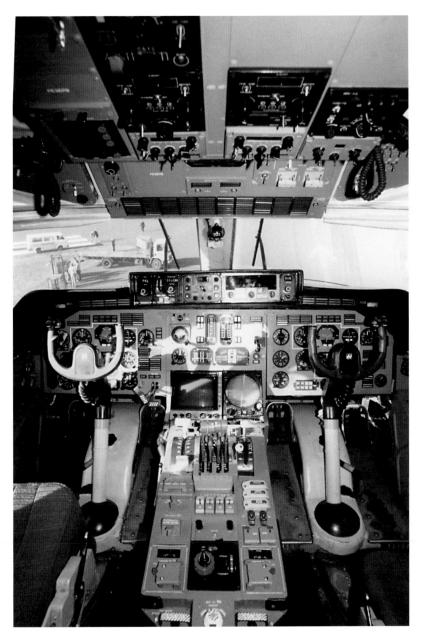

Far left: *Soviet aviation design produced one of the largest jet-powered transport aircraft ever in the Antonov An-124 Ruslan.*

Above: *This Antonov An-124 was flown in a cooperative arrangement by the Russian cargo carrier Volga Dnepr and the UK-based cargo carrier HeavyLift.*

Left: *The cockpit of the An-124 is mounted high above the main cargo deck, behind the hinged-nose cargo door.*

(16,500km). Like the Galaxy, passenger seating is available on the upper deck, but with capacity for 88 passengers as opposed to the 73 conveyed by its American cousin. On July 26, 1985, the An-124 set a new world record, lifting 377,473lb (171,219kg) to 35,269ft (10,750m).

The An-124 was the basis for the even larger Antonov An-225 Mriya (Dream), which first flew on December 21, 1988, and holds the current title of the largest aircraft in the world. Originally designed to carry the Russian Space Shuttle "Buran" on its back, its designers had hoped that the aircraft would also be able to transport bulky oil and gas exploration equipment around Russia's northern territories. The Mriya is longer than the Ruslan, needing a 32-wheel undercarriage and six turbofans to propel it on the ground and through the skies. The fuselage is extended by 49ft (15m) to 275ft (84m), and its maximum take-off weight is a remarkable 1,322,750lb (600,000kg).

New designs from Europe

The Nord Noratlas worked hard for the French Armée de l'Air and the West German Luftwaffe,

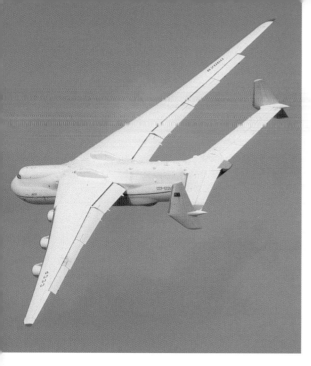

Flying the "dream"

The Mriya—so far only one has been built—is an aircraft of impressive statistics. Its 107ft (32.65m) horizontal tail is wider than the wingspan of a Boeing 737-300. The tail has two vertical fins at its tips to give the aircraft better handling when carrying a load on its back.

The sheer size of the aircraft can make it temperamental on the ground. Its undercarriage has four nose wheels, and a special tow bar is needed for a tug which in turn has to be powerful enough to move the aircraft out of its parking space. The nose then has to be lifted and the tow bar stowed back inside the aircraft using an internal crane. When on the ground the heavy aircraft can sometimes sink into tarmac taxiways and runways warmed by the sun.

When the plane takes off, it creates a massive disturbance in the air, causing violent vortices. Other aircraft waiting to depart after the Mriya have to wait for fifteen minutes for the air to settle. As a consequence, the An-225 is normally seen at quiet airfields rather than major airports, where there is constant pressure to keep aircraft landing and departing.

Since the aircraft first began commercial flights with Stansted-based Antonov Airlines, there has been no shortage of pilots from around the world seeking vacancies to fly this amazing aircraft. But their approaches are often unsuccessful. The crews flying both the Mriya and the Ruslan tend to be Russian or Ukrainian, and any would-be Antonov pilots must be fluent in Russian to work with the crews and to read the instruments in the aircraft's cockpit.

As well as moving heavy cargoes around the world, the aircraft has performed important humanitarian missions. On December 11, 2002, the Mriya left New York bound for Africa, filled with toys and games for Ugandan children as part of the "Operation Christmas Child" humanitarian initiative. Seeing off the flight, Bono, lead singer of rock band U2, was overheard saying that the aircraft was "bigger than a rock star's ego."

Top: *The scale of the Antonov An-225 "Mriya" can be seen by the massive span and surface area of its wings.*
Bottom: *A giant comes to rest as the sole An-225 in service comes to land at the Farnborough Air Show in 1990.*

Above: *The prototype Fiat/Aeritalia G222. The type has also seen service with the USAF as the C-27 Spartan.*

and its replacement also had its work cut out transporting troops and equipment around the world. The Transall C-160 was the product of the Franco-German Transport Allianz consortium, formed to develop a twin-engined turboprop freighter. In 1987 the last Transall rolled off the production lines, after a total of 160 had been built for the French and German air forces. The aircraft can carry a 35,275lb (16,000kg) payload, 93 soldiers or 62 stretchers. Like the C-5 Galaxy, the aircraft's undercarriage can be lowered to ease loading and unloading.

Three years later another European-developed cargo aircraft entered service with the USAF, a variant of the Fiat G.222 known as the C-27 Spartan. Built by the Italian Alenia company, ten

were purchased and stationed at Howard AFB, Panama, for operations with USAF Southern Command in Latin America. The aircraft was not especially popular with the force, however, and all of the Spartans were in storage by 1999.

Antonov followed their successful series of cargo aircraft with the An-70. This medium-sized STOL freighter made its first flight in 1994. Development of the aircraft was slowed following a crash on February 10, 1995, when a prototype collided with an An-72 chase-plane during a test-flight. Unlike its Ruslan, Mriya, and "Coaler" counterparts, the An-70 is powered by state-of-the-art turboprop engines featuring contra-rotating propellers. They give the aircraft high-speed performance at a low fuel cost, while

Below: *The Transall C-160 is a rugged, twin-engined tactical freighter. It was a joint collaborative project between France and Germany. It serves with the Armée de l'Air and the Luftwaffe as well as the Turkish Air Force.*
Right: *Up to 110 fully-equipped paratroopers or 300 regular soldiers can be carried in Antonov's latest generation freighter, the An-70, which is powered by four contra-rotating prop fans.*

composite materials used in the construction of the propellers help to save weight. With a maximum take-off weight of 135 tons (137 tonnes), the aircraft can cruise efficiently at between 466 and 497mph (750–800km/h) and operate from unprepared dirt airstrips.

They may look ungainly and lack the glamour of fast military aircraft, but the cargo plane has been an unsung hero. In under a century, air freight has gone from transporting small bundles of fabric across a country, to moving railway locomotives across the world. Lives have been saved through the speedy movement of food and aid supplies to disaster areas, and armies have won wars through the rapid movement of troops and matériel by air.

Aircraft like the Ruslan, Galaxy, and Belfast have pushed speeds and payloads upwards, but it remains to be seen whether the size of cargo aircraft will continue to increase, or whether the Russians have reached the limit with the Ruslan and its even bigger cousin, the solitary Mriya.

military aviation in the cold war

superpower stand-off

The defeat of fascism in World War II left the Soviet Union under Joseph Stalin as the most powerful state in Europe. Nervous of Soviet expansion the Western powers, including the United States, Canada, France, and the United Kingdom, signed the North Atlantic Treaty Organisation (NATO) Treaty in 1949. NATO would be a mutual defence pact in which an attack on one nation would be treated as an attack on the whole alliance.

Left: *An RAF Boeing E-3 AWACS in formation with an RAF Panavia Tornado.*
Top: *Wave upon wave of bombers take to the skies. Such displays were valuable propaganda exercises during the Cold War as both sides demonstrated the resolve and power of their deterrent.*

While the Western powers were establishing NATO, the Soviets were busy establishing a similar alliance. Following World War II, Moscow had kept a tight grip on several of the countries it had liberated from Nazi rule. Puppet communist governments were installed, and a mutual defence organization known as the Warsaw Pact was formed.

Air power proved vital in deterring each alliance from attacking the other, as legions of warplanes faced each other across Europe. In the early days of the Cold War, before the advent of Intercontinental Ballistic Missiles (ICBMs), long-range bombers were the only "platform" able to deliver nuclear weapons. Early atomic and hydrogen bombs

The egg-shaped killer

Bomber and fighter development accelerated after the end of World War II. It became clear to the United States and the Soviet Union that their bombers would be vulnerable to high performance fighters. In America, a novel idea was developed to allow a bomber to defend itself during an attack by carrying its own fighter plane.

In 1945 a project under the leadership of the McDonnell Aircraft Company began to develop a bomber-portable fighter plane, which could attack enemy fighters before returning to its host aircraft. To this end, the XF-85 "Goblin" was developed. This egg-shaped fighter would be stored in the bomber's weapons bay. It had a pressurized cockpit, an ejector seat and four machine guns. It could be launched from the bomber to engage the enemy and would be retrieved by a retractable "trapeze."

A specially-configured Boeing B-29 Superfortress bomber was used to test the concept. On 23 August 1948 an XF-85 was successfully launched from a B-29, but its return to the bomber proved difficult. The trapeze smashed into the cockpit, tearing off the Goblin pilot's oxygen mask. Putting the remains of the hose in his mouth, he made a 200mph (321km/h) emergency landing on special skids fitted to the aircraft for this kind of emergency.

In 1949 the project was canceled. Improvements in refueling technology meant that conventional fighters could now accompany the bomber force. Secondly, the return docking procedure was judged to be so difficult, even for highly trained test pilots, that it was uncertain how many squadron pilots could perform such a feat. Finally, the Goblin's performance was judged to be markedly inferior to the fighters that would soon be entering service.

Top: *McDonnell's tiny and basic XF-85 Goblin was a far cry from today's state-of-the-art warplanes.*
Below: *A pilot surveys an XF-85 Goblin prior to a test flight. The rationale behind this aircraft was eventually rendered obsolete by the appearance of air-to-air missiles and the demise of dogfighting.*

Above: *Two USAF McDonnell Douglas F-4 Phantoms keep a close eye on a Soviet Tupolev Tu-95 "Bear" reconnaissance aircraft as it strays into NATO airspace.*

were heavy—the first American hydrogen bomb, the Mk. 17, weighed 41,997lb (19,050kg)—and these weapons required large aircraft with enough fuel to carry them to their targets.

SAC and the B-29

Bombers were flexible. They could take off when ordered, and "loiter" before being sent to their targets. Communications allowed targets to be changed in flight. Bombers were also thought to be the most accurate of the nuclear delivery systems available. But how many bombers would have made it to their targets in wartime is uncertain. Inevitably some aircraft would have been shot down, and some would have been in maintenance as hostilities broke out. Bomber bases were vulnerable to attack and some might have been destroyed by the opening salvo of nuclear weapons before their aircraft had even taken off.

For a few years, the USAF had to rely on the Boeing B-29 Superfortress to deliver its atomic bombs. The B-29 was the only plane to have dropped atomic bombs in anger at the close of World War II. But with a range of 5830 miles (9382km), there was a limit to the targets in the USSR that the aircraft could reach. This was partially remedied by the USAF's use of British airfields. After the NATO Treaty was signed, up to eight nuclear-armed B-29s, codenamed "Silver Plate," were deployed to the UK to strike targets in southern Russia. Strategic Air Command (SAC)—in charge of the USAF strategic bomber force throughout the Cold War—also had access to bases in Alaska, the Azores, Guam, Libya, Morocco, Okinawa, and the Philippines.

Ironically, the B-29 design was also the first nuclear bomber to enter Soviet service. Three B-29s had landed in the USSR during World War II. They were retained and copied by the Tupolev

Left: The Boeing B-29 Superfortress, America's first nuclear bomber and the only aircraft to drop an atomic weapon in anger.

Left bottom: In an effort to improve the range of the B-29, Boeing developed the B-50 as a replacement. Note the fuel tanks beneath the wings.

Above: *Originally designed to bomb Europe from the USA during World War II, the Convair B-36 Peacemaker was reconfigured to carry nuclear weapons.*

design bureau, which produced the aircraft as the Tu-4 "Bull." The Chinese People's Liberation Army Air Force (PLAAF) also acquired 13 Bulls from the Soviet Union. However, these aircraft had a range of only 2224 miles (3580km) with a load of 19,841 lb (9000kg), which did not allow a round trip to their likely targets.

The USAF solution to the range issue was to order Boeing to develop an improved version of the B-29, the B-50. This aircraft had a 4650 mile (7483km) range and featured Pratt and Whitney R-4360-35 piston engines, which gave 50 percent more power than the Wright Double Cyclone 2200hp (1641kW) engines of its predecessor. However, the USAF soon realized that the B-50 was only a stop-gap—a new, even larger and more powerful bomber would be needed.

Bigger is better

The Convair B-36 Peacemaker was designed in the early 1940s to bomb targets in occupied Europe should the UK have been invaded by the Nazis. The development program slowed down once it became clear that Hitler's invasion of Britain was no longer imminent. Entering service in 1948, the Peacemaker was one of the largest aircraft ever built, with a wingspan of 230ft (70m). It was powered by six rearward-facing piston engines and four turbojets—nicknamed "six turning and four burning." The B-36 had a range of 6800 miles (10,944km), and its size prompted one pilot to remark that it was "like flying an apartment building."

By 1950 the Boeing B-47 Stratojet had followed the Peacemaker into SAC service. 1200 of these aircraft equipped 28 bombardment wings. The numerous gun-turrets of previous bombers were dispensed with, along with their large crews. A crew of three flew the B-47. Top speeds of 557mph (896km/h) at altitudes of 40,500ft (12,344m), coupled with sophisticated electronic countermeasures and a single aft-facing gun, comprised its defence.

But the 4,000 mile (6440km) range of the

Stratojet was disappointing. Air-to-air refueling was vigorously pursued as a way to address the short range of these aircraft. Tankers played a vital strategic role in the Cold War. Refueling at high altitude mid-mission allowed warplanes great and small to extend their range without having to divert to airfields. It meant the bomber forces of the world's nuclear powers (USA, USSR, UK, France, and China) could in theory reach anywhere on earth.

Air-to-air refueling

Entering service in the early 1950s, the first tanker to serve with the USAF was the Boeing KC-97.

Based on the Boeing Stratocruiser airliner, the plane used the so-called "flying boom" refueling system in which the tanker carried a long rigid boom to link up with a fuel receptacle on another aircraft. This system was also used nearly 20 years later by the French for a time.

The British and the Soviets preferred the "hose and drogue" method, by which a long hose with a basket at the end was trailed from a tanker. The receiving aircraft steered a probe into the basket, triggering the fuel flow. For a time, the Soviets used a wingtip-to-wingtip method with their Tupolev Tu-16 "Badger" bombers, but this was later abandoned. The USAF followed the KC-97

Above: Boeing's B-47 Stratojet was America's first jet-propelled strategic nuclear bomber. Some aircraft were equipped with additional rocket packs to enable a swift take-off in the event of a sudden attack.
Right top: The Soviets experimented with a wingtip-to-wingtip refueling method for the Tupolev Tu-16 "Badger."
Right bottom: USAF F-15s refueling using the "flying boom" method.

Nuclear-powered aircraft

In the 1940s the relatively new science of nuclear physics was not just engaged in developing bombs, but was also being investigated as a means of propelling aircraft. To this end, the Nuclear Energy Propulsion for Aircraft (NEPA) program began in the spring of 1946 under USAF auspices. The USAF was interested in developing a long-range nuclear powered bomber with an endurance unhindered by fuel consumption.

In a 1947 paper, Kelly Johnson and F.A. Cleveland of Lockheed wrote: "It appears that the strategic bomber, by requiring both high speed and great endurance and because of the inherent low-altitude potential advantages over similar chemical airplanes, will be the first candidate for a nuclear power plant." By 1948 the Fairchild Engine and Airframe Company was contracted to investigate the concept.

In 1952 a B-36H bomber was procured as a testbed for a nuclear propulsion system for the proposed X-6 bomber. Known as the Nuclear Test Aircraft (NTA), it was redesignated the "NB-36H" and modified to carry a nuclear reactor in its aft weapons bay. Shielding surrounded the reactor to protect the aircraft from radiation and a nose section with 12 tons of shielding was added to protect the crew. The aircraft performed a number of flights during which the reactor was used, but the X-6 program ran into trouble and was scrapped in 1953.

Not to be outdone, the Soviets began their own initiative in 1954. One proposal mooted the construction of a 1000-ton (1016 tonne) flying boat with four nuclear-powered turboprop engines and carrying 1000 passengers or 100 tons (101.6 tonnes)of cargo at 621mph (1000 km/h).

The USAF project was restarted in 1955, and the NB-36H made more test flights. Those involved were confident of the concept's safety and it was decided that "the risks caused by radiation were no greater than the risks that had been incurred during the development of steam and electric power, the airplane, the automobile, or the rocket." That year, having given up on the idea of a nuclear-powered flying boat, the Soviets began developing a nuclear-powered version of one of their existing bombers. The turboprop-powered Tu-95LAL (Letavshaia Atomnaia Laboratoriya—Flying Atomic Laboratory) also featured a nuclear reactor and tons of shielding for the crew.

Yet the renaissance of the NB-36H was short-lived. On March 28, 1961, President John F. Kennedy cancelled the project, commenting that "nearly 15 years and about $1 billion have been devoted to the attempted development of a nuclear-powered aircraft, but the possibility of achieving a militarily useful aircraft in the foreseeable future is still very remote." By August 1961 the Soviets had also pulled the plug, having learned of the demise of the US project. Moscow felt that the cost of developing a fleet of nuclear-powered bombers—estimated at the value of the entire Soviet national budget for the next two years—was a little expensive.

Right: *The sole NB-36H test aircraft in flight. Developing a nuclear powered bomber was always going to be difficult at best, and the Nuclear Energy Propulsion for Aircraft (NEPA) project was scrapped in 1961.*
Below: *Note the redesigned nose and cockpit of the NB-36H. This was necessary to protect the crew from radiation.*

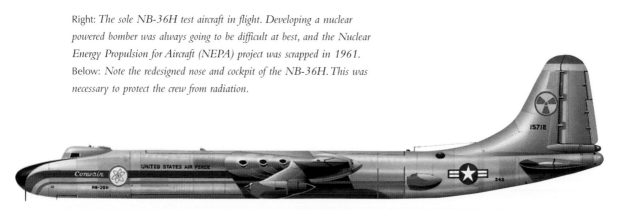

Below: *The MiG-15 "Fagot" made life difficult for*
U.S. pilots over the skies of Korea.
Bottom: *A MiG-17 "Fresco" on display alongside*
other Warsaw Pact military technology.

Left: *A pair of Sukhoi Su-7 "Fitters" in flight. Note the high angle at which the wings are swept back.*

with other airliner designs adapted as tankers, including the KC-135, based on the Boeing 707, and the KC-10, modelled on the McDonnell Douglas DC-10. The RAF also used airliner conversions, including the Vickers VC-10 and the Lockheed L-1011 Tristar, although Avro Vulcan and Handley Page Victor bombers were also converted to tankers toward the end of their service lives. Not all nuclear bomber crews would benefit from refueling. French Dassault Mirage IVA bombers with a 2485 mile (4000km) range had an insufficient endurance for a return journey after attacking targets deep in the Soviet Union, even with tanker support, given that the tankers would have been too vulnerable to accompany the Mirages over enemy territory.

Soviet forces

After the formation of the Warsaw Pact in May 1955, the Soviets began to organize their air power in Eastern Europe under the command of Frontsaya Aviatsiya (Frontal Aviation). At its zenith, the force included over 4000 aircraft facing NATO, organized into one fighter division, two fighter-bomber divisions, two mixed fighter and fighter-bomber formations and five helicopter assault regiments. In wartime Frontsaya Aviatsiya would have attacked targets 248 miles (400km) into enemy territory, provided cover for advancing

troops, performed reconnaissance, and airlifted troops and supplies, tightly coordinating all of these operations with the Army. Their battlefield targets would have included NATO artillery systems, command and control sites, enemy airfields and tactical "battlefield" nuclear weapons.

The elite unit in Frontsaya Aviatsiya was the East Germany-based Soviet 16th Air Army, which would also have been reinforced with aircraft from the East German air force. This unit used many different designs of warplanes through the period of the Cold War. Among the earliest was the MiG-15 "Fagot," which made its name in Korea. This was followed in 1952 by the MiG-17 "Fresco" which could carry 1102lb (500kg) of bombs and had a combat radius (the distance to and from the target) of 434 miles (700km). The "Fresco" was joined in 1956 by the Sukhoi Su-7 "Fitter" fighter bomber, which could reach speeds of up to Mach 1.6 and could carry a 5511lb (2500kg) bomb load. Due to high fuel consumption, the Su-7's combat radius was half that of the MiG-17. Realizing this limitation, Sukhoi developed the original design into the swing-wing Su-17 "Fitter-C." This increased the payload to 7716lb (3500kg), but gave the aircraft a maximum range of 1430 miles (2300km).

The most successful US aircraft of the Korean War had been the North American F-86 Sabre,

Left: *North American F-86 Sabres on a temporary airfield in Korea. Note the kit and equipment behind the aircraft, and the open canopies, to enable a quick take-off.*
Below: *They called it the missile with a man in it. Lockheed's F-104 Starfighter was one of the fastest and most dangerous of the Cold War fighters.*

which was capable of speeds over 707mph (1137km/h). The prototype flew in 1947 and the Sabre entered service in 1949. From November 1950, the USAF began to realize that their aircraft could not match the MiG-15's speed, although the superior dogfighting skills of the American pilots, coupled with the higher maneuverability of their Sabre aircraft, meant that the MiG-15 usually came off worse in combat. Over Korea, the Sabres were outnumbered one to four against the MiGs, but Sabres downed 792 MiGs, losing only 78 of their own.

Soviet designers realized that they needed a new, faster short-range fighter. The result was a robust, simple aircraft, which could reach speeds of Mach 2—the MiG-21 "Fishbed."

By far the most numerous fighter to serve both in the Soviet air force and in Soviet-aligned countries around the world, the MiG-21 entered service in 1956. Several versions of the aircraft were produced, including the MiG-21bis, which could perform ground attack missions, delivering a 4409lb (2000kg) payload over a 1118 mile (1799km) combat radius.

Fast fighters

Several air forces contributed aircraft to NATO, including the Royal Air Force, which had large numbers of warplanes based in West Germany. It was tasked with air superiority, ground attack, and reconnaissance missions. In the 1950s and 1960s, the RAF deployed English Electric Canberra bombers

Pushing the envelope

How fast could an aircraft fly? In the late 1940s, the United States sought to find out under the auspices of the Bell Aircraft Company's X-1 experiments. Of those involved in the design and piloting of these fearsome rocket-powered aircraft, two stand out: General Charles E. "Chuck" Yeager and Major Arthur "Kit" Murray.

Chuck Yeager joined the Army Air Corps straight out of High School in September 1941. In July 1942 he was accepted for flight school and received his pilot's wings seven months later as a flight officer. During World War II he flew 64 combat missions and was credited with shooting down 13 German aircraft. Over the course of his service career he flew 201 different aircraft designs and accumulated 14,000 hours flight time. But of all these one flight is remembered above all others—that of October 14, 1947, in the Bell X-1.

US experts were impressed by the speed and performance of the jet engine, but the Bell X-1 project was commissioned to build a rocket-powered airplane in order to push the maximum speed of an aircraft past the seemingly impenetrable "sound barrier." The initial aim was to fly as close to the speed of sound as possible (which at sea level is approximately 760mph or 1223km/h, but decreases in the thinner air of higher altitudes) and measure the effect of the shock waves on the aircraft and pilot.

In August 1947 Chuck Yeager went to Muroc Air Base in California as the Bell X-1 project officer. Two months later, on October 14, 1947, Chuck Yeager and the X-1 were attached to the underside of a B-29 bomber and carried to 25,000ft (7620m) before being released. Free of the bomber, Yeager powered the X-1 up to 40,000ft (12,192m) at a speed of 662mph (1065km/h), breaking the speed of sound at that altitude and becoming the first man to go supersonic. For this achievement, the Bell project was awarded the 1948 Collier Trophy, but the X-1 was not finished yet. In December 1953 Yeager took the X-1A up to 1650mph (2655km/h): two-and-a-half times the speed of sound.

In June 1954 Kit Murray set another record for the X-1 project when he took the X-1A up to 90,440ft (27,566m), the highest altitude achieved by man to that time. The success of the X-1 project paved the way for later rocket-propelled aircraft tests, and for the NASA space program.

Above: The Bell X-1 was the first manned aircraft to break the sound barrier.
Left: *Bombers such as this B-29 would often be used as carriers for experimental aircraft such as the X-2 pictured here, a development of the X-1 with swept wings.*

armed with nuclear weapons, alongside Hawker Hunter fighters. The Hunter was the successor to the British Gloster Meteor and de Havilland Vampire jet fighters, and over 1500 Hunters were produced in the UK, Belgium and the Netherlands. The Canberra attracted the attention of the USAF and over 400 were built under licence in the United States as the Martin B-57.

American warplane design executed a quantum leap with the introduction of the Lockheed F-104 Starfighter, which became operational with the USAF 83rd Fighter Interceptor Squadron on February 20, 1958. Although it was very fast, with a maximum speed

of 1,447mph (2,330km/h), the Starfighter was also highly dangerous, given its difficult handling and high landing speeds. The aircraft also became unstable if the manufacturer's recommended "safe flying" guidelines were exceeded by inexperienced or badly trained pilots. Although the USAF purchased a small number of Starfighters, they were withdrawn from service by 1975 due to unacceptably high accident losses. By far the largest operator of the Starfighter was the West German Luftwaffe, which operated over 900 of the type. The Starfighter was exported to several countries including Italy, Japan, Jordan, Pakistan, and Taiwan.

Below: *The fastest manned aircraft ever to fly, the North American X-15, tucked under the wing of its B-52 launch vehicle prior to release. The X-15 reached 4534mph (7297km/h) in 1964.*

Northern frontier

The Royal Canadian Air Force (RCAF) also provided an important contribution to NATO, flying an interesting mix of aircraft. Using warplanes designed by its continental neighbor but built in Canada, during the Cold War it deployed the CF-104 (the Canadian-built Starfighter), the CF-116 (originally the Northrop F-5 Freedom Fighter) and the CF-18 Hornet, (a Canadian-built version of the US carrier aircraft). In the immediate postwar period, Canada was at the forefront of fighter aircraft design. By 1947 Canada was working on a home-grown design for a long-range, twin-engined interceptor, which eventually became the Avro Canada CF-100 Canuck. Deliveries of this effective aircraft to the RCAF began in 1951.

Keeping the momentum, Canadian engineers forged ahead with the CF-105 Arrow, another large, twin-engined interceptor, this time with delta wings and a maximum speed of 1523mph (2453km/h). By 1959, five prototypes of this formidable warplane were undergoing tests. The CF-105 was way ahead of its time, but this sophistication was its downfall. Around C$400 million was necessary to finish the project and this was too much for the Canadian government to bear, particularly at a time when many were saying that manned aircraft would soon be made obsolete by the development of ballistic missiles. The project was terminated and Canada's ability to build home-grown warplanes with it. No sooner had the project been cancelled than the government ordered 66 McDonnell Douglas F-101 Voodoo interceptors to be built in Canada.

Jet bombers

The first Soviet bomber to truly mirror the B-47 Stratojet's attributes was the Tupolev Tu-16 "Badger," which entered service in 1954. Powered by two turbojets as opposed to the B-47's six engines, the aircraft nonetheless had a speed of 484mph (780km/h) and a range of 2980 miles (4800km) when carrying two missiles—enough to threaten Europe, Alaska, and Japan but not America. The aircraft could also carry two nuclear bombs, and the Soviets kept 287 in service until 1987. The Tu-16 also entered service with China's People's Liberation Army Air Force as the Hong-5.

Left: *A Canadair-built CF-86 Sabre and CF-104 Starfighter flank the unique CL-41R, the prototype of a Canadian-designed trainer for CF-104 pilots.*

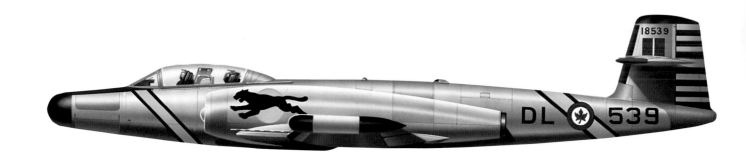

One year later the USAF unveiled the classic Cold War bomber: the Boeing B-52. Lending its name to a rock band and a cocktail, the B-52 also provided the USAF with an awesome striking force. The Stratofortress could carry eight nuclear bombs over an unrefueled range of 8800 miles (14,161km), and could also deploy the one-megaton "Hound Dog" air-to-surface missile. Over 700 Stratofortresses were built in various versions. The B-52 has served as a high-level bomber, a low level bomber, and even as a maritime strike aircraft armed with AGM-84

Harpoon missiles. In the 1980s, 98 B-52Gs were converted to carry AGM-86 Air-Launched Cruise Missiles (ALCMs). Current US Air Force plans envisage the B-52 remaining in service until at least 2016.

During the 1960s, the United States had become embroiled in the Vietnam War, providing at first military advisors, and then troops, ships, and aircraft to the government of South Vietnam, as it sought to prevent communist North Vietnam from taking over the country. The B-52 was seen on television pounding the jungle to devastate the Ho

Left top: The Canadair CF-100 Canuck was the only Canadian-designed fighter to enter mass production.

Left bottom: A Boeing B-52 Stratofortress thunders into the skies during the Cold War.

Below: The Vickers Valiant, first of the British V-bombers.

Chi Minh trail, the supply routes from North Vietnam that supported the communist Vietcong guerrillas in their struggle. An array of listening devices and sensors monitored the trail for unusual activity. A B-52 air strike would then be ordered. The bombs would be dropped and several square kilometers of jungle would be flattened. With hindsight, the bombing campaign is now thought to have been largely ineffective. As many tons of bombs were dropped on the Ho Chi Minh trail as were dropped during the whole of World War II, but on average 100 tons (101.6 tonnes) of bombs were needed to kill a single guerrilla.

V-bombers and the "Bear"

The same year that the B-52 entered service, the RAF began operating its Vickers Valiant nuclear bombers—the first of the "V-bombers." A Valiant dropped the first British hydrogen bomb on April 28, 1958, in a test over Malden Island in the Pacific. The Valiant was joined from 1958 by the Handley Page Victor. The Victor had a high-placed "T"-tail and a crescent-shaped wing, with engines mounted in the wing roots. The Victor was able to exceed the speed of sound in a dive. The Valiant and Victor were augmented in 1957 by the Avro Vulcan. One of the most elegant aircraft ever to

grace the skies, the massive delta-winged Vulcan was tasked, along with the Victor and the Valiant, with delivering Britain's nuclear deterrent.

Several new bombers appeared in 1955—and not just from the NATO allies. The Soviets brought out their legendary Tupolev Tu-95 "Bear" long-range bomber in that year too. It was the only swept-wing turboprop aircraft in widespread use, and the fastest propeller-driven plane in the world, reaching speeds of 575mph (925km/h). It entered service fully in 1956. Numerous versions were built, including the Tu-142 "Bear-F" maritime patrol aircraft. A civilian airliner version, the Tu-114, was also built. Like its old adversary, the B-52 Stratofortress, the Tu-95 remains in service.

Global arms race

The French were also working on a strategic nuclear bomber. The Mirage IVA was a supersonic, delta-winged bomber based on the Dassault Mirage III fighter. It first took to the air in 1959, beginning service on a 24-hour deterrent alert on October 1, 1964. Thirty-six aircraft were deployed around France with the Force de Frappe at nine separate bases, supported by Boeing KC-135F tankers. The limitations of the Mirage IVA led to the improved Dassault Mirage IVP, which had a range of 2486 miles (4000km) and entered service in 1986.

In 1955 intelligence revealed the existence of a new Soviet four-engined bomber, the Myasischchev M-4 "Bison." This caused some panic in the USA where fears of a "bomber gap" gripped

Below: *The striking Avro Vulcan would perform one of the longest bombing sorties in history during the "Black Buck" bombing raids on the Falkland Islands in 1982.*
Right: *The sleek Handley Page Victor, with its crescent shaped wing design, could exceed the speed of sound in a dive.*

Right: *The rakish Dassault Mirage IV performs a spectacular rocket-assisted take-off. The Mirage IV was France's first dedicated nuclear bomber.*

Left: *The prototype Convair YF-102 all-weather interceptor (top) was extensively modified according to the area-rule principle after testing. The end result was the supersonic production F-102 (bottom).*
Top: *The single-seat F-102A.*
Above: *The F-5A was designed as a low-cost, easy-to-maintain fighter-bomber for America's allies.*

defence planners, and boosted production of the B-52. Yet the Bison was never built in large numbers and its performance as a bomber was disappointing. The aircraft was eventually converted to reconnaissance and electronic warfare missions.

If these Soviet aircraft had ever headed towards America in anger, they would almost certainly have encountered USAF fighters like the Convair F-102 Delta Dagger. The prototype YF-102 made its first flight in 1953, and after a

disappointing series of tests, in which it failed to reach supersonic speeds, it was completely redesigned. Eventually 875 single-seat and 111 twin-seat aircraft were purchased by the USAF. The Dagger was replaced in USAF service by the Convair F-106 Delta Dart, which entered service in 1958 after a similarly problematic development. The F-106 had a service ceiling of 53,000ft (16,154m) and controversially lacked guns, relying on Anti-Aircraft Missiles (AAMs) for defence.

The cost of military aircraft was a major problem for NATO during the Cold War. Military aircraft never seemed to get any cheaper. Attempts were made to produce low-cost warplanes, one example being the Northrop F-5 Freedom Fighter which was produced as a private venture. Northrop advertised it as a cheap high-performance plane. First flying in 1959, the aircraft attracted little USAF interest, but it was a phenomenal success abroad, equipping several air forces around the world.

Reconnaissance aircraft

For nuclear-armed bombers to be a deterrent, they needed targets to strike. One way of gathering target information, apart from using satellites, was to use sophisticated spy planes. The Lockheed U-2R, which entered USAF service in 1956, could fly at altitudes of 24,385m (80,000ft) over the Soviet Union, photographing military facilities. However, one such flight greatly embarrassed the United States, when a U-2 flown by Central Intelligence Agency (CIA) pilot Gary Powers was shot down over Sverdlovsk in the USSR on May 2, 1960. U-2 reconnaissance flights were swiftly discontinued.

The U-2 was later augmented in the controversial intelligence-gathering role by the immensely fast Lockheed SR-71 Blackbird, capable of sustained flight at Mach 3.2. It was

Below: *The Lockheed TR-1 reconnaissance aircraft flies at such high altitudes that pilots must wear special pressurized suits similar to those worn by astronauts.*

The King of Bombs

"A powerful white flash appeared over the horizon, then a remote, indistinct and heavy blow, as if the earth had been killed" was one description of the world's biggest man-made explosion, when the 58 megaton Tsar Bomba ("King of Bombs") was tested by the USSR in October 1961. This single bomb had more explosive power than the total of all the armaments used in World War II combined.

In June 1961, Soviet President Nikita Khrushchev met with his senior nuclear weapons scientist Andrei Sakharov and ordered him to develop a 100-megaton hydrogen bomb. By mid-October, a giant bomb, weighing 27 tons, was ready for testing.

On a cold fall day, Major Andrei Durnovtsev steered his Tu-95 bomber towards the Arctic island of Novaya Zemlya ("New Land.") The bomb dropped towards the island attached to a nylon parachute so large that its construction had seriously disrupted the Soviet hosiery industry.

The bomb exploded 12,138ft (3700m) above the island with a yield of 58 megatons (42 megatons below its promised strength). Its shockwave circled the Earth three times. One observer noted that "in districts hundreds of kilometers from ground zero, wooden houses were destroyed, and stone ones lost their roofs." The flash could be seen 600 miles (965km) away despite the fact that the island was covered by heavy cloud. The mushroom cloud rose over 43 miles (69km) into the sky.

Nuclear bombs produce an electronic disturbance known as an electro-magnetic pulse, which severely damages or destroys electronic circuits. Tsar Bomba knocked out all long-range communications around the Arctic sea for over an hour. Staff at the Olenya air force base where Durnovtsev's bomber was scheduled to land had no radio confirmation that the aircraft was safe or that the bomb had exploded. As regards Novaya Zemlya, the area below the explosion was transformed from a rugged snow- and ice-covered landscape into "an immense skating rink."

The Soviet military were largely unimpressed, unconvinced that the weapon had real military value. They believed it was more effective to destroy a city with many small hydrogen bombs targeted on its periphery, rather than one large bomb dropped on the center. But despite this, a few of the giant bombs were stockpiled.

Above: *A Tupolev Tu-95 "Bear" pictured from a NATO interceptor.*
Right: *The power and speed of the "Bear" is owed in no small part to the aircraft's powerful turboprops, which turn eight-bladed contra-rotating propellers.*

Left: *The Lockheed SR-71 Blackbird was capable of speeds in excess of Mach 3.2.*
Below: *Although it only remained in USAF service for a decade, the Convair B-58 Hustler was the holder of no fewer than 19 speed and altitude records.*
Bottom: *The rakish Tupolev Tu-22 "Blinder."*

thought that the speed of the SR-71 would render it invulnerable to Soviet air defences, but the USSR developed the MiG 25 "Foxbat"—which remains as the fastest fighter aircraft ever built—to fend off the Blackbird.

Multi-role development

Although aircraft like the SR-71 and the MiG-25 were designed for specific roles, the US aircraft industry was turning its attention to "multi-role" warplanes by the early 1960s—aircraft that, differently configured, could perform a variety of different combat tasks. To this end, McDonnell Douglas produced versions of the F-4 Phantom, for the US Navy and Air Force, entering service in 1958 and 1961 respectively. With a top speed of 1485mph (2389km/h) the aircraft outperformed many of its USAF contemporaries and gave impressive service over Vietnam. The Phantom was highly respected by the Soviets.

To keep up with fighter aircraft development in the West, the Soviets produced the variable-geometry (or swing-wing) MiG-23 "Flogger." Swing-wings became a feature on many combat aircraft throughout the Cold War. The wings would be swept back when the aircraft traveled at high speeds, affording a more aerodynamic "delta" shape. At lower speeds, the sweepback would be decreased, giving greatly improved handling compared to that enjoyed by a delta winged aircraft at slow speeds. Entering service in 1971, the Flogger carried powerful interception radar and was adaptable enough to operate from hastily-prepared airfields near the front line.

Above: *The Tu-22M "Backfire" was an extensive redesign of the Tu-22 "Blinder." In came swing-wings and an improved cockpit; out went the tail-mounted engines.*

Left: *Perhaps the most audacious aircraft ever to the reach the prototype stage, the North American XB-70 Valkyrie bomber was designed for sustained flight at Mach 3.*

Bomber development

US bomber development continued with the hugely costly Convair B-58 Hustler, which entered service in 1960. The aircraft could fly at Mach 2 and the B-58B model had a 4603 mile (7408km) range. A large pod below the fuselage contained a combined fuel tank and nuclear bomb. The fuel in the pod was used for the aircraft's outward flight, and the pod was jettisoned along with the accompanying weapon once the aircraft reached its target. Fuel stored in the body of the aircraft before the flight was used on the return journey.

The Soviets responded to the threat of the US military's fast bombers with the rakish Tu-22 "Blinder." Two huge turbojets on either side of the tail propelled the aircraft to Mach 1.4, although its range was only 1926 miles (3100km). Its payload of 19,841lb (9000kg) was similarly disappointing. Crews also complained that the cockpit was badly designed. Pieces of string were attached to some switches and levers to make them operable.

With top speeds accelerating with each new combat aircraft, the USAF sought to develop a bomber which could outperform anything else in the sky. The result was the North American XB-70, the fastest and arguably the finest bomber never to have been built. Nicknamed the "Valkyrie," this massive twin-tailed aircraft was designed for

Above: *The General Dynamics F-111 design saw service in the fighter, bomber, reconnaissance, and electronic warfare roles.*

sustained flight at Mach 3. But such capabilities did not come cheap. Although two prototype aircraft were constructed, one was lost in a collision with an F-104 Starfighter during a demonstration flight. The project was abandoned in 1969.

The Soviets were having more luck with their new designs. In 1969 American spy satellites photographed a new bomber, which became known as the Tupolev Tu-22M2 "Backfire-B." Based on the Tu-22 design, this aircraft had engines built into its fuselage rather than on the tail, and variable geometry wings.

The "Backfire" bomber controversially hit the news during the second round of the Strategic Arms Limitation Talks (SALT-II) in June 1979, designed to limit the huge stockpiles of nuclear weapons and aircraft held by the superpowers. The US claimed that the bomber was a "strategic" system, because, despite the Tu-22M2 version having a range of 3169 miles (5100km), it could refuel in flight. Soviet President Leonid Brezhnev ordered that the bombers' refueling equipment be removed. This was largely a

cosmetic gesture as the refueling equipment could have been put back within 30 minutes.

The "Backfire-B" was followed in Red Army service by the Sukhoi Su-24 "Fencer" strike aircraft, which entered service in 1974 and was one of the finest attack aircraft of its generation. It could deliver its 17,636lb (8000kg) almost anywhere in Central Europe. At a stretch, this could include targets in Spain and the United Kingdom.

NATO alert

In any confrontation, the USAF could draw on large numbers of its aircraft stationed in the UK. This included General Dynamics F-111 fighter-bombers, and Fairchild A-10 Thunderbolt II close air support/anti-tank aircraft. The F-111 was dogged with difficulties during its development, including aerodynamic problems and spiraling costs. Deliveries began from July 1967 and seven variants of the aircraft were built including the two main versions—the F-111 fighter and the FB-111 bomber. The FB-111 could carry either six AGM-69 Short Range Attack Missiles (SRAMs), each with a 200kT nuclear warhead, or 37,500lb (17,010kg) of nuclear bombs. The aircraft would fly at low level and high speed towards heavily defended large "area" targets, such as airfields in the western USSR.

Meanwhile, the ungainly A-10 would set out to destroy armored vehicles. Entering service in 1977, this aircraft had a robust airframe and an armored cockpit protecting the pilot. A seven-barrelled 1.18in (30mm) cannon, and a mix of other weapons up to a maximum 16,000lb (7200kg) payload would have sliced through Soviet and Warsaw Pact armored columns. Like its Soviet rival, the Su-25 "Frogfoot," the A-10 could fly from hastily prepared airstrips near the front line. The Su-25 also had an armored cockpit, but its payload was only 9700lb (4400kg). The aircraft entered service during the Soviet invasion of Afghanistan and from 1981 it gave an impressive performance.

Close air support

A similarly versatile close-air support aircraft to the A-10 was the British Aerospace (originally Hawker Siddleley) Harrier, which was the only foreign military aircraft, apart from the English Electric Canberra medium bomber, to be purchased by the United States during the Cold War. A highly innovative design capable of vertical take-off and landing, the Harrier attracted the interest of the United States Marine Corps in 1968 for use on the decks of its assault ships. McDonnell Douglas produced the aircraft as the AV-8A. An improved version, the AV-8B, would later be designed as a collaborative venture between McDonnell Douglas and British Aerospace. The maritime Sea Harrier achieved an impressive combat record defending Royal Navy ships during the Falklands War with Argentina in 1982, and variants of the Harrier design remain in service with several air forces today.

Below: *A McDonnell Douglas/BAe AV-8B of the US Marine Corps.*

High-speed, low-level

Despite suffering a setback with the XB-70, the USAF lobbied hard for a new bomber. Critics said that bombers were rendered anachronistic by the advent of ICBMs. Undeterred, SAC placed an order for four new Rockwell B-1A bombers in 1971. This was a promising four-engined variable-geometry bomber, capable of Mach 2. But in 1977 further development was canceled by President Jimmy Carter. The bomber project was resurrected in 1985 by the Reagan administration, and the electronic systems in the aircraft were greatly improved. The new aircraft, which could achieve speeds of up to Mach 1.2 at low level, was redesignated the B-1B Lancer. A phalanx of electronic countermeasures (ECMs) protected the plane against missiles while a radar signature one hundredth that of a B-52 concealed it from radar. The B-1B forms a key part of the USAF bomber inventory today.

Ready for war

By the 1980s, the USAF had a robust deployment of aircraft in Europe, which included McDonnell Douglas F-15 Eagles, three squadrons of F-4 Phantoms and General Dynamics F-16s to suppress enemy air defences, two squadrons of General Dynamics EF-111 Raven and Lockheed EC-130 Commando Solo/Rivet Rider aircraft for electronic warfare, and two reconnaissance squadrons of Phantoms.

Boeing E-3 Sentry Airborne Warning and Control System (AWACS) aircraft could watch the skies of Europe and North America for intruders. Inside the fuselage, teams of operators drawn from across NATO would gaze at radar screens looking for the first tell-tale movements of Soviet aircraft which could have been the overture to World War Three.

If war had ever broken out over Europe these "eyes in the sky" would have sent "strike packages" of warplanes towards Soviet and Warsaw Pact

Below: A group of Fairchild A-10s line up on the taxiway. Although an ungainly aircraft, it has proved its worth in several conflicts following the end of the Cold War.

NATO names for Soviet planes

Where could you find a "Bear" and a "Badger" sitting happily side-by-side? On a Russian air force base housing Tupolev Tu-16 and Tu-95 bombers, which had these animals as their respective code-names. NATO reporting names were devised during the Cold War to give easily-memorable "tags" to help pilots, sailors and soldiers identify aircraft or missiles. NATO invented the system because it was not always possible to get an aircraft's name from the Soviets. Even when pictures of new Soviet planes were publicly released, Moscow would often neglect to provide a name for the aircraft in question.

Above: *A Sukhoi Su-7 "Fitter"— a jet-engined fighter—of the Indian Air Force.*
Below: *The Antonov An-72 "Coaler"—a jet-engined transport.*

There was a certain logic to NATO's code-names. All bombers were given a code-name beginning with "B"; hence the Tupolev Tu-22M "Backfire." Freighters were designated with a "C"; for example, the Ilyushin Il-76 "Candid"; "F" was unsurprisingly reserved for fighters; "H" for helicopters, and "M" for everything else. The last designation helps to explain aircraft such as the Il-78 "Midas" tanker, which closely resembled the Il-76 freighter, but which had a different role.

There was also a logic to the actual code-names. For instance "Farmer," "Bounder," and "Cossack:" (the MiG-19; Myasischchev M-50/52 and Antonov An-225 respectively) are two-syllable names. Why? Because jet aircraft were always given two-syllable code-names. Propeller aircraft like the "May," "Mail," or "Coke" (Ilyushin Il-38, Beriev Be-12, and Antonov An-24) received a single syllable designation.

To ensure the most precise designation possible, NATO would attach a letter to the end of the code-name denoting the aircraft model. For example, the "Fitter-K" (Sukhoi Su-17 ground attack variant) designation indicates that this is the eleventh variant—the first variant being the Fitter-A.

Since the end of the Cold War the system has fallen into disuse. New Russian aircraft are no longer given code-names and are often known by their actual Russian designation, as with the prototype MiG-35 fighter, known as the Mnogofunksionalni Frontovoi Istrebiel (MFI - Multirole Front-Line Fighter).

Supercarrier

Throughout the Cold War the US Navy's aircraft carriers were self-contained air forces sailing the world's oceans ready to undertake reconnaissance, air superiority, and strike missions. Each US Navy carrier air wing could include 80 aircraft of various types. With its 50 strike aircraft an aircraft carrier could perform 150 strikes per day, using up to 4000 bombs stored on the ship.

The carrier aircraft included McDonnell Douglas F/A-18 Hornet fighter and attack aircraft, Grumman F-14 Tomcat fighters, Sikorsky SH-60 Seahawk helicopters, Lockheed S-3B Viking anti-submarine planes, Grumman E-2C Hawkeye AWACS aircraft, and Grumman EA-6B Prowler electronic warfare aircraft. In a typical mission to support either troops on land or Marines making an amphibious landing, F/A-18s would attack ground targets. They would be protected from enemy aircraft by the Tomcats, which would also protect the ships of the accompanying Carrier Battle Group (CBG) from air attack. The Tomcats would obtain information on enemy aircraft from AWACs, while the Prowlers would jam enemy radars. Meanwhile, the Vikings and Seahawks would watch the depths for submarines—potentially the most deadly threat to the CBG.

In the Cold War, the CBGs were a source of major concern for the Soviet navy. Although it had five carriers: the *Minsk, Kiev, Novorossiysk, Baku,* and *Leonid Brezhnev,* the size of the ships and their air wings were smaller than their American counterparts. For example, the *Kiev* carried 20 Ka-25 "Hormone" anti-submarine helicopters but only 12 Yak-36 "Forger" Vertical Take-Off and Landing (VTOL) fighter-bombers. The Soviets instead favoured using long-range, land-based aircraft deployed with Aviatzia VMF (Soviet Naval Aviation) to counter NATO shipping and US Navy CBGs. To this end it had over 60 Air Regiments and Squadrons to guard Soviet waters against enemy shipping.

Above: *A McDonnell Douglas F/A-18 Hornet is prepared for a catapult launch from the the USS* Constellation.
Right: *The USS* Nimitz*, a nuclear-powered carrier, saw action against Libyan aircraft in 1981.*

Left: *Despite a troubled and
protracted development, the B-1B
Lancer eventually entered service in
1986, five years before the end of
the Cold War.*

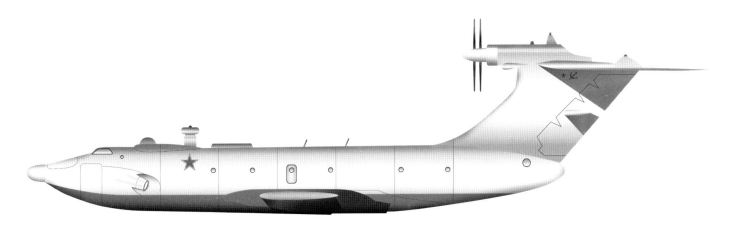

Top left: *Rostislav Alekseev, the father of the Soviet Ekranoplan program.*
Bottom left: *The A-90 Orlyonok could cruise at 249mph (400km/h) just 6ft 7in (2m) above the waves.*
Above: *The A-90 Orlyonok, the most successful design to emerge from the CHDB's experiments into military WIG craft.*

targets. The packages would include bombers, with an array of support aircraft like Boeing KC-135 tankers and General Dynamics EF-111 aircraft packed with ECMs to jam enemy radar systems and prevent SAMs and Anti-Aircraft Artillery (AAA) from countering the attack. Protection was also available from "Wild Weasel" F-4 Phantoms armed with anti-radar missiles which could home in on the beam of a SAM or AAA radar. The entire package would also be protected by fighters.

The last bomber to enter service during the Cold War was the Tupolev Tu-160 "Blackjack." Widely regarded as the finest bomber ever built, the aircraft had a range of 8699 miles (14,000km) and a dash speed of Mach 1.9. A swing-wing design allowed the aircraft to perform high-speed, low level attacks. Bearing a striking resemblance to the B-1B, the Backfire-A was in fact 30ft (9m) longer than its US counterpart.

During the Cold War, huge numbers of fighters, bombers, electronic warfare, and reconnaissance aircraft on either side helped to deter the superpowers from starting a war, conventional or otherwise. Yet the advances in technology which allowed military aircraft to leap from subsonic speeds to Mach 3 in less than 15 years following the end of World War II were cripplingly expensive. Both Soviet and American administrations were happy to throw money at the problem of defence. For the Soviets this overloaded their relatively underdeveloped economy, contributed to the bankruptcy of the Soviet system and led to the end of the Cold War itself. For the Americans, the days of designing expensive aircraft for one specific mission, such as air superiority, reconnaissance, or ground attack, finished as the Iron Curtain lifted.

The Development of Wing-in-Ground Effect (WIG) Craft

The Cold War spurred the Soviet Union to develop an unconventional form of transport known as Wing-in-Ground Effect craft. "Ground effect" is the term used to describe the effect on an aircraft as it flies near to the ground. As the air below is compressed, drag is reduced and lift is increased. This phenomenon has been known since the 1920s, but only received the financial backing necessary for research and development in the 1960s.

Although taking off from water and flying in the air, WIG crafts are neither boats nor aircraft, but incorporate the advantages of both. Flying at a height of no more than ten percent of its wingspan for reasons of stability, a WIG craft's drag is vastly reduced while lift is increased to around 80 percent more than a regular aircraft. The result of this greater efficiency equates to fuel consumption of about half that of normal airplanes and one-fifth that of a fast boat.

Ground effect was utilized long before specially designed WIG craft were built. The pilots of the Dornier Do X flying boats noticed that the plane's efficiency increased the closer to the surface of the Atlantic they flew. Air crews in World War II knew that if they had to return from a bombing operation with low fuel, consumption would be reduced if they flew low over the sea.

Rostislav Alekseev began true WIG research and development in the Soviet Union during the 1960s. Alekseev was the head of the Central Hydrofoil Design Bureau (CHDB) and had a history in ship design. Naming his craft "ekranoplans" (in Russian, "ekran" means screen

and "plan" means plane), Alekseev constructed a series of experimental models that could use ground effect to skim just above the surface of the water. The CHDB's most successful craft was the A-90 Orlyonok, built in the late 1970s for the Soviet military. This huge transport, of which only four were built, had a maximum speed of 249mph (400km/h) and the capacity for a 33,069lb (15,000kg) payload. Come the break-up of the Soviet Union, the Orlyonoks retired to Kaspiisk Naval Air Base to await their fate.

Today, manufacturers are looking to the commercial market to develop WIG craft. Compared to ships, WIG craft offer a smoother and faster journey. Compared to aircraft, they are more fuel-efficient and produce less pollution. The CHDB began to look at the possibilities of civil WIG craft in the mid-1980s with the production of the Volga-2. Financial difficulties and a split in the CHDB led to Dmitri Sinitsyn departing and

establishing the Asian-funded Technologies and Transport with other like-minded members of the Bureau. T&T is now developing the Amphistar, or Xtreme Xplorer. Various other American companies have also attempted WIG craft designs, but without previous experience of the technology their efforts have so far been unsuccessful.

The most interesting developments of WIG technology are taking place in Australia and China. In Australia, Radacraft and Incat are just two companies looking to improve ferry services with WIG systems. Although there are no true WIG craft in service yet, the future of this technology looks bright in the South Pacific. Further north, in China, work is also underway on WIG craft.

Although the KM ekranoplan demonstrated a definite military transport role, a WIG craft would be vulnerable to more maneuverable aircraft in wartime. If there is a future for WIG vehicles, it is now most likely to be in the commercial arena.

Above: *The Lun Spasatel ekranoplan in rescue configuration.*
Top right: *Airfish 8, an 8-seat WIG craft designed and built by FischerFlugmechanik/AFD Airfoil Development GmbH, Germany.*
Bottom right: *The CHDB Volga-2 concept in model form.*

The Caspian Sea Monster

In the late 1970s Western intelligence experts received satellite photographs of a large vehicle being transported from Gorky (now Nizhny Novgorod) to the Caspian Sea. It looked like nothing they had ever seen before and so was dubbed the "Caspian Sea Monster."

The life of this almost mythological craft began in 1963 when Rostislav Alekseev, the head of the CHDB, designed a huge ekranoplan which could be used by the Soviet military to transport large amounts of equipment over long distances very quickly. The KM, or as it was later known, the Caspian Sea Monster, was built in the closed city of Gorky. The KM was powered by ten engines; eight mounted on the fuselage just behind the cockpit, and one on either side of the tail. The former would aid the aircraft in getting airborne, and the latter would provide extra power when cruising. At 540 tons (548.5 tonnes) fully laden, it was nearly 200 times heavier than its predecessor, the SM-2, and even today seems an ambitious undertaking. With its cargo, the 328ft (100m) long KM could travel at over 480km/h (300mph) a few meters above the surface of the water. Once the Sea Monster was airborne, it could skim over land just as easily.

So successful was the KM that Alekseev developed a smaller, armed version called Project 903 Lun (or "Dove.") The Lun was approximately one-fifth smaller than the KM, with 8 engines instead of the latter's 10 and with a maximum take-off weight of 400 tons (406 tonnes). Aside from the number of engines, the greatest visual difference between the two was the positioning of three twin cruise missile launchers on the fuselage of the first Lun. The second, and only other, Lun was converted into a six-engine SAR ekranoplan and renamed Spasatel.

The sheer size of these ekranoplans caused problems for their designers during testing and thereafter. The KM required a huge amount of power to get airborne. Once in the air, the pilot had a vast amount of power but slow acceleration, and little stability or control of the aircraft. In addition, a massive turning circle was needed to change direction. This would have been a great problem for the Lun if ever faced with heavily armed opposition, and in this sense, the dove was more like a sitting duck.

At the time of the break-up of the Soviet Union, the KM and the first Lun were in operation and the second Lun was nearing completion, although the KM was subsequently damaged and sank in the Caspian Sea. The subsequent reduction in the Russian Navy budget effectively ended the career of Alekseev's ekranoplans, although the Spasatel may yet be reprieved if a plan to complete it as a rescue craft goes ahead as planned.

Left: *The first Lun was configured to fire anti-ship missiles. Here it is pictured test-launching a 3M80 "Moskit" missile.*

Above: *A rare image of the ten-engined KM, nicknamed the "Caspian Sea Monster."*

Right: *The second Lun ("Dove") which was intended to be converted into the Spasatel rescue craft.*

helicopter

During the Cold War the United States and the Soviet Union fought proxy wars in uncompromising terrain. The helicopter proved a vital tool in Korea, Vietnam, and Afghanistan, fulfilling reconnaissance, transport, and assault roles. The helicopter has also become a regular sight around the world in police, ambulance, and other civilian uses.

Left: The WAH-64 Longbow Apache. The fire control radar above the rotors gives the Longbow an even greater potency.
Top: The father of the modern helicopter, Igor Sikorsky (right), stands with one of his VS-300 rotor test stands.

The concept of rotary-wing aviation dates back to the fourth century AD when a Chinese book titled *Pao Phu Tau* described flying vehicles made of wood and leather that were powered by rotating blades. A millennium later Leonardo da Vinci designed an "Aerial Screw", which worked on the principle of compressing the air below the craft to obtain lift. To be accurate, Leonardo's 1483 design was an autogiro, an aircraft with unpowered rotating blades. Although the aerodynamics are similar, true helicopters have powered rotor blades.

Leonardo's design was not widely published until the 1700s, at a time when several other engineers in western Europe were grappling with vertical flight. One of the most prominent experimenters was the British engineer Sir George Cayley. Cayley was already well known for his writings on the principles of flight and for his invention of

Right: *A model of Sir George Cayley's "Aerial Steam Carriage" design of 1843.*
Below: *The first true helicopter. Paul Cornu was the first man to achieve vertical flight, in 1907. Controlled flight was another matter, however.*

an "aerial steam carriage". Turning his attention to vertical flight, in 1796 Cayley made reference to a helicopter design in his research papers, although the available steam-driven powerplants would have been too heavy to allow it to fly.

In September 1863, Viscount Gustave de Ponton d'Amécourt combined the Greek words *elikoeioas* (spinning or turning) and *pteron* (feather or wing) in the first use of the word *hélicoptère*.

Vertical flight pioneers

In November 1907, the first true helicopter took off when Paul Cornu's aircraft rose vertically and made a free flight. However, his helicopter had very little means of control and was instead stabilized by men on the ground with sticks. The first successful flight of a rotary-wing aircraft was Juan de la Cierva's C30A autogiro in 1923, but the controllable helicopter still eluded designers.

Controlling the Helicopter

One unavoidable problem associated with rotary-winged aircraft is the torque effect of the main rotor. If the rotor turns in a clockwise direction when viewed from above, the torque tends to make the fuselage rotate in an anti-clockwise direction. To counter this, the tail rotor pushes air to the right, keeping the helicopter straight by imparting a clockwise moment. Increasing the thrust of the main rotor increases the torque, so the thrust of the tail rotor needs to be adjusted to compensate. The pitch of the tail rotor blades, and thus the thrust, is controlled by the pilot's yaw pedals.

When a helicopter's rotor blade disc is "flat," the total rotor thrust acts vertically, as lift. The helicopter will climb vertically into the air with no forward or backward movement. To travel forwards, the pilot tilts the whole rotor disc forward, applying some of the rotor lift as forward thrust. When the pilot tilts the rotor disc to the left, right or backward, the aircraft will move in that direction. This is known as adjusting the cyclic pitch. Because some of the total thrust available is now acting horizontally, the share of the thrust dedicated to lift is reduced. For this reason, more lift must be applied using the pilot's third method of control, the collective. The collective increases the angle of pitch on all the rotor blades

collectively—hence the name. More air is passed through the rotor system, producing more lift, as long as the rotors keep turning at the same speed.

The first helicopter designer to incorporate collective and cyclic controls was the Argentine Marquis Raul Pateras Pescara, when his No.3 helicopter took off and travelled at 8mph (13km/h) in 1924. But it was not until Juan de la Cierva invented the hinged rotor blade that these controls could be truly effective and the first practical and fully controllable helicopters could get airborne.

Left: *The complex rotor control system can be clearly seen in this image of a Kaman SH-2G Super Seasprite.*
Below: *Pescara's No.3 helicopter was the first to incorporate collective and cyclic controls in 1924.*

The first practical helicopter was the twin-engined Focke Wulf Fw 61, which was controlled accurately enough to be flown indoors. To show its controllability, the famous German test pilot Hanna Reitsch hovered the Fw 61 inside the Deutschlandhalle Stadium in Berlin in February 1938. Proving the helicopter's effectiveness and reliability, the Fw 61 set a number of records by climbing to 11,243ft (3427m), reaching a maximum speed of 76mph (122km/h) and making a 143 mile (230km) non-stop flight in 1938.

Igor Sikorsky

As the Fw 61 was setting these records, the world's most successful helicopter manufacturer was perfecting his own designs. Igor Sikorsky was born in Kiev and trained as a chemist before turning to engineering after attending the Naval Academy in St Petersburg. Before the Russian Revolution, Sikorsky had designed a number of fixed-wing aircraft including the huge Ilya Murometz bomber. During World War I he briefly worked in France before crossing to the United States in 1919 and establishing the Sikorsky Aero Engineering Corporation. More fixed-wing airplanes followed before a merger with Chance Vought and a move into rotary-wing design. Sikorsky's first major breakthrough came with the VS300 in 1939, the first practical single-rotor helicopter. This design included one key innovation: a tail rotor to counter torque.

The first Sikorsky production model was the VS316, introduced in 1941. Designated XR-4 by the US military, it was more than twice as

Left: *Vought-Sikorsky's first
successful helicopter was the
VS300, which included a tail rotor
for torque control.*
Right: *The first production model
followed—the side-by-side seat
VS316. Pictured is the US Army
version, designated the XR-4.*

powerful as the VS300 and had dual side-by-side controls. In 1943 Sikorsky introduced his first passenger-carrying model, the R–5. Although designed for the military, a civil version of the four-seater R–5 was made, and designated the S–51. The first proper troop-carrying Sikorsky was the S–55, which could transport ten people and saw service in the Korean War. Sikorsky helicopters have gone on to become a mainstay of armed forces around the world.

British collaboration

In 1946 the British Westland aircraft company began talks with Sikorsky to licence-build versions of its designs. Britain developed and operated other rotary wing aircraft in the early 1950s, such as the small Saro Skeeter and Bristol Sycamore, but these were eclipsed by the new Sikorsky-Westland models. The first collaborative production was the Westland version of the S–51, the Dragonfly, which entered service with the Royal Navy in 1950 and equipped the RAF's first helicopter squadron. A second successful Sikorsky variant was the Westland Wessex, based on the S–58. The Wessex was employed by the Royal Navy on anti-submarine duties when it entered service in July 1961, while the RAF used the Wessex for troop

transport and medical evacuations (MedEvac). Such collaboration and contract-sharing has become common as US and European helicopter manufacturers share the huge cost of development. Another successful joint venture was the agreement between Westland and Aérospatiale in the late 1960s which resulted in the SA341 Gazelle and its variants.

Civil advances

Although the development of the helicopter has been driven by the military, there is a large market for civil helicopters. The first helicopter to be granted a US Federal Aviation Authority certificate was the Bell Model 47 in 1946. The type would remain in continuous production by Bell until 1973, and was also licence-built by Agusta, Westland and Kawasaki. Just as Sikorsky designs and their derivatives dominated the military helicopter market, Bell Helicopters Textron and the Eurocopter Group have dominated the civil market. Bell produces around 150 civil helicopters per year with the Model 206 JetRanger, first delivered in 1967, making up almost a third of that figure. The JetRanger is the most successful civil helicopter design ever, with sales of all variants topping 7500.

Bell has a long history of collaborating with international partners, and one recent result of the company's relationship with Italy's Agusta is the AB 139, which made its first flight in February 2001 and began to be delivered to customers in 2002. Such collaborative projects now seem to be the norm. Eurocopter was formed in 1992 from a merger between the helicopter sections of Aérospatiale and DaimlerChrysler Aerospace AG, and now accounts for 40 percent of the worldwide market for helicopters. Eurocopter's most popular model is the Ecureuil, or Squirrel, which incorporates a tail rotor enclosed in the tail, known as a fenestron, which is much safer than an exposed tail rotor. Other manufacturers have experimented with the NO TAil Rotor (NOTAR) system, in which air is blown through a nozzle in the tail to counter torque. With an increasing demand for civil

helicopters in countries like China (where current numbers are only around 100), industry experts predict demand for roughly 500 new helicopters per year over the next decade.

Birth of the military helicopter

Although conceived in China 1500 years earlier, the military helicopter was truly born in Korea, where it revealed its potential and made itself indispensable to the army, particularly in the MedEvac role. But the full potential of the helicopter in combat was not realized until the Vietnam War.

Although helicopters are most often used by the military to transport troops and other equipment close to the front line, the military first became interested in their use as reconnaissance aircraft to replace air balloons over the battlefield. During

Above: *A Sikorsky S-51 of the US Navy.*
Right top: *A US Navy HSS-1 (SH-34G) Seabat of training squadron HT-8.*
Right middle: *The SA341 Gazelle was the result of Westland-Aérospatiale co-operation. This is one of approximately 100 Gazelles sold to Iraq in the 1980s.*
Right bottom: *The Cierva W.9 used an innovative system to counter torque. This experimental helicopter used jet thrust instead of a tail rotor to control its stability.*

Above: *The Bell H-13E Sioux (the military version of the Model 47) was used to great effect in Korea in the MedEvac role.*

World War I a team led by Theodore von Kármán attempted to introduce primitive helicopters in place of kite balloons for the Austro-Hungarian Army. Their PKZ-2 design performed relatively successfully in experiments, but was not used in combat. During World War II, Germany again used basic helicopters for observation, but it was in Vietnam that the reconnaissance helicopter truly came into its own. For this role, the US Army deployed one of the smallest military helicopters to see service, the Hughes OH-6 Cayuse. The prototype of the Cayuse first flew in February 1963. The original production model was completely unarmed, but gunship, anti-armor, and civil versions have since been built, with licences granted for the aircraft to be built in Japan and Italy. In total, over 1400 examples of all variants were produced. Also employed in the reconnaissance role in Vietnam was the Bell OH-58 Kiowa, along with an armed version designated the Kiowa Warrior.

Fewer specialist observation and reconnaissance helicopters are employed today because gunship and transport helicopters can carry technology that enables them to fulfil this role in addition to their main function. Unarmed or lightly armed observation helicopters are not needed on the modern battlefield. Information from frontline helicopters, UAVs, and satellites can now be viewed and analyzed in real-time to build a picture of the electronic battlefield for military commanders located far from the battle.

Tandem rotor

After the Korean War, the US Army and Marines issued a requirement for a new troop transport and MedEvac helicopter. Although Sikorsky was the dominant force in this market, other manufacturers presented effective alternatives. The Piasecki (later Vertol) H-21 Shawnee, or "Flying Banana", was the first tandem rotor helicopter employed by the US armed forces, and could carry 14 soldiers or 12 litters (stretchers) plus medical staff. The Shawnee saw service well into the Vietnam War before it was phased out in favor of more modern helicopters.

Above: *The Hughes OH-6 Cayuse saw service with the US Army in Vietnam.*

Above: *As well as carrying artillery and equipment, the CH-54 Tarhe, or Skycrane, could carry a 10,000lb (4535kg) bomb to drop and clear areas as landing zones.*

Previous pages: *The Bell UH-1 Huey summed up everything that the US forces needed in Vietnam— mobility, flexibility, and power.*

One of the most famous helicopters in the world was and still is the Bell UH-1 Huey. In February 1955, the Army awarded Bell a contract for a utility helicopter and in October the following year the XH-40 made its maiden flight. The new compact gas turbine engine used in the XH-40 was more reliable, more powerful, and had a simpler drive system than those used in other contemporary helicopters. With Army orders from March 1959, the Huey was born. The UH-1 was an effective troop transport, accommodating up to 12 men or six litters, but a bigger helicopter was also needed to transport large numbers of troops more effectively. Boeing developed two such troop transports for the war in Indochina. The first was the CH-47 Chinook, which entered service with the army in 1961 and could accommodate up to 55 troops. The second was the 25-troop CH-46 Sea Knight, which was first used by the Marines in 1964. Both designs went on to achieve substantial export sales,

although the Sea Knight has sold significantly fewer than the larger and more powerful Chinook. A contemporary of the Chinook and Sea Knight was the Sikorsky CH-54 Tarhe or "Skycrane" heavy lift helicopter, which could haul a maximum 47,000lb (21,319kg) payload.

Sikorsky did not challenge the large Boeing troop transports until the late 1960s, when it introduced the heavy-lift CH-53 Sea Stallion and the medium-lift UH-60 Black Hawk. The Sea Stallion first flew with the Marines in 1966, and with its 37-man or 24-litter capacity proved a valuable asset in the Vietnam War. The CH-53 was upgraded with a third engine in the early 1980s to create the CH-53E Super Stallion, one of the most powerful helicopters in the world. In 1978 the US Army took delivery of its first UH-60 Black Hawk, which has since seen action all over the world, including the infamous Mogadishu raid in 1993 that later became the subject of the film *Black Hawk Down*.

Above: *The $26 million three-engine CH-53E Super Stallion is one of the most powerful helicopters in the world.*

Left: *The UH-60 Black Hawk is the US military's primary medium-lift helicopter and has seen action all over the world.*

Top: *The Mil Mi-26 "Halo" was the first successful
helicopter with eight rotor blades.*
Above: *An Aeroflot Mi-6P "Hook" civil transport,
with accommodation for up to 80 passengers.*

Soviet weightlifters

As the United States was developing powerful helicopter technology for use in Vietnam, the Soviet Union developed its own heavy lift capability. When it appeared in 1957, the Mil Mi-6 "Hook" was the largest helicopter in the world, and set the standard for heavy lift rotary aircraft, carrying a 12,000kg (26,450lb) payload, 65–75 soldiers or 41 litters with two attendants. In 1961, the "Hook" was also the first helicopter to reach 186mph (300km/h). The Mil Mi-12 that followed was an even larger, and stranger-looking, helicopter. It had twin rotors at the ends of fixed wings, a layout which the Soviets believed to be more stable and durable than the tandem design used on large American helicopters. The Mi-12 helicopter was designed to be the rotary-wing equivalent of the Antonov An-22, and set a payload record by lifting 88,633lb (40,204kg) up to 7398ft (2255m). Although the next Mil helicopter, the Mi-8 "Hip", was a mere 24-troop transport with a payload capacity of 8820lb (4000kg), the Soviet Union retained the crown for heavy lift capability with the Mil Mi-26. The Mi-26 "Halo" entered Soviet Army Aviation service in 1985 as the most powerful helicopter in the world, with the lift

Below: *Based on the UH-60 Black Hawk, the HH-60 Jayhawk is an important element of the US Coast Guard's medium range rescue capability.*

capacity of a C-130 Hercules. With two turboshaft engines each providing 11,240hp (8500kW), the "Halo" can carry 44,090lb (20,000kg) cargo, 80 soldiers or 60 litters.

SAR and ASW helicopters

During World War II, the US military introduced makeshift search-and-rescue (SAR) helicopters to find its downed aircrews. The US Army received its first R-4 in 1941, which proved its worth in the jungles of Burma. Two years later, the Coast Guard considered adding the helicopter to its fleet for rescues off the US coast.

Until 1964 SAR missions for the retrieval of pilots shot down in Vietnam were undertaken by civilian organizations like Air America,

Continental Air Services, and Bird & Son. However, in June 1964 the Air Rescue Service (ARS) was established with two helicopters at Nakhon Phanom. The Kaman HH-43 Huskie was the first designated combat SAR helicopter to be used by the ARS. As the ARS (later renamed the Aerospace Rescue and Recovery Service, or ARRS) flew its maiden rescue missions, Sikorsky was already designing a replacement for the HH-43 Huskie. The USAF had been impressed by the US Navy's SH-3A Sea Kings and wanted to procure a similar, larger version for combat SAR. The CH-3C arrived on July 6, 1965, with the capacity for 5000lb (2270kg), 30 men or 15 litters. However, the USAF CH-3Cs were unarmed at first and needed an A-1 Skyraider to escort them.

This escort stayed even when armed HH-3Es were introduced.

The US Coast Guard also procured the Sea King in its HH-3F Pelican variant. These aircraft continued in Coast Guard service for 20 years, until the HH-60 Jayhawk was introduced in the 1980s. The Jayhawk provides the modern Coast Guard with a reliable medium-range rescue helicopter. For shorter-range duties, they operate the Aérospatiale HH-65A Dolphin.

Contemporary US military SAR is conducted by UH-60 Black Hawks and CH-53 Sea Stallions. The Marines' Sea Stallions have been used for many dramatic rescues in recent years, including the retrieval of pilots in the 1991 Gulf War and the rescue of Scott O'Grady after his F-16 was shot down over Bosnia in 2000. Even more recently, during Operation Iraqi Freedom, Black Hawks were used in the rescue of Private Jessica Lynch after the maintenance convoy she was part of was captured.

Around the time of the Vietnam War, the U.S. Navy also became heavily involved in helicopter development. In 1956 a specification was outlined for a defensive rotary-wing aircraft to patrol the skies around aircraft carriers. Kaman answered the call with the UH-2 Seasprite, the prototype of which first flew in July 1959. The US Navy began taking delivery of the basic Seasprite in December 1962, and Kaman went on to introduce the more powerful twin-engined UH-2B and armed HH-2C.

Another key requirement for any modern navy is the anti-submarine warfare (ASW) helicopter. In late 1957 the US Navy approached Sikorsky for an anti-submarine helicopter and in March 1959 the YHSS-2 prototype first flew. It was introduced to the Navy as the SH-3 Sea King just 18 months later. A valuable Navy asset, the Sea King could carry up to 840lb (381kg) of munitions including torpedoes and depth charges. It set a distance record in March 1965 when it took off from the USS *Hornet* in San Diego and flew 3486km (2166 miles) to land on the flight deck of the USS *Franklin D. Roosevelt* in Jacksonville, Florida. To compete with Sikorsky, Kaman upgraded the Seasprite to the SH-2D

Left: *The Sikorsky SH-3 Sea King is one of the most familiar SAR helicopters, but is now being replaced by aircraft such as the EH.101 Merlin.*
Below: *A Westland Wasp HAS 1 of 829 Naval Air Squadron fires a wire-guided AS.11 air-launched anti-tank missile during exercises.*

285

variant, offering greater over-the-horizon reach and strike capabilities.

In 1977 Sikorsky won a further Navy contract for a light multi-purpose helicopter, and six years later the SH-60 Sea Hawk entered service. This versatile helicopter is capable of ASW and combat SAR missions, and by the end of 2002 395 had been built or ordered, including the Japanese and Australian SH-70B variants.

British developments

In Britain, the development of naval helicopters was slow but steady. In July 1958 Westland unveiled the prototype of its P.531, intending it as a scout for the British Army. But the Royal Navy took over the design and in mid-1963 began receiving the first of the production helicopters, now renamed "Wasp". From the mid-1960s through to the mid-1980s, the Wasp was the primary shipborne helicopter of the Royal Navy, capable of carrying

Left: *The Westland Lynx has been a stalwart of the British Army for more than 25 years.*
Below: *The EH.101 Merlin is replacing the Royal Air Force and Royal Navy's Sea Kings and Lynxes. Other operators are set to include Canada, Denmark, Italy, and Japan.*

out a range of roles including ASW, reconnaissance, SAR and general utility. It was a Wasp based on the Royal Navy's HMS *Endurance*, piloted by Lieutenant Commander Tony Ellerbeck, which scored the first British naval success of the Falklands War in 1982, when the submarine *Santa Fe* was disabled by his AS.12 missiles. But the real helicopter success of the Falklands campaign was the Wasp's successor, the Westland Lynx.

The Lynx was another product of the 1967 Westland-Aérospatiale agreement. Westland tabled the design in the late 1960s and carried out two thirds of the manufacturing work. The British Army took delivery of the first AH-1 Lynx in 1978, but there was no real international interest. The true Lynx success was the navalized version, of which over 430 have been built for or ordered by the Royal Navy and 12 other countries worldwide. Like the Wasp, its success is built on its flexibility. The Navy Lynx is a potent ship and submarine killer armed with Sea Skua missiles for the former or Sting Ray torpedoes

Left: *The adapted Bell UH-1D Iroquois was the first gunship and paved the way for the formation of US airmobile units in Vietnam.* Above: *The United States Marine Corps AH-1W SuperCobra was originally conceived to meet an Iranian requirement.*

for the latter. The upgraded HAS.8 Super Lynx boasts more powerful Rolls-Royce engines, thermal imaging sensors and an improved electronic warfare suite.

The Anglo-Italian EH.101 Merlin is currently replacing the Super Lynx and Sea King as the Royal Navy's ASW helicopter. The Merlin started out as the Westland WG.34 in 1978. Italian interest led to the signing of a contract between Westland and Agusta to build what would be called the European Helicopter Industries EH.101, and the first prototype flew in Britain in 1987. The required capabilities of the Merlin are wide, calling for ASW, airborne early warning (AEW), SAR, utility and civil versions. The first four production models were delivered to the

Royal Navy for testing and training in December 1998, and the Merlin began trials on the aircraft carrier HMS *Ark Royal* in early 2002. At present, other operators look set to include the RAF, the Italian Navy, Denmark, Canada (civil version), and the Tokyo Police. As can be seen, British naval helicopters gain their strength from their adaptability and durability, offering the Royal Navy reliable aircraft with a long service life.

Helicopter gunships

Providing a stable and maneuverable platform, it is unsurprising that one of the helicopter's key roles in recent conflicts has been as a dedicated gunship. The heavily armed helicopter gunship came of age in Vietnam, when unarmed transport

helicopters began to be fired upon by Vietcong guerrillas. The US Army wanted to arm its utility helicopters, but faced opposition from the USAF, as ground support was their responsibility. The Army won out, and began to use the ubiquitous Bell UH-1 Huey as a mobile artillery platform, organized into "Air Mobile" offensive units. Gunship support reduced troop transport casualties by around a quarter when it was introduced in 1963.

In US military designations the letter "O" stands for "observation", as in OH-6, and the "U" in UH-1 "utility". In 1966 the Army ordered the Bell AH-1 HueyCobra, the "A" signifying "attack". The HueyCobra was the first to introduce the tandem-seat cockpit layout that has been used in many subsequent gunships. Over 2000 AH-1 variants were built, some with the capability to deploy TOW anti-tank missiles, and the aircraft has seen action in the Middle East, Somalia, Haiti, Bosnia, and twice in the Gulf. A naval version was built as the AH-1J SeaCobra, which has been intermittently upgraded, and the US Marine Corps is currently awaiting delivery of the AH-1Z SuperCobra.

In 1976 Hughes (now part of Boeing) Helicopters were declared the winners for a US Army contract to develop an Advanced Attack Helicopter. Six years later the first order for AH-64A Apaches was made, and the first Apache was delivered in 1984.

The Apache first saw action in Panama in 1989, but truly showed its worth in Operation Desert Storm in 1991 when it destroyed over 500 Iraqi tanks, 120 artillery pieces, 120 armoured personnel carriers, 325 other vehicles, 30 air defence installations, 10 radars, 50 bunkers, 10 helicopters, and 10 aircraft on the ground. With this level of success, willing buyers for the Apache have not been hard to find, and over 1000 AH-64A and the improved-radar AH-64D and WAH-64D Longbow Apaches have been built or ordered.

The Soviet Union introduced its own heavy gunship in 1972, the Mil Mi-24 "Hind", which was first deployed in East Germany in 1974. Unlike the HueyCobra and later Apache, the "Hind" is heavily armored, weighing 18,078lb (8200kg) to the Apache's 11,225lb (5095kg). The "Hind" is capable as an air-to-air combat helicopter, but excels in the ground support and anti-armor role. First seeing action in the war in Afghanistan between 1979 and 1989, the "Hind" has since been mostly used against rebels in the Caucasus region.

Left: *A US Army AH-64 Apache of the 18th Airborne Corps during Operation Desert Storm, 1991.*
Below: *More than 2500 examples of the Mil Mi-24 "Hind" and its variants have been sold, operated by over 40 countries worldwide.*

V-22 Osprey: A Tilt-Rotor Ahead of its Time

It is clear that airplanes and helicopters have distinct strengths and advantages over each other. Helicopters can access the most remote parts of the globe, but lack the high speed of fixed-wing aircraft. But what if the strengths of both could be combined into just one aircraft? This was the proposition that many manufacturers like Vertol, Kaman, Hiller, and Bell took on in the 1950s. Bell Helicopter Textron began experimenting with tilt-rotor research aircraft in the late 1950s, but it was not until the XV-15 first flew in 1977 that the concept was proven in a practical design. The two-seat XV-15 was the result of US Army and NASA funding. Resembling a normal fixed-wing airplane, the difference was that at the end of each wing was a rotor capable of a 90-degree tilt to allow it to lock into a vertical or horizontal position. Only two examples of the XV-15 were built, but they are still used as testbeds and for training pilots to fly tilt-rotors.

Bell Helicopter Textron then combined with Boeing Helicopters to submit a proposal based on the XV-15 for a Joint Services Advanced Vertical Lift Aircraft, which the services designated JVX, for troop transport to the battlefield. The renamed V-22 Osprey made its first flight in vertical helicopter mode and in level flight, in March and September 1989 respectively. Conversion from rotary to fixed-wing mode takes place when the Osprey has enough forward speed to provide the necessary lift. It takes just 12 seconds for the rotors to tilt from vertical to horizontal flight configuration. At 57ft (17.5m), the V-22 is roughly the same length as a Black Hawk helicopter, with a payload roughly half that of a C-130 Hercules. In April 1997 the United States Government ordered the first five production models at a total cost of just over $400 million. The first US Marine Corps MV-22B flew in April 1999.

Above left: *In just 12 seconds the Osprey can convert from vertical to horizontal flight.*
Above right: *The Bell XV-15 project, initiated in 1973, was a major success, and paved the way for the joint Bell-Boeing program to develop the V-22 Osprey.*
Below left: *The Bell-Boeing Osprey has had a fault-plagued history thus far, but it is likely that the U.S. Marines will receive their first MV-22 in 2005.*

But despite the early technical success of the Osprey, enthusiasm waned. In 1989 the Defense Department required a provisional 663 V-22s in three variants: the MV-22 for the Marine Corps, the CV-22 for USAF special operations and the HV-22 for US Navy SAR. By 1996 this had been reduced to just 523 aircraft. One of the main reasons for hesitancy and lower order numbers has been the cost of the Osprey. Those opposed to the V-22 project see it as too expensive, and believe its role can be met well enough with existing aircraft. Supporters of tilt-rotor aircraft argue that the US armed forces' helicopters should be replaced with something that can deliver more. In horizontal flight, the V-22 is faster and can fly further and higher than any helicopter could, while retaining the advantage of vertical landing. The V-22 could be the end result of the lessons learned from the failed attempt in 1980 to rescue 53 American hostages being held in Iran. En route, a C-130 military transport collided with a special forces helicopter, with eight US servicemen losing their lives in the desert.

Production of the V-22 was temporarily halted in 2001 after four fatal crashes raised questions over safety. After investigations revealed the technical faults responsible, the Osprey project continued, with a firm order for 11 MV-22s being placed in March 2002. These first aircraft are expected to enter front line service in 2005.

One argument for the mass production of the V-22 has largely been passed over, or at least been given little credence by all but a few—the opportunities for commercial use. In early 1988 the FAA and NASA published a study into tilt-rotors and their effect on air congestion. It was concluded that these hybrid aircraft would reduce overcrowding in the skies over major cities as passengers could fly from smaller "vertiports" rather than flock to the large commercial airports. In 1996 Bell and Boeing announced a nine-seater commercial tilt-rotor designated D-600, the prototype of which flew at the Paris Air Show in 1997. However, in 1998 Boeing withdrew from the tilt-rotor team and Bell found a new partner in AgustaWestland, developing the D-600 into the renamed BA609. The 10 to 12 million dollar BA609 first flew in March 2003 and is expected to gain its flight certification in 2007.

A history of space travel

to the stars

To say that space has fascinated humans for centuries is both a cliché and an understatement. Ever since our earliest ancestors looked to the night skies, stars have been a talisman for the superstitious and a practical guide to navigators. Philosophers and scientists have ruminated on what is "out there" for centuries, while fundamental discoveries like Galileo's principle of planetary motion brought wonderment from his contemporaries and disgust from the clergy.

Left: The Space Shuttle Orbiter, attached to its booster rockets and fuel tank, sits atop the giant crawler vehicle which will transport it to the launch site.

Top: Dr Robert Goddard, designer of the world's first liquid propellant rocket.

It was in the twentieth century that space travel became a reality. The launch of a satellite or a Space Shuttle mission is now relegated to the "and finally" part of a news bulletin, but in the 1950s and 1960s each space flight by the United States or the Soviet Union was an extra point in the tense game of political one-upmanship that was central to the Cold War.

Space flight arose from humble beginnings. In the late nineteenth century, Russian physicist Konstantin Tsiolkovsky theorized that the most effective way to propel a person into space was by rocket, prophetically suggesting liquid oxygen as a possible fuel. Writing a paper entitled "The Exploration of Space with Reaction Propelled Devices," Tsiolkovsky expanded his ideas—although his audience was confined to a small academic journal.

Left: *Konstantin Tsiolkovsky, Soviet spaceflight theorist, in his study.*
Right: *Yuri Gagarin became the first man in space on April 12, 1961.*
Below: *Robert Goddard in his rocket workshop in Hawaii. The facilities used by the early rocket pioneers were a far cry from NASA's cutting edge technology.*

Robert Goddard

In the west, Robert Goddard helped to fuel America's hunger for space travel. Beginning his research in 1903, this postgraduate student at Clark University, Massachusetts, calculated the speeds which a rocket would need to achieve to escape Earth's vice-like gravity. In 1920 he published a paper, "A Method of Reaching Extreme Altitudes," which set out many of the basic principles of rocketry and space flight for the first time.

Around the same time, some important research was happening in Germany. In 1923 Hermann Oberth published *The Rocket into Interplanetary Space*, developing Tsiolkovsky's liquid-fuelled ideas and arguing for a multi-stage rocket system—another important contribution. Several "stages" would provide continual thrust for the rocket, and as the fuel in each stage was spent it would be discarded until the payload reached orbit.

By 1926 Goddard had built his first liquid oxygen and gasoline-fuelled rocket, which reached a height of 41ft (12.5m). Not the most auspicious flight—but it was an important start. Continuing his research in Roswell, New Mexico, in 1930, Goddard launched two rockets reaching 2000ft (600m) and 7500ft (2300m). Goddard later went on to develop gyroscopic control systems for rockets, but despite his breakthroughs his work was ignored by the US military establishment. In 1938 the American Rocket Society was founded, dedicating itself to the practical development of spacecraft.

Wartime experiments

A similar society in Germany, the *Verein für Raumschiffahrt* (Society for Space Travel), had been performing research along the same lines as Goddard. Between 1931 and 1932 the Society made around 100 rocket launches, reaching altitudes of over 4921ft (1500m). A year later, the German army approached one of the Society's members, Wernher von Braun, and asked him to design rockets for the army. With huge military investment,

von Braun's enterprise grew into a massive undertaking at Peenemünde on the Baltic coast, using slave labor as the workforce. Within eleven years, the V-2 rocket was raining terror on Europe.

The Soviet Union was also fully aware of the military potential of rockets. In 1932 Sergei Korolev was "red" rocketry's most distinguished scientist. He began working for Marshal Mikhail Tukhachevsky, the First Deputy People's Commissar of Defence, to develop the rocket as long-range artillery. Korolev and his boss would soon fall victim to the paranoia of Soviet Premier Joseph Stalin, ending up in the Gulag and the execution room respectively.

In America Theodore von Karman, a professor at the California Institute of Technology, had been carrying out research into rocket propulsion, mainly for aircraft. To this end, in 1941 the American Rocket Society became Reaction Motors Inc, whose engines would propel the Bell X-1, the world's first supersonic aircraft, into history.

The final two years of World War II netted two major benefits for the Soviets and the Americans. Korolev was released from the labor camps and was

Right: Officials of the US Army Ballistic Missile Agency pictured in 1956. Rocket scientist Hermann Oberth sits in the foreground, flanked left to right by Dr Ernst Stublinger, Major General H.N. Toftoy, Werner von Braun, and Dr Eberhard Rees.
Below: A German V-2 rocket sits on its launcher during World War II.

Above: *Tail units for V-2 rockets await assembly at the Nordhausen facility, a combined Nazi death camp and rocket factory.*

free to develop rockets; he would soon be directing the Soviet space program. The Soviets also captured a V-2 facility and the accompanying concentration camp at Nordhausen, taking several German scientists in the process. In the scramble to carve up German assets at the end of the war, the Americans succeeded in capturing von Braun and members of his team, and put them to work on rockets at White Sands, New Mexico. Both Cold War rivals now had what they needed to start the "space race." Von Braun went on to become the technical head of NASA.

The space race

Following Marshal Tukhachevsky's lead, the Soviets continued to explore the military potential of the rocket. From 1952, the cordite and fuse wire of the *Katyusha* ("Little Katie") rockets which had

devastated the German army during the war were replaced in research by nuclear warheads. Marshal of the Soviet Air Force Pavel Zhigarev knew what he wanted: long-range reliable rockets capable of hitting North America.

Although it was concentrating its efforts on long-range bombers like the B-36 Peacemaker and B-47 Stratojet, the strategic value of the nuclear-armed rocket was not lost on the US Government —or the German expatriates in the desert sun. By 1953 the first American nuclear missile was being prepared for a test launch at Cape Canaveral, Florida. This launch facility on the Atlantic coast had been reclaimed from the Florida swampland. The weather was warm and the beaches plentiful and it was considered a pleasant posting by the astronauts and scientists who worked there. The Soviets, on the other hand, had the Baikonur

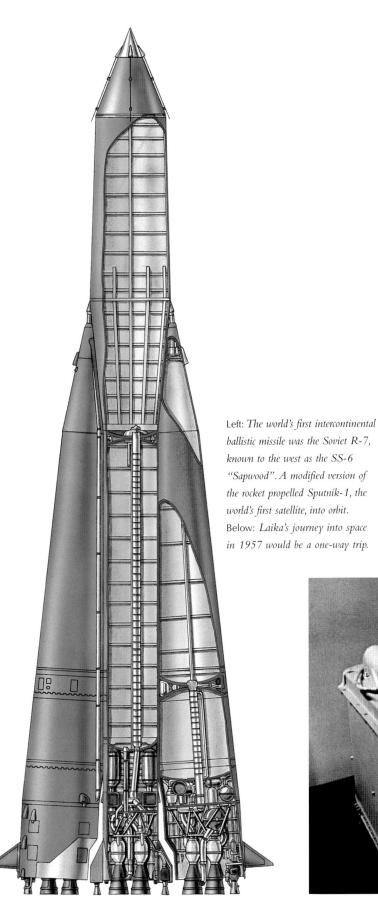

Cosmodrome in modern-day Kazakhstan, in the center of a barren inland wilderness.

Korolev had a secret weapon for the race into space. Although the first Soviet rocket, the R–7/SS–6 "Sapwood," was designed to carry a nuclear warhead, its real strength was its power. With 1,000,000lb (455,000kg) of thrust, it could lift up to 11,684lb (5300kg) into space. Test flights began in May 1957, with the first successful flight on August 21. Soviet Premier Nikita Khrushchev, a keen advocate of space travel, then gave the order for the first satellite to be launched. On October 4, Sputnik entered space. Ostensibly designed to study Earth's upper atmosphere, Sputnik transmitted its characteristic "bleep" for 21 days, and eventually left orbit on January 4, 1958. The Soviets had performed a dramatic coup, becoming the first country to place an artificial satellite in space.

Not content with stoking McCarthyist fears of communism with Sputnik, the Soviets decided to put an animal in space. A small dog called Laika— Russian for "little barker"—was propelled into orbit on November 3, 1957, aboard Sputnik II. "Muttnik!" screamed the headlines as Laika circled the earth for seven days. But she would never see Earth again. Although the Soviet Union claimed that Laika was put to sleep by Russian scientists during her flight, evidence emerged after the Cold War suggesting that she was killed as her capsule overheated after launch.

Left: *The world's first intercontinental ballistic missile was the Soviet R-7, known to the west as the SS-6 "Sapwood". A modified version of the rocket propelled Sputnik-1, the world's first satellite, into orbit.*
Below: *Laika's journey into space in 1957 would be a one-way trip.*

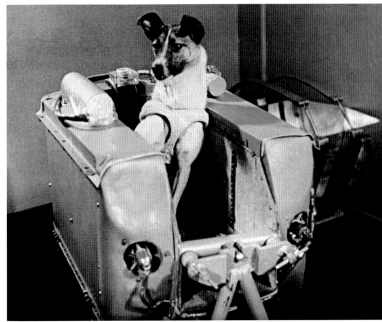

The Sputnik Scare

The Russian word for "fellow traveler," Sputnik was anything but benign for the United States. Weighing 84kg (184lb), it orbited Earth once every 90 minutes. Not only had Moscow stolen a lead in the space race, but the USSR could now fire a rocket which could reach the United States and which might carry a nuclear warhead.

Immediately after the launch, sound bites and reactions streamed across the news wires. Edward Teller, the father of the Hydrogen Bomb, said that: "America has lost a battle more important and greater than Pearl Harbor." Von Braun promised that any nuclear missile would have "line of sight" accuracy. Future President Lyndon B. Johnson mixed outrage and indignation, commenting that Sputnik caused "the profound shock of realizing that it might be possible for another nation to achieve technological superiority over this great nation of ours." Senator Syles Bridges, a Republican from New Hampshire, argued for an all-out effort to win the Space Race, insisting: "The time has clearly come to be less concerned with the depth of pile on the new boardroom rug or the height of the tailfin on the new car and to be more prepared to shed blood, sweat, and tears."

But Sputnik was not bad news for all Americans. For Richard Jackson, a NASA engineer, the Sputnik launch launched his career, thanks to the cash that the US administration now ploughed into space research: "Thanks to Sputnik, I had a wonderful career ... After that, we wanted to do something, we felt we had a duty to the country to fight back. The people I worked with were extremely dedicated to doing their best as fast as they could."

But that Christmas was tinged with apprehension. Would the Soviet Union now drop atomic bombs on America from space "like kids dropping rocks from a highway overpass?"

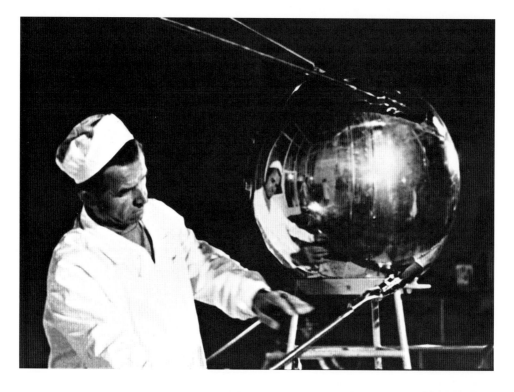

Above: *A Soviet technician attends to Sputnik I. Its characteristic bleeping transmission would strike fear into the hearts of many in the United States who feared that the next Soviet satellite might contain a nuclear warhead.*

Right: *America's first attempt to launch a satellite atop a Vanguard rocket ends in disaster as the entire ensemble explodes on the launch pad at Cape Canaveral.*

One month later, on December 6, 1957, the United States prepared their riposte. A 3lb (1.4kg) satellite stood on top of a Navy Vanguard rocket ready for launch. America held its breath—the countdown seemed to last for ever. On the stroke of "zero," the rocket lifted a few feet off the launch pad and violently exploded. The press splashed "Kaputnik!" and "Flopnik!" across the front pages. Von Braun and his colleagues trudged back to their drawing boards. Adding insult to injury, the Soviet Union politely enquired whether their American counterparts would like any help.

Finally, on January 31, 1958, Explorer I became the first US satellite in orbit. Launched from Cape

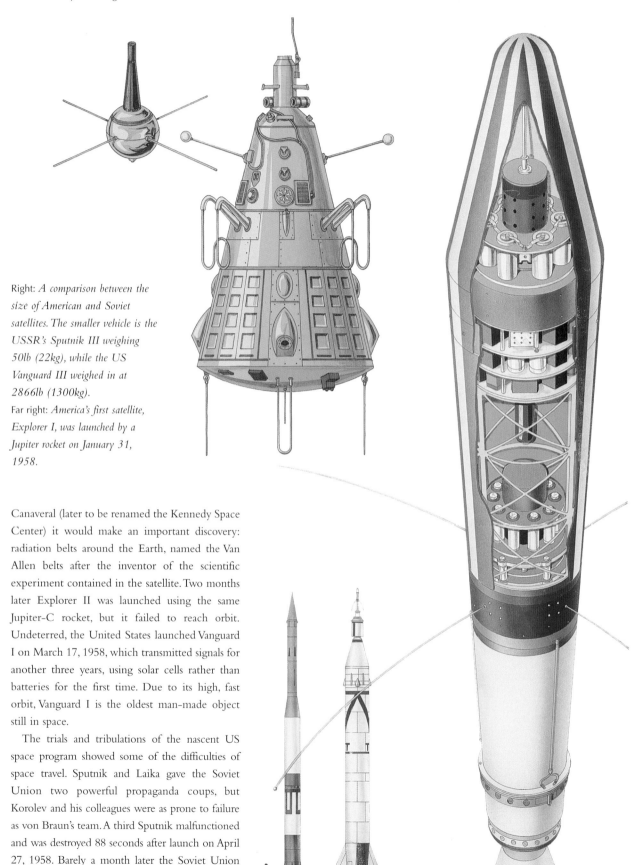

Right: *A comparison between the size of American and Soviet satellites. The smaller vehicle is the USSR's Sputnik III weighing 50lb (22kg), while the US Vanguard III weighed in at 2866lb (1300kg).*
Far right: *America's first satellite, Explorer I, was launched by a Jupiter rocket on January 31, 1958.*

Canaveral (later to be renamed the Kennedy Space Center) it would make an important discovery: radiation belts around the Earth, named the Van Allen belts after the inventor of the scientific experiment contained in the satellite. Two months later Explorer II was launched using the same Jupiter-C rocket, but it failed to reach orbit. Undeterred, the United States launched Vanguard I on March 17, 1958, which transmitted signals for another three years, using solar cells rather than batteries for the first time. Due to its high, fast orbit, Vanguard I is the oldest man-made object still in space.

The trials and tribulations of the nascent US space program showed some of the difficulties of space travel. Sputnik and Laika gave the Soviet Union two powerful propaganda coups, but Korolev and his colleagues were as prone to failure as von Braun's team. A third Sputnik malfunctioned and was destroyed 88 seconds after launch on April 27, 1958. Barely a month later the Soviet Union successfully launched a third satellite, called Sputnik III, to gloss over their previous failure. It was an

orbiting laboratory which conducted research into the Earth's atmosphere.

Wary of the power of his military–industrial complex, on October 1, 1958, President Dwight D. Eisenhower consolidated the disparate parts of the American space program into a single, civilian-controlled body called the National Air and Space Administration (NASA). Ten days later the fledgling NASA launched Pioneer I 70,700 miles (113,777km) into space in an unsuccessful attempt to reach the moon.

The Soviets were also extending their reach, albeit by accident. Luna I was launched on January 2, 1959, to land on the lunar surface, but a miscalculation caused it to overshoot at high speed, bypassing the moon and heading towards the sun, becoming the first artificial satellite to conduct a solar orbit. However, Korolev and his team could obtain little data from their machine as

Left: *A Jupiter-C rocket heads for the heavens.*
Below: *A replica of the Soviet Luna 1 probe, which overshot the moon and ended up in solar orbit.*

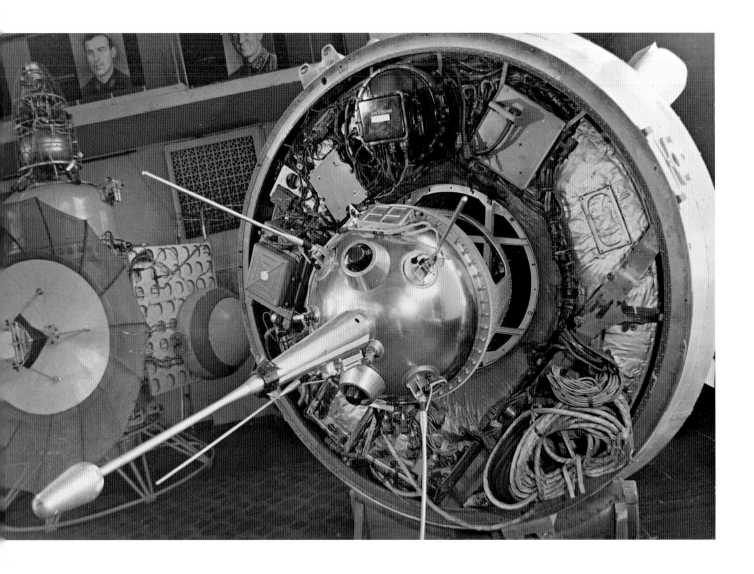

Above: *The Soviet Union's Luna II was the first spacecraft to crash onto the moon in September 1959.*

its batteries ran out 62 hours after launch. Luna I was followed by NASA's Pioneer IV, becoming the first US probe to enter a solar orbit—the mission for which it was designed.

Undeterred by the failure of Luna I, Luna II became the first man-made object to grace the lunar surface on September 12, 1959. Designed to crash-land, its cargo included a copy of the Soviet coat of arms. One month later, the Soviets followed their success with Luna III, an orbital satellite which photographed 70 percent of the moon.

Exploring the cosmos yielded important information for scientists on Earth. In April 1960, the Americans launched Tiros I, the world's first successful weather satellite, which helped revolutionize weather forecasting and hurricane prediction. In August of that year, the US launched Discoverer 14, a Corona spy satellite equipped

with reconnaissance cameras to photograph missile bases in the Soviet Union. The capsule was successfully recovered in mid-air by a C-119 aircraft fitted with a special capture net.

A man in space

By the 1960s the space race had become a desperate struggle for technological primacy and political one-upmanship between the superpowers. The Soviets won another "first" on April 12, 1961. After sitting on the ground in his Vostok capsule listening to Russian love songs for 50 minutes, cosmonaut Yuri Gagarin was lifted into orbit atop an R-7 rocket, becoming the first man in space. Gagarin orbited the Earth only once and was technically a passenger floating in a tin can. Flight instruments were operated by mission control, though Gagarin had a key which could override the controls, allowing him to fly Vostok in an emergency. When Gagarin entered the Earth's atmosphere, he had to jump out of Vostok with a parachute. This was concealed from the Fédération Aéronautique Internationale (FAI) to qualify for the record, which stipulated that the occupant had to land in the spacecraft to be officially recorded as the first person in space. This was to be Gagarin's only trip. He died on March 27, 1968, when his MiG-15 crashed near Moscow.

Gagarin's flight threw down the gauntlet for the United States, who were desperately trying to keep up with Soviet space "firsts." On May 25, 1961, at Rice University stadium in Houston, President John F. Kennedy announced that the US would land a person on the moon and bring them back to Earth safely, before the end of the decade. Prior to Kennedy's announcement no American had spent more than 15 minutes in space. This had been accomplished twenty days earlier by Alan Shepard, performing one suborbital flight aboard Mercury Freedom VII.

Sheppard's flight was the consequence of much hard work and many discouraging setbacks. In July

Below: *The Tiros satellite carried 9260 solar cells which powered the 64 batteries on the satellite. Its cameras could capture 32 images during each of the craft's earth orbits.*

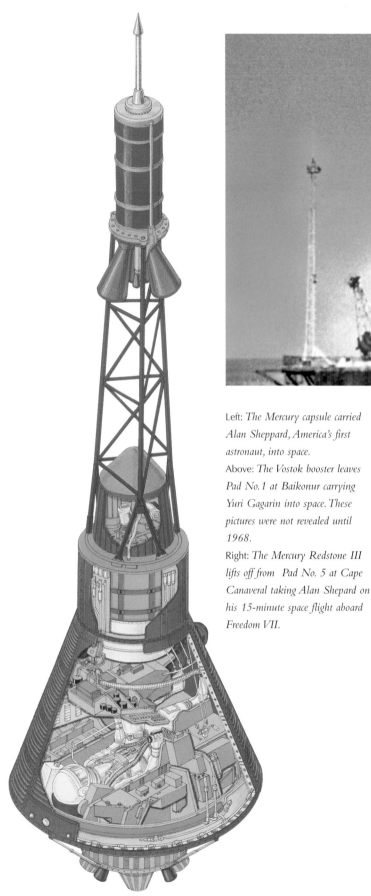

Left: *The Mercury capsule carried Alan Sheppard, America's first astronaut, into space.*
Above: *The Vostok booster leaves Pad No. 1 at Baikonur carrying Yuri Gagarin into space. These pictures were not revealed until 1968.*
Right: *The Mercury Redstone III lifts off from Pad No. 5 at Cape Canaveral taking Alan Shepard on his 15-minute space flight aboard Freedom VII.*

1960, a test launch was carried out using an Atlas rocket in combination with a Mercury capsule. Seconds after launch, it exploded. The Soviets suffered a similar fate in October 1960 when a rocket carrying an unmanned probe to Mars exploded on the launch pad, incinerating several of the scientists and technicians who were inspecting the vehicle. Valentin Bondarenko met a similar fiery fate on March 23, 1961. This earthbound 24-year-old cosmonaut was performing tests inside a pressurized oxygen chamber. He accidentally put an alcohol-soaked cotton bud on an electric hot plate, turning the oxygen-rich atmosphere into a fireball.

America lags behind

Meanwhile in the United States, the Mercury program was proceeding slowly. A second test launch in November barely lifted 6in (15cm) off the launch pad before again exploding. Finally, on January 31, 1961, the United States got a living creature into space. Eschewing the Soviet choice of propelling a dog into the cosmos, they opted for a chimpanzee, Ham, who, unlike his Soviet canine cousin, survived the experience. The success of Ham's flight emboldened NASA to proceed with Shepard's successful manned mission.

But the United States always seemed to be one step behind. It seemed that no sooner had Alan

Shepard splashed down than Vostok 2 was launched on August 6, 1961, carrying Gherman Titov. Titov made 17 Earth orbits, becoming the first person to spend a day in space and also the first to sleep there. Yet the trip was not all plain sailing. Titov's journey was punctuated with nausea, disorientation, and heart trouble, which would later be diagnosed as "space sickness."

On February 20, 1962, a Mercury capsule took John Glenn into the history books as the first American to orbit the Earth. But US efforts were not just yielding manned orbits of the planet, chasing up the Soviets' firsts. The first ever transatlantic satellite television broadcast occurred on July 10, 1962, courtesy of Telstar. The satellite would lend its name to a US number one hit for The Tornadoes on January 5, 1963, and would mark the beginning of the satellite communications revolution.

Building on their successes with unmanned space vehicles, the United States launched Mariner 2 on August 27, 1962, on the first successful mission to explore Venus. The probe sent back valuable data, including the information that the surface of the planet was a scorching 425°C (797°F).

Not satisfied with putting the first satellite, dog and human into space, and notching up endurance records, the Soviet Union soon became the first nation to put a woman into space. On June 16, 1963, Vostok VI carried Valentina Tereshkova into

Left: *John Glenn becomes the first American to orbit the earth, on February 20, 1962.*
Right: *Gherman Titov, the Soviet Union's second cosmonaut, spent more than a day in space in August 1961, suffering the first ever bout of space sickness.*

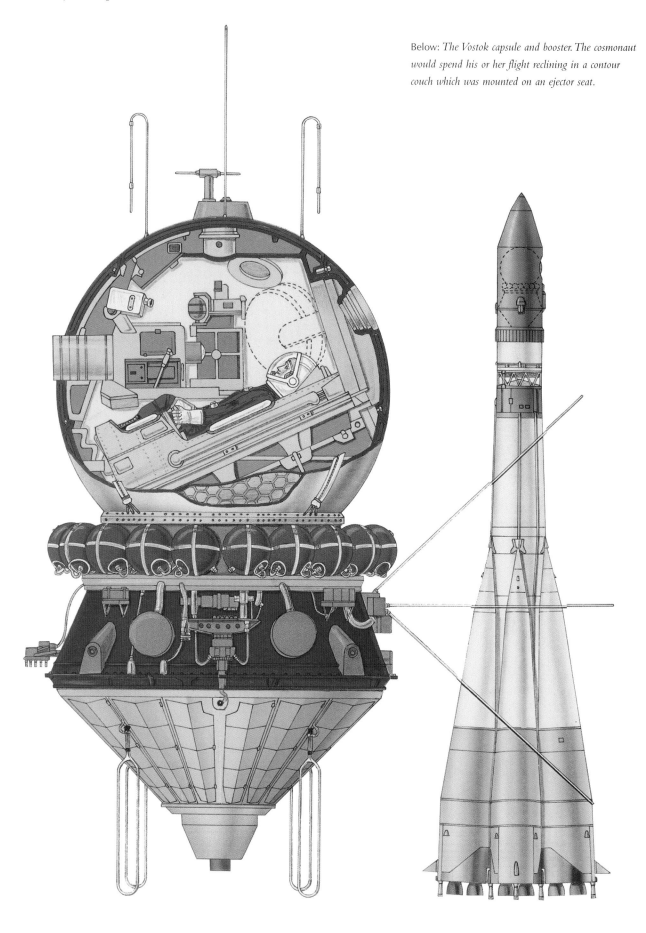

Below: *The Vostok capsule and booster. The cosmonaut would spend his or her flight reclining in a contour couch which was mounted on an ejector seat.*

Earth orbit. Although this was trumpeted as a great triumph for equality and communism, it would be another 19 years before Svetlana Savitskaya would become the second Soviet woman in space, aboard Soyuz T-7. Later that year, Tereshkova married fellow cosmonaut Andrian Nikolayev. Their daughter Elena was the first child of two parents who had both traveled in space.

The Vostok series of spacecraft could carry only one cosmonaut, and the Soviets were keen to improve on the planned American Gemini craft, which could carry two. Accordingly, the Voskhod module was developed. Basically a Vostok capsule with equipment removed, Voskhod could carry three cosmonauts in extremely cramped conditions. Space suits, ejection seats, and the escape tower were removed, giving extra room at the expense of safety. The first mission, Voskhod I, left the Baikonur Cosmodrome on October 12, 1964, carrying

Vladimir Komarov, Boris Yegorov, and Konstantin Feoktisov. On the next Voskhod mission, the first ever spacewalk was undertaken by Alexei A. Leonov in Voskhod II on March 18, 1965. He remained outside for 20 minutes, but getting back into the spacecraft was difficult. His suit had swelled and he had to deflate it slightly to reduce its size. After 26 orbits, Leonov and his colleague Pavel Belayev landed in a pine forest in the Ural Mountains. Rescue workers did not find them for some time and the crew spent a night surrounded by wolves.

Always seeming to play catch up, NASA equalled this Soviet feat on June 3, 1965, when Edward White made a 22-minute spacewalk outside Gemini IV. Some months earlier, Virgil "Gus" Grissom and John Young had undertaken the first manned flight of the Gemini program, orbiting the Earth three times in Gemini III. However, this mission was not without

Below: *The Soviet Voskhod II capsule allowed the cosmonaut to perform a spacewalk via an inflatable airlock.*

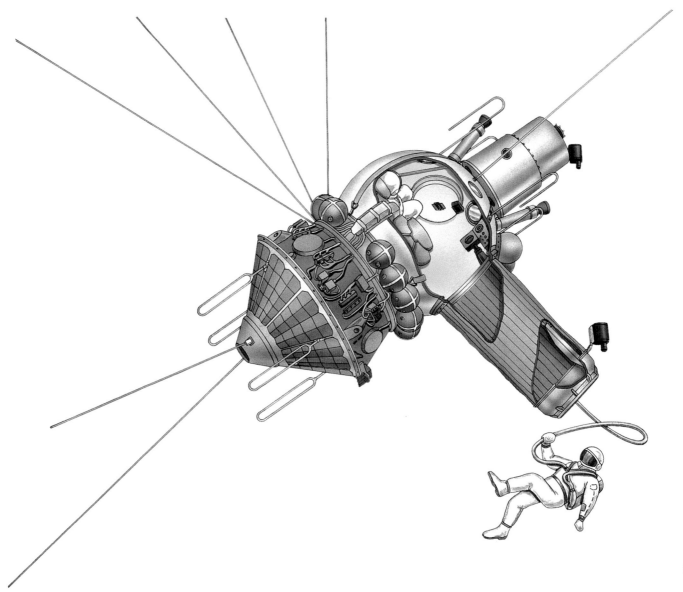

Above: *The spectacular sight of Gemini VII, viewed from Gemini VI, as the two spacecraft rendezvous in orbit on December 15, 1965.*
Right: *The ill-fated Apollo I crew of Roger Chaffee, Edward White, and Gus Grissom, who were killed in a launch pad fire during a training exercise.*

controversy. Young had smuggled a corned beef sandwich on board. During the flight Grissom complained that he was hungry and the sandwich duly appeared. Crumb and meat debris was soon drifting through the capsule, causing an unpleasant odor. NASA was criticized for the incident in a stony-faced official hearing.

Space technology was also bringing images of the cosmos into people's homes. While Telstar and its successors beamed TV pictures around the world, from March 24, 1965, Ranger IX sent back pictures of the moon, which were relayed by television into people's homes, mesmerizing audiences worldwide. Three months later, Mariner IV returned close-up pictures of Mars.

Shooting for the moon

In many ways, the Gemini program was a testing ground for the technology which would be used on President Kennedy's promised moon missions, soon to be named Apollo. In December 1965,

Frank Borman and James Lovell in Gemini VII remained in orbit for almost two weeks, demonstrating that a space flight of the duration necessary to reach the moon was possible. The craft also made a rendezvous with Gemini VI, proving that spacecraft could meet and eventually dock while in orbit. The moon was now the ultimate prize in the superpower space race. In March 1966, the USSR's Luna X became the first spacecraft to orbit the moon. That June, the American Surveyor I was the first spacecraft to soft-land on the lunar surface.

The USSR suffered two major blows to its space program during the next two years. In 1966 Sergei Korolov, the father of the Soviet space program, died of cancer. One year later, space claimed its first explorer. Vladimir Komarov was killed on April 24, 1967, when his Soyuz I craft crashed after its parachute failed to open properly after re-entry. That same year, astronauts Gus Grissom, Edward White, and Roger Chaffee died when fire swept through their oxygen-filled Apollo I capsule during a launch test on January 27. The Apollo

program was halted whilst the capsule's faults and deficiencies were ironed out.

The program's self-examination yielded results. On October 11, 1968, Apollo VII was launched into earth orbit, carrying Walter Schirra, Donn Eisele, and Walter Cunningham. A remarkable and historic mission followed in December 1968, when Apollo VIII carried out ten orbits of the moon during a six-day mission. The craft's crew, Frank Borman, James Lovell, and William Anders, were the first humans ever to reach the moon. The success of Apollo VIII emboldened NASA to attempt the ultimate goal: a lunar landing. After two more proving flights to the moon and back, on July 16, 1969, Apollo XI was launched. Four days later, the lunar lander touched down on the moon. Watched by millions of people around the world, Neil Armstrong set foot on the lunar surface, followed by Edwin "Buzz" Aldrin. Michael Collins remained in the orbiting Command Module.

Despite the triumph of setting foot on the moon, NASA was still set on exploring the rest of

Above: US astronauts Tom Stafford and Eugene Cernan congratulate each other as they emerge from the Gemini IX capsule onboard the aircraft carrier USS Wasp after a 72-hour space flight.

the solar system. Mariner VI and Mariner VII returned impressive pictures of the Martian surface as they passed the red planet. In November 1971 Mariner IX became the first Mars orbiter, photographing over 70 percent of the Martian surface. But American fascination with the god of war was equalled by Soviet fondness for the god of love, and in December 1970 the Soviets succeeded in landing Venera 7 on Venus, revealing an atmospheric pressure over 90 times that on Earth.

Traveling the quarter of a million miles to the moon and back was a dangerous business. The unlucky Apollo XIII was launched in April 1970. Although a moon landing had been planned, an explosion in an oxygen tank on the command module curtailed the mission, and almost cost James Lovell, John Swigert, and Fred Haise their lives.

Far left: *Buzz Aldrin emerges from the Apollo XI lunar module on June 20, 1969.*
Left: *The Apollo XI module sits atop its giant Saturn V rocket as it prepared for launch from Kennedy Space Center's Pad No. 39A.*
Below: *The Soviet Union's Salyut I space station was fitted with photographic and movie cameras as well as a telescope.*

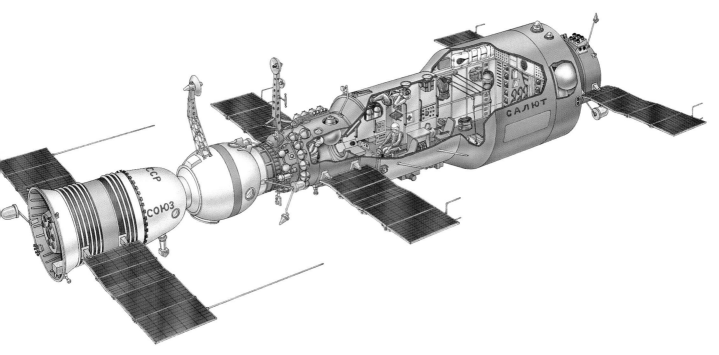

Earth's ambassadors

Fascination with space travel has always carried with it the desire to discover what or who is "out there." Pioneer X was fitted with a plaque to give intelligent life an introduction to Earth and the human race. The plaque contained information encoded into a binary language including the position of the sun in our galaxy, our neighboring planets and their relative distances. Pioneer X is currently heading towards a red star called Aldebaran, which is 68 light years from Earth.

The Voyager I and Voyager II probes (launched on September 5 and August 20, 1977, respectively) were more ambitious. The celebrated astronomer Carl Sagan and several of his colleagues at Cornell University were asked to design a 12in (30cm) gold-plated record containing sounds from Earth. The record included a stylus and symbolic instructions for use.

Musical extracts included a Zairian pygmy girl's initiation song, Chuck Berry's hit "Johnny B. Goode," Azeri bagpipe music, "Melancholy Blues" by Louis Armstrong and his Hot Seven, Beethoven's Fifth Symphony, and a Peruvian wedding song. Greetings from Earth in 55 languages were also recorded. There were a few omissions: for example, the Swahili speaker missed the recording. Pictures were also included in an information pack depicting Heron Island in Australia's Great Barrier Reef, a "Forest Scene with Mushrooms," a supermarket, a Chinese dinner party, and a Turkish man with glasses.

These postcards from Earth are now travelling through deep space. The late Carl Sagan noted that: "The spacecraft will be encountered and the record played only if there are advanced space-faring civilizations in interstellar space. But the launching of this bottle into the cosmic ocean says something very hopeful about life on this planet."

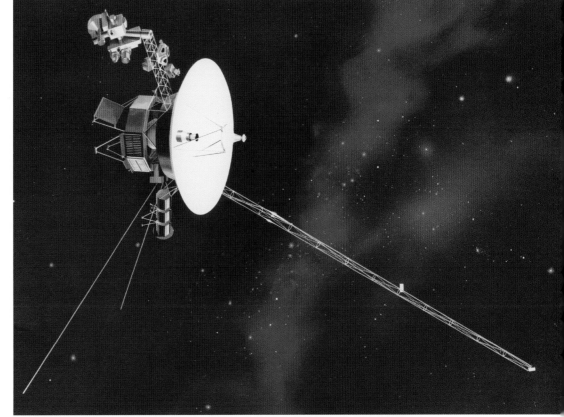

Left: *Pioneer X was launched in 1972. It passed close to Jupiter before heading out into the unknown beyond the Solar System.* Right: *Voyager II explored the planets of Jupiter, Saturn, Uranus, and Neptune before following Pioneer X out of the Solar System.* Below: *The surface of Io, one of Jupiter's moons, is constantly disturbed by volcanic eruptions.*

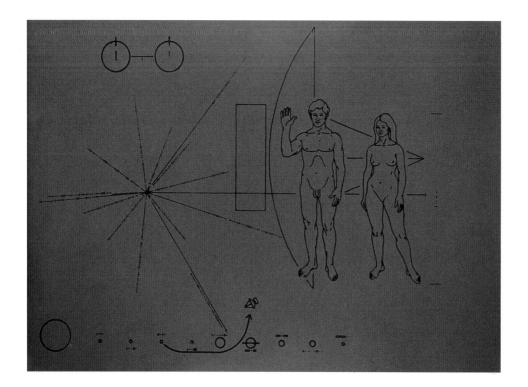

Only the ingenuity and skill of mission control and the astronauts, watched with bated breath by the world's media, brought them safely back home.

The moon landing was arguably the pinnacle of the space race, and a feat which has been unequalled since. In the 1970s, both the Americans and the Soviets began to spend more time in space. In the USSR, the first of the highly successful Salyut series of space stations was launched on April 19, 1971. But the first attempt to dock with the craft by Vladimir Shatalov, Alexei Yeliseyev, and Nikolai Rukavishnikov was unsuccessful. The crew almost lost their lives on re-entry when the air in their Soyuz X capsule became toxic. On June 6, 1971, Soyuz XI carried Georgi Dobrovolsky, Vladislav Volkov, and Viktor Patsayev on a round trip to the space station. This time the cosmonauts managed to gain entry, although tragedy struck on their return journey. As their capsule re-entered the atmosphere, a

Left: *The plaque carried by the Voyager spacecraft was designed to provide information about Earth and its place in the cosmos to extraterrestrial life.*
Below: *Scientist-astronaut Edward Gibson is seen floating aboard the roomy Skylab space station.*

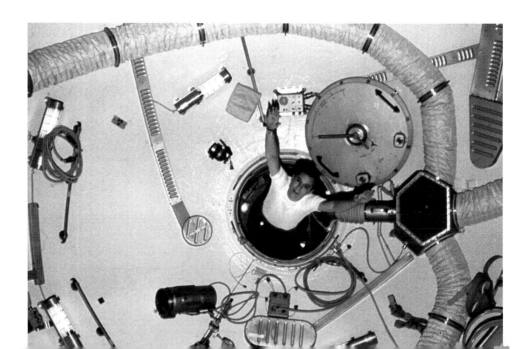

Above: *The Apollo-Soyuz Test Project was an ambitious experiment in space cooperation between the superpowers. Here US astronaut Tom Stafford greets one of his Soviet counterparts.*

faulty valve caused their craft to depressurize 25 minutes before it landed, killing the occupants. It seemed that Salyut I was jinxed.

Endurance and exploration

In America the 1970s saw a renewed push into deep space. The last lunar mission had taken place in December 1972, and NASA now began to focus on exploring the outer reaches of the solar system. The first interstellar diplomat was Pioneer X, launched on March 2, 1972, on a mission that would take it past Jupiter. Its sister ship Pioneer XI followed, reaching Jupiter in December 1974 before being flung in the direction of Saturn, from which it would send back remarkable close-up images of the planet's ring system.

As Soviet cosmonauts settled into life onboard Salyut, the US launched its own Space Station, Skylab, on May 14, 1973. A heat shield failed to open after launch, causing the interior

temperature to rise to 126°F (52°C), although a spacewalk and improvised parasol soon solved the problem. One year later, the Soviets launched Salyut III, a military space station tasked with spying on the West's military bases. The space station even had a 0.9in (23mm) Nudelman gun in case it was attacked by an armed Apollo module. Civilian missions resumed with Salyut IV on December 26, 1974. Continuing the Soviet fascination with long-term space endurance, Pyotr Klimuk and Vitali Sevastyanov spent 63 days in space.

Back on Earth, the Cold War was thawing slightly, and an early example of "shuttle diplomacy" was seen in July 1975, when an Apollo module and a Soyuz vehicle docked in space. Astronauts Tom Stafford, Deke Slayton, and Vance Brand exchanged greetings and gifts with their Soviet counterparts Alexei Leonov and Valery Kubasov. During their re-entry, the Apollo crew were exposed to nitrogen tetroxide gas, causing some breathing difficulties, but they managed to return safely to earth on July 24, five days after the Soviets. The American visit had given the Soviets a taste for stellar hospitality, and by July 1979 astronauts from Czechoslovakia, Poland, East Germany, Bulgaria, Hungary, Vietnam, Cuba, Mongolia, and Romania had all set foot on Salyut VI, launched in September 1977. The mid-1970s also witnessed some of the most striking images of our nearest planetary neighbors to date, when NASA's Viking I and Viking II probes landed on Mars in 1976.

The Space Shuttle

Space travel has always been as expensive as it is glamorous. By the late 1970s, NASA was under increasing pressure, in the words of President Richard Nixon, to "take the astronomical cost out of astronautics." The proposed solution was a reusable spaceplane which would be launched by recoverable rocket boosters, perform missions in orbit, and land like a normal aircraft. The Space Transportation System, as it was originally known, eventually became known as the Space Shuttle. The first space shuttle, *Enterprise*, was constructed for tests only and did not fly in space. The first manned space mission was launched on April 12, 1982, and undertaken by *Columbia*, named after an eighteenth-century merchant sloop. The Soviets, sticking with traditional non-reusable rockets and space stations, launched Salyut VII on April 19, 1982, in which Soviet cosmonauts Anatoli Berezovoi and Valentin Lebedev set a duration record of 211 days in space.

Below: *Valles Marineris, a giant canyon etched into the Martian surface, taken from one of the Viking orbiters.*
Right: *Under a brilliant moon, the Space Shuttle Columbia is prepared for its second mission in November 1981.*

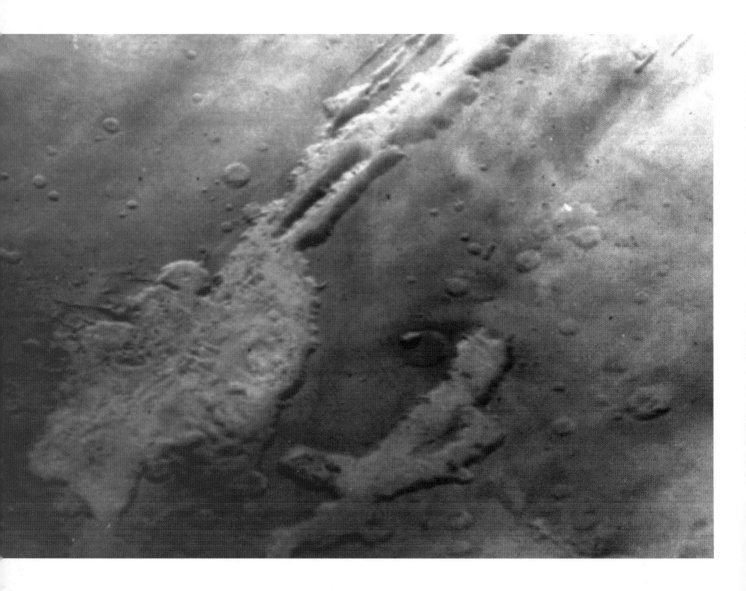

One year later the second NASA shuttle, *Challenger,* took to the skies. On April 4 the crew performed the first US spacewalk for nine years, and two months later Sally Ride became the first American woman to travel in space. In November 1983, Ulf Merbold, a German astronaut from the European Space Agency (ESA), became the first western European in space, aboard *Columbia.* In reality, the Shuttle was not as cheap as had been hoped. Nonetheless, in 1984 Rockwell International, the Shuttle's constructors, unveiled their fourth vehicle, called *Discovery. Discovery* was followed by *Atlantis* which took to the skies for its first mission on October 3, 1985.

In October 1984 the Soviets smashed another duration record when Leonid Kizim, Vladimir

suffered a fatality since the Apollo I accident of 1966. But on January 28, 1986, Gregory Jarvis, Christa McAuliffe, Ronald McNair, Ellison Onizuka, Judy Resnik, Francis Scobee, and Michael Smith were lost when *Challenger* exploded 73 seconds after launch. Cold weather and the failure of an O-ring seal on one of the solid rocket boosters were blamed for the accident. It would be two years and eight months before a Shuttle would fly again, after safety procedures had

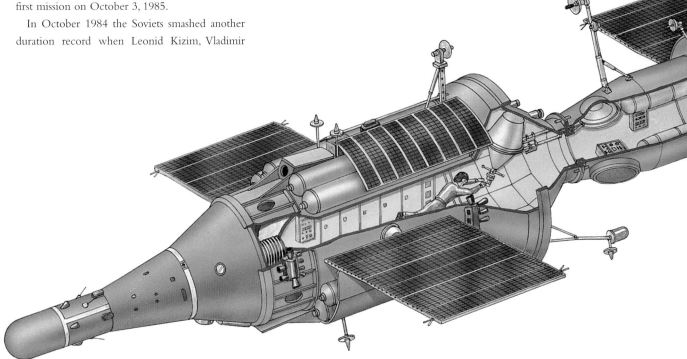

Soloyyov, and Oleg Atkov spent 237 days onboard Salyut VII. This space station also hosted the first Briton in space, the former confectionery scientist Helen Sharman, who made a space-walk—the first woman to perform this feat. The vehicle accumulated an astonishing nine years in orbit, facilitating the many improvements in medical, biological, and exercise technology that were necessary for long duration flights. This important work would be carried over onto the Mir space station, which would be launched in 1986.

The United States' space program had not

been tightened and equipment redesigned. A sixth Shuttle, *Endeavour,* was subsequently built to replace *Challenger.*

Discovery continued to push back the frontiers of space exploration. On April 24, 1990, the Shuttle launched the Edwin P. Hubble Space Telescope, giving astronomers a greater insight into the distant depths of our universe than ever before.

Space station development

The end of the Cold War heralded cooperation between Russia and the United States not seen

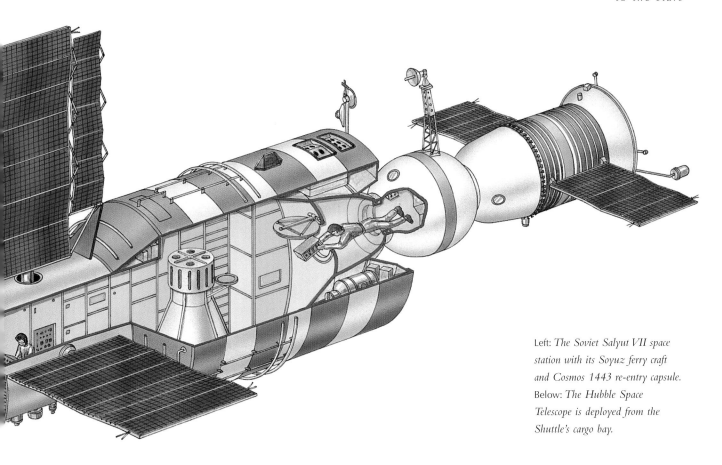

Left: *The Soviet Salyut VII space station with its Soyuz ferry craft and Cosmos 1443 re-entry capsule.*
Below: *The Hubble Space Telescope is deployed from the Shuttle's cargo bay.*

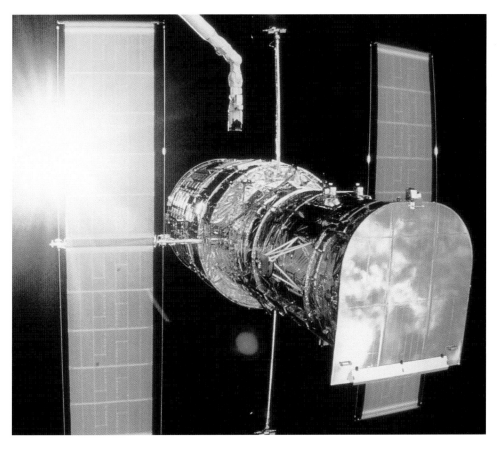

Buran over Baikonur

Uncannily resembling its American cousin, Buran ("Snowstorm") was the Soviet Space Shuttle. Authorized in 1976 in response to the American Shuttle program, construction of Buran began in 1980. By July 1983 sub-orbital flight tests were underway using a scale model. A completed vehicle was rolled out in 1984 and a series of atmospheric and aerodynamic test flights began. In one test, the giant Energia booster rockets which were to carry Buran aloft began to overheat and the entire city of Leninsk (now Baikonur) went without running water for ten days to provide liquid for the cooling system.

On November 15, 1988, Buran performed its first and only orbital test. The vehicle flew unmanned by remote control because several avionic and life-support systems were yet to be installed. Buran orbited the Earth twice, making a near-perfect landing at Baikonur. The Soviet technicians declared the flight a complete success.

Sadly, Buran never hosted a crew. The end of the Cold War and the economic collapse of the former USSR made the program unsustainable and it was canceled in 1993. Two additional airframes were left incomplete at Baikonur, and the vehicle's birthplace has since diversified into making buses, syringes, and diapers. The only complete Buran is now a theme café in Moscow's Gorky Park.

Below: *Russia's Buran space shuttle made only one orbital flight, without a crew of cosmonauts.*

Right: *Much as the US Space Shuttle is piggybacked on a Boeing 747 for trips back to the launch pad after it has landed, the Buran was carried on top of a giant Antonov An-225 cargo aircraft.*

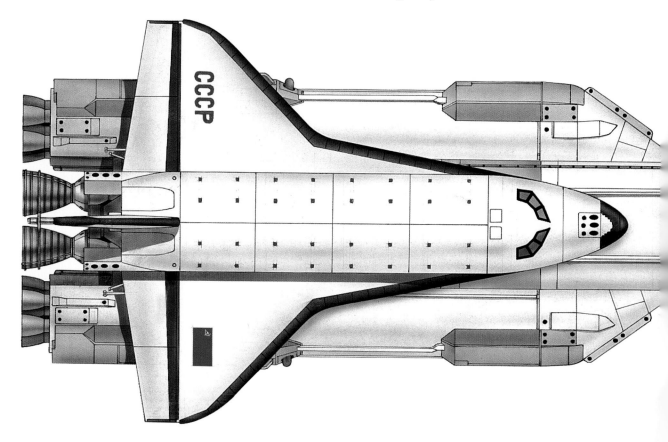

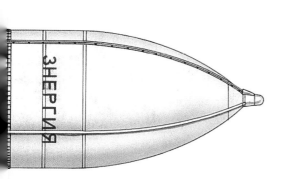

Right: *Seen on the back of its Energia booster rockets,*
the Buran is moved towards the Baikonur launch pad
on a massive traveling frame.

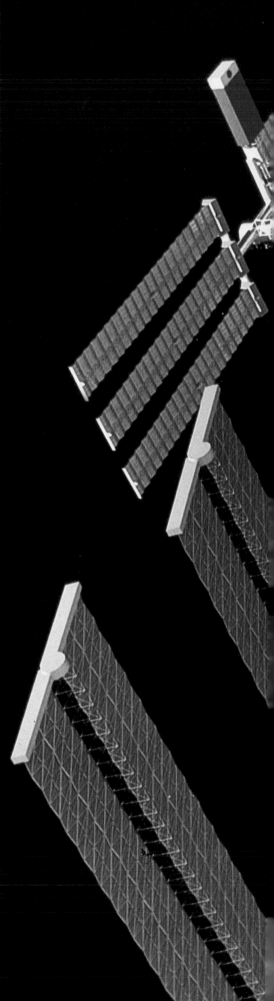

since the Apollo-Soyuz mission of 1975. For example, in 1984 Russia was invited to participate in the International Space Station along with Canada, Brazil, the European Space Agency, and Japan. In February 1994, cosmonaut Sergei Krikalev became the first Russian to fly on a US mission, as part of the *Discovery* crew. One year later, *Discovery* would continue its diplomatic role, maneuvering within 37ft (11m) of Mir in preparation for an eventual joint mission. This flight included Eileen Collins, the first female Shuttle pilot. Collins's mission was observed from Mir by cosmonaut Valeri Polyakov, who returned to Earth the next month having spent a continuous 438 days on Mir.

Discovery's "dry run" that February led to the real thing on June 26, 1995, when *Atlantis* docked with Mir on a ten-day mission. Astronaut Norman Thagard returned to Earth on the Shuttle having arrived on Mir via a Soyuz TM-21 capsule. He took with him an American space endurance record of 115 days.

Above: *The Space Shuttle Atlantis docks with Russia's Mir space station in 1995. Note the relative size of the two vehicles.*
Right: *The International Space Station (ISS) will be the largest man-made structure in space when it is finally completed.*

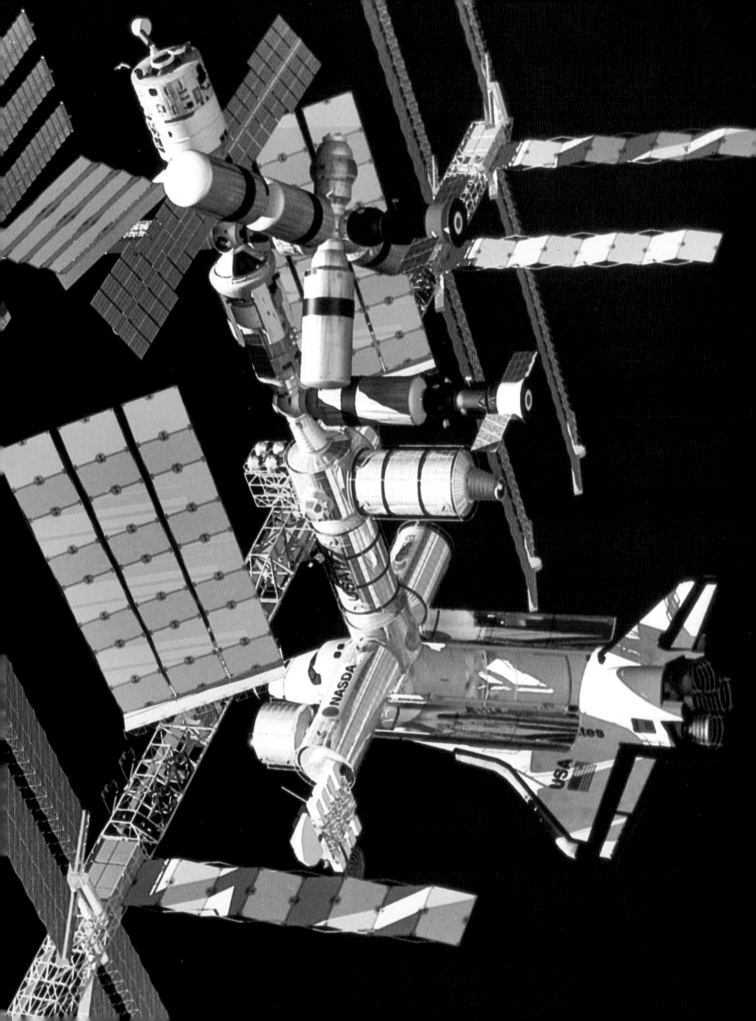

Left: *Seen here in 1999, the Unity and Zarya modules, the foundation for the ISS, await their attachments which will eventually grow into the space station.*

Right: *The ISS suffered a major setback in February 2003 when the Space Shuttle* Columbia *was incinerated during re-entry with the loss of its crew. Here a scientist examines fragments of the wreckage.*

But as one era of space travel was beginning, another ended. In November 1995 contact with Pioneer XI was lost when its power source finally ran out. Pioneer XI was later overtaken by Voyager I, which on February 18, 1999, became the farthest man-made object from Earth. When last in contact, it was heading towards the Lambda Aquila star, which it will reach in around four million years time.

On July 4, 1997, the American Mars Pathfinder landed on the red planet, sending back information which led scientists to believe that life might once have existed there. Two years later, a further pair of US probes, Mars Climate Observer and Mars Polar Lander, were lost because of a design fault confusing metric and imperial measurements.

The world's largest space project finally got under way on November 20, 1998, after a Russian Zarya module became the first component of the International Space Station. On May 29, 1999, the module was joined by *Discovery*, which became the first Shuttle to dock with the fledgling station. As Russia increased its participation in the ISS, it was finding it too expensive to keep Mir in orbit. After a series of high profile accidents, including computer crashes and a collision with a cargo craft, Michael Foale (an astronaut who had spent 145

days onboard) commented that it resembled "someone's very old garage where stuff's just been put away for years on end and nobody's moved it." The problems led to a decision to terminate the space station. The last crew departed in August 1999, thirteen years after the first piece of Mir was launched. It met its demise on March 23, 2001, re-entering the Earth's atmosphere and breaking up after being nudged out of orbit by ground controllers. Russian participation in space exploration would now be largely confined to the ISS.

However, the cash-strapped Russian space industry did have a couple of money-making schemes. In April 2001 a reported $20 million (£12.7 million) bought Dennis Tito, an American entrepreneur, a ticket to the ISS as the world's first space tourist. He was followed on April 25, 2002, by another millionaire, Mark Shuttleworth from South Africa.

Work on the ISS was expected to be completed by 2004, but this date is now likely to be set back after the tragic loss of astronauts Ilan Ramon, Rick Husband, William McCool, Michael Anderson, David Brown, Kalpana Chawla, and Laurel Clark on February 1, 2003, when *Columbia* was destroyed during re-entry.

The China Challenge

Xinhua, the official Chinese news agency, announced on April 24, 2002, that three chickens had successfully hatched from nine eggs which had orbited the earth 108 times, during China's Shenzhou III (Divine Vessel) space mission, which landed on April 1 in Inner Mongolia. The chickens join a monkey, rabbit, dog, and several snails which have successfully orbited the earth in Chinese spacecraft. China is no stranger to dreams of rocket flight. In the sixteenth century, inventor Wan Hu developed a rocket-powered chair which was intended to take him to heaven. The contraption was fitted with 47 rockets and two kites. Wan may have got his wish as both chair and occupant seem to have been vaporized during the launch.

China's space program formally began in the late 1960s. Several Chinese scientists, including the program's father, Tsien Hsueshen, had been expelled from the United States during the McCarthy witch hunts. They returned to China with their expertise, and began to develop China's space program.

The program lacked the luxurious subsidies of its Soviet and American cousins and was often bereft of important materials such as aluminium alloy. At one point, 70 percent of the scientific team were said to be suffering from malnutrition.

The efforts of Tsien and his colleagues resulted in the launch of China's first satellite, Dong Fang Hong I (The East is Red) on April 24, 1970. Since 1985 China has exploited the lucrative satellite launch market, placing 27 foreign-built satellites into orbit for clients including Pakistan, Australia, Sweden, and the Philippines.

The manned space program was launched in 1992. In November 1999 Shenzhou I orbited Earth 14 times in a 12-hour flight designed to test launching and re-entry systems. Shenzhou I was followed by a second mission which used animals and microbes to test the capsule's life support systems.

The efforts of the scientists paid off on October 15, when a Shenzhou V craft took "taikonaut" Yang Lwei—a 35-year-old fighter pilot with the Chinese People's Liberation Army Air Force—into earth orbit. He landed safely the following day after a 21-hour flight, making China only the third nation to have sent a human into space using one of their own rockets. During his flight he is reported to have eaten vacuum-packed dried pork and garlic sauce. One Beijing resident commented: "Now the world will realize that we don't only make clothes and shoes."

Beijing also has plans to conduct a manned lunar landing within a decade. At Expo 2000, in Hanover, visitors were shown scale models of a Chinese lunar rover and taikonauts planting the Chinese flag on the moon's surface. Preparations are already under way and China is designing a new range of rockets called the Chang Zheng V (Long March) which will have the capacity to lift a 55,115lb (25,000kg) payload into orbit.

Left: *China blasted into the exclusive space club in 2003 with its remarkable Long March 2F rocket, carrying a manned Shenzhou capsule.*

Top: *An artist's impression of a Shenzhou capsule of the type which carried China's first taikonaut, Yang Lwei, into space.*

This has caused the grounding of all NASA Shuttles until the cause of the accident is determined and preventive measures taken.

The days of a Space Race turbo-charged with Cold War rivalry have been replaced by a spirit of co-operation. Advances on Earth in genetics and communications have eclipsed the giant leaps which are still being made as we explore our celestial backyard. But spaceflight will certainly continue to excite and amaze future generations. The next big event may be the first manned flight to Mars. But no matter how routine it may become to orbit the earth, whether en route to the moon or one of the planets, or even as a space tourist, nothing can compare to the emotions experienced by those who see the earth from space. In the words of astronaut Thomas Stafford: "The white twisted clouds and the endless shades of blue in the ocean make the hum of the spacecraft systems, the radio chatter, even your own breathing disappear. There is no cold or wind or smell to tell you that you are connected to Earth. You have an almost dispassionate platform— remote, Olympian and yet so moving that you can hardly believe how emotionally attached you are to those rough patterns shifting steadily below."

Above: *A spacewalk is performed during the early stages of the construction of the ISS to build a communications antenna.*
Right: *A montage showing the bodies which spacecraft have so far explored in our solar system.*

The future of flight

over the horizon

In the future, technological development will undoubtedly continue to transform flight. For commercial aircraft, bigger has usually meant better; but in the military context, small and maneuverable has often proved superior. Will those formulae continue to be valid in the twenty-first century?

Left: The 480- to 656-seat Airbus A380 is the next generation super-jumbo jet, due to enter service at the end of 2005.

Top: A Lockheed Martin F-117A "stealth" fighter refuels from the boom of a USAF tanker. This aircraft has been a key weapon in several post-Cold War conflicts.

In the early years of the twenty-first century, it is clear that the heavyweights of airliner manufacturing are reduced to just two: Boeing and Airbus. Ahead for many years, Boeing is now feeling the heat from its competitor. But both companies may find that the wide-bodied "jumbo" jet has reached the limit of its development, restricted by airline economics and airport facilities.

With the benefit of advanced technology, the latest jumbo jets promise to be the best in terms of size and performance. Of the two, Airbus will fly its A380 first, with its maiden flight planned for mid-2004. The A380 is the result of consultation between Airbus and international airports on the easing of congestion over the first half of the new century. The airliner began its life as the A3XX when it was announced at the 1997 Paris Air Show to challenge the Boeing 747. The widest airliner in the world, the A380 will offer almost 50 percent more floor space and 35 percent more seats than the 747-400. The cabin was designed after interviewing 1200 frequent flyers of all ages and backgrounds.

Above: *The proposed interior of the A380 will have 50 percent more floor space and 35 percent more seats than the Boeing 747-400.*

The two decks will accommodate between 481 and 656 passengers, and there are plans to convert compartments on the cargo deck into shops and lounges. One question that has arisen is how the pilots will cope with the transition to these mammoths. The A380 has a larger cockpit, positioned higher up, than any other Airbus. This is where "commonality" plays an important role. Commonality is the similarity between different aircraft regardless of size and role, and the similarity between the cockpits of the A380 and other Airbus aircraft means that pilots can transfer to the type in considerably less time than that needed to convert between aircraft that share no commonality.

The A380 is expected to enter service with its eight current customers from late 2005 at a cost of $275 million each, compared to $215 million for the latest Boeing 747-400. Initial operators include Air France, Qantas, and Virgin Atlantic, but the A380 is expected to appear in many different variants, which include folding wings for parking at smaller airports, a converted cargo deck option for larger long-haul airlines, and a freighter version.

Boeing 7E7

While Airbus has concentrated its efforts on size with the A380 "super-jumbo," Boeing has directed some of its energy into faster and more efficient airliners. In early 2001 Boeing announced the Sonic Cruiser, which was to fly just below the speed of sound, taking just under two hours off the transatlantic crossing time for current passenger jets. Rising costs and a lack of interest have prompted Boeing to postpone the design indefinitely in favor of the more traditional 7E7 Dreamliner, where the "E" stands for "Efficient." The 7E7 will offer the speed, range, and comfort

Right: *The one to beat: this Air India 747-400 represents the phenomenally successful competition to the Airbus A380.*
Below: *Airbus is considering a number of A380 versions, including freighter examples.*

Above: *Boeing's Phantom Works and NASA are currently working together to develop an 800-seat Blended-Wing Body (BWB) aircraft for both civil and military use.*

Previous: *Boeing promised that the Sonic Cruiser would cut transatlantic crossings by two hours, but rising costs have led to the project being postponed.*

a wide-body airliner, but for just 200 to 250 passengers, and will use around 20 percent less fuel than other aircraft of a similar size. Boeing expects to be able to offer a final design to airlines in early 2004, with production beginning in 2005 for deliveries in 2008. It remains to be seen whether the 7E7 will excite airlines in today's depressed commercial aviation industry.

New airliner concepts

Looking further ahead, Airbus and Boeing are just two of the companies researching alternative wing and fuselage designs for more efficient and higher capacity airliners in the future. Airbus have carried out studies into wing shape and size that have resulted in two concept aircraft, the "Joined Wing Concept" (JWC) and "Three Surface Aircraft" (TSA). The JWC has a slightly taller fuselage and shorter wings than contemporary airliners, and

incorporates a second wing attached to the top of the fuselage, connected to the lower wing by struts at the tips. The idea is that the greater wing area will give more lift, and although a small increase in drag is inevitable, the aircraft will be more fuel-efficient. The TSA is again based on the conventional airliner design, but has a pair of "canard" wings positioned high on the fuselage just behind the cockpit. Although a naturally unstable airplane in flight, it will be stabilized by complex computer systems that monitor the TSA's performance and make tiny adjustments. As with the JWC, the increased wing surface area will make the airliner more fuel-efficient.

Flying wing airliners

The flying wing design, employed successfully in the Northrop-Grumman B-2A Spirit bomber, is only now gaining more credence in commercial

Above: *Designed to be the world's first full double-deck commercial airliner, the 500-seat McDonnell Douglas MD-12 project was cancelled in the mid-1990s.*
Below: *Two A300-600ST Belugas parked alongside two examples of the first Airbus outsize transporter, the Super Guppy.*

circles. The B-2A made its maiden flight in 1989, and shortly afterwards McDonnell Douglas (MDD) and Aérospatiale separately began research into a flying wing or "blended-wing-body" (BWB) airliner. The French study began in the mid-1990s and looked at designing an aircraft for introduction around 2050. The result was a design for a 1000-seat aircraft with four huge turbofan engines above the wing, making it capable of speeds up to Mach 0.85 (552mph or 910km/h) over a 7547 mile (12,000km) range. The MDD project was on a smaller scale, but continued through Boeing's buyout of the company in the mid-1990s. The

outcome of these initial studies has led to Boeing and Airbus developing more concrete designs for future aircraft. Airbus presented their progress with the flying wing design at the 2002 Berlin International Aerospace Exhibition. Although ambitiously aiming for entry into service between 2020 and 2030, some structural and logistical problems remain. For example, it is still undecided which materials are to be used, and their strength and weight. There is also still no solution to the conundrum that only a small proportion of the 1000 travelers will have a window seat, the rest staring ahead down the long, wide cabin.

Above: The first of the Belugas was flown in September 1994 and delivered the following year.

The Boeing BWB is more advanced, because the design team at Boeing's Phantom Works have joined forces with NASA and several research universities. While Boeing have solved the passenger window seat problem by proposing television monitors showing the view outside, other safety issues present themselves, such as the question of how the 800 passengers on two decks would be evacuated in an emergency. In addition, there are technical problems to overcome, not least the issue of pressurizing such a huge area. These questions need to be answered before the general public will feel comfortable flying in this new shape of aircraft. Another concern is convincing airline companies to take a risk and purchase BWB airliners. Because of the shape of the flying wing, new sections cannot be added to stretch the airliner to accommodate more passengers, and the proposed 295ft (90m) wingspan will cause even more problems at airports than the 262ft (80m)

A380. If commercial production of a BWB design succeeds, it may outstrip all competition, but for now it still seems a long way off.

Outsize air cargo

As a multinational corporation, Airbus's aircraft parts are constructed in different parts of Europe before the final aircraft is assembled in Toulouse or Hamburg. Initially, Airbus would transport its parts by road, but this proved too slow and impractical, so four modified Boeing Stratocruisers were converted, with extended fuselages to accommodate the large wings of the aircraft. Known as Guppies, these ageing aircraft became too expensive to operate in the 1990s, and so in October 1991 Aérospatiale and Deutsche Aerospace AG (DASA) formed the Special Air Transport International Company (SATIC) to build a replacement to transport outsize parts. In September 1994 the Airbus

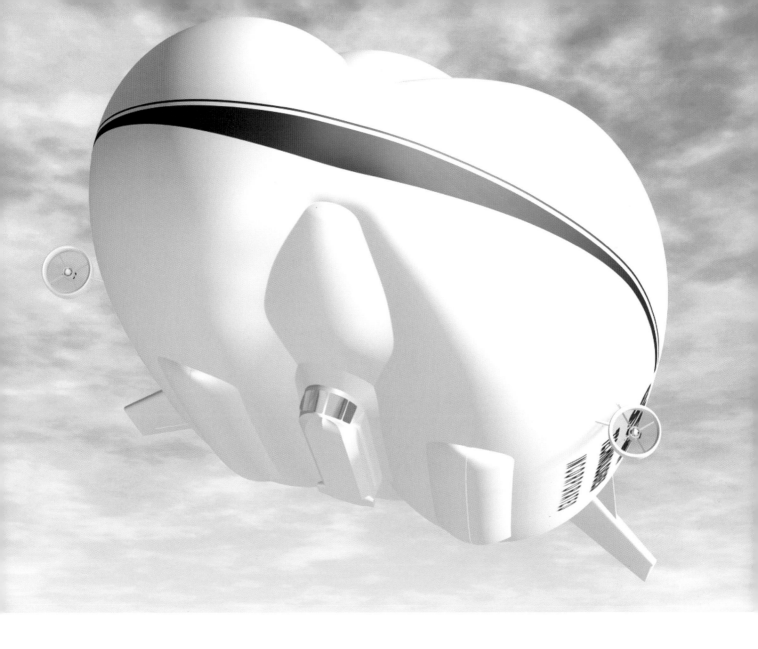

Above: *The SkyCat 1000, the largest of the intended SkyCat family, would be capable of transporting a payload of 984 tons (1000 tonnes).*

A300-600ST Beluga made its first flight, and the first of five was delivered to Airbus the following year. Aircraft like the Boeing 747, Lockheed C-5 Galaxy and Antonov An-124 can carry heavier loads, but none can match the Beluga's internal volume with its 123ft 8in (37.7m) length and 24ft 3in (7.4m) diameter.

Return of the airship?

With greater emphasis being put on efficiency and volume rather than speed, the future of freighters appears to be pointing towards an aircraft not seen for 60 years: the airship. When it comes to freight, airships are faster than ships and cheaper than airplanes, and could prove attractive to a wide market. There are a number of companies vying to obtain a piece of the market, which is estimated at

$1 billion a year in the United States alone. Zeppelin, or Friedrichshafen Zeppelin Luftschiff GmbH as it is now known, unveiled its LZ N07 at the Aero International Flight Fair in 1997. The Friedrichshafen, as it is known, is not specifically designed for freight, nor for reopening the passenger routes of the 1920s and 1930s, but will instead focus on sightseeing tours.

The future freight airships will be unlike the previous rigid dirigibles. Instead these will be hybrids, with qualities of both heavier and lighter-than-air craft. These new airships are slightly heavier than air and remain airborne through a combination of natural buoyancy and aerodynamic lift created by their shape.

One example of the new breed of airship is the SkyCat concept. Developed by the Advanced

Technologies Group (ATG), the SkyCat is only semi-rigid, and incorporates two hulls, hence its name. ATG proposes three models: the SkyCat 20, with a 44,100lb (20,000kg) payload, the SkyCat 200, able to carry 441,000lb (200,000kg), and the SkyCat 1000, with a capacity for 2,205,000lb (1,000,000kg). Despite its commercial attraction, the biggest customer of the SkyCat may well be the military. At present it takes about ten days for the US Army to deploy two light divisions (20,000 men), using up to 600 conventional aircraft, while 20 SkyCats could perform the task in just two days. It is this sort of potential that military planners are relishing. An obvious benefit of airships is that they do not need a runway to land, although some need a ground crew and others like the CL-160 need a water supply for ballast. The SkyCat needs neither as, although it needs water for permanent landings, for unloading at its destination it uses a vacuum to literally suck it to the ground, even on an uneven surface.

A major concern for commercial and military procurement is the risk involved in operating airships in a period of heightened terrorism. ATG has foreseen this and allayed fears with tests that measure the airship's tolerance to attack. One airship remained airborne despite more than two hours of continuous small arms fire, and ATG asserts that the envelope can also endure missile attack. As for the payload gondola, this is made of a Kevlar composite which offers tremendous strength and impenetrability.

Future airships are not limited to military and commercial freight use. ATG promotes over a dozen uses of its hybrid aircraft, from SkyLift for emergency relief, to FireCat for fire fighting, and from SkyFerry for ferrying passengers and their cars to SkyYacht, an airship version of the executive jet. The potential for airships is great, and perhaps ATG will be the company to seize the opportunity and turn that potential into reality.

Advanced freighter design

Despite the appeal of airships, the end of conventional cargo airplanes is not yet upon us, and advanced technology promises to prolong the life of more conventional freighter designs. On January 17, 1995, the Boeing C-17 Globemaster entered USAF service with the 17th Airlift Squadron. The Globemaster is arguably the most advanced cargo aircraft ever. A specially-designed "supercritical" wing is more aerodynamic, giving less drag and causing fewer shock waves as the aircraft travels at high speed, thereby reducing stress to the airframe.

It should also improve the aircraft's fuel efficiency. The aircraft's wing flaps permit the Globemaster to perform steep landings on runways as short as 3000ft (914m) in length, even with a total weight of 585,000lb (265,352kg). The aircraft has a range of 5984 miles (9630km) and a cruising speed of approximately 517mph (833km/h).

In the same way that airliner designs are being rethought for the twenty-first century, so aircraft designers are experimenting with new freighter designs. The Lockheed Martin Advanced Mobility Aircraft (AMA) team is currently developing a response to the USAF "Air Mobility Master Plan" specification. The most innovative design to come from the team is the Box-Wing, in which two sets of wings, one set attached to the fuselage at the center of the aircraft and the other near the nose, meet at their tips. If accepted, the Box-Wing will have the capacity to refuel twice as many aircraft as is possible with the current Boeing KC-135 Stratotanker. Such designs are still at an early stage and the Box-Wing is just one of a number of

Left: *SkyCat variants will include SkyLift for emergency relief and FireCat (pictured) for fire fighting.* Below: *One of the most likely customers for the SkyCat is the military. 20 SkyCats could deploy 200,000 military personnel in just two days.*

CargoLifter CL-160: End of the Giant Airship?

One company which has conducted extensive research into airship design is CargoLifter AG of Germany. In October 1999, CargoLifter's "Joey" made its maiden flight, the scaled-down testbed for the company's flagship CL-160. At 853ft (260m) long, the CL-160 design is three-and-a-half times longer than a Boeing 747, Unlike earlier zeppelins it has no frame and is only semi-rigid, with a keel running the entire length of the airship to provide the necessary rigidity. The sheer size of the CL-160 requires a huge hangar, which was completed in Brand in November 2000.

The CL-160's proposed 352,000lb (160,000kg) payload would be highly attractive to civil and military operators. Although only travelling at 56mph (90km/h), the airship has a range of 6214 miles (10,000km), and at $100 million costs a little over half the price of a Lockheed C-5 Galaxy. These advantages should have made the CL-160 a very desirable proposition. However, in June 2002 CargoLifter was forced to file for an application for insolvency proceedings. The future appeared bleak for CargoLifter as administrators took over, but soon afterwards Boeing stepped forward with a lifeline. As part of a design proposal for a stratospheric airship, Boeing offered a contract to CargoLifter to jointly explore viable concepts. At present, CargoLifter is maintained by partnership deals and a continuation of smaller airship development. Although not officially cancelled, the CL-160 project is on hold for the foreseeable future.

Below: *An artist's impression of the CL-160 CargoLifter in action.*

possibilities, but the face of military transport is changing. Boeing's Phantom Works has presented a revolutionary design for a future transport aircraft based on ground effect. To meet the US Army's "Deployment Transformational Goals" that require the deployment of a division within five days, Boeing has conceived the Pelican Ultra Large Transport Aircraft, or ULTRA. If built, the Pelican will have a capacity of 3,086,420 lb (1,400,000kg), which could include up to 17 M-1 main battle tanks. The most attractive aspect of the Pelican, aside from the obvious payload benefit, is its

efficiency. With a 500ft (152.4m) wingspan—giving a surface area of more than an acre—the Pelican can use ground effect without being a designated WIG craft. It will skim 20ft (6m) over the seas and oceans with a range of 11,200 miles (18,025km), or soar to 20,000ft (6096m) over land for 7300 miles (11,748km). Unlike a similarly oversized transport from an earlier era, the *Spruce Goose*, the Pelican will be land-based, but will require 38 fuselage-mounted landing legs and 76 wheels to spread its weight evenly. The future of the project is not yet certain, but if it is

Above: *The Boeing C-17 freighter is a "go anywhere" aircraft able to operate from rough strips. Here it is seen landing at Charleston Air Force Base, South Carolina.*

approved, the Pelican will become the world's largest aircraft.

Desert Storm

Despite being billed as one of the most technologically modern wars ever fought, Operation Desert Storm, the US-led military campaign to evict Iraq from Kuwait in 1991, was mostly fought using old, unguided bombs—"dumb" munitions in military parlance. But the laser- and satellite-guided weapons that were used, known as "smart" munitions, changed the face of warfare forever, making them without doubt the weapon of choice for many wars to come.

At 0238 local time on January 17, 1991, a team of US Army AH-64 Apache attack helicopters from "Task Force Normandy" attacked a radar station in southern Iraq, paving the way for an armada of combat aircraft, including those of the United States, Britain, France, and Saudi Arabia, to

attack targets in Iraq. Hot on the heels of the Apaches were the USAF's F-117A Nighthawk "Stealth" attack aircraft, which hit another air defence radar center in southern Iraq, en route to their main targets in downtown Baghdad. The Nighthawks were joined by older aircraft like the Boeing B-52G Stratofortress, firing advanced AGM-86C/D Air Launched Cruise Missiles (ALCMs). This gave a glimpse of future conflicts in which old aircraft have been and will be given a new punch by using ultra-modern bombs and missiles. Several ageing combat aircraft made their final combat missions, including USAF McDonnell Douglas F-4 Phantoms, which carried AGM-88 High Speed Anti-Radiation Missiles (HARMs) to smash Iraqi radar installations, as well as US Navy Vought A-7 Corsair carrier-based attack aircraft, and RAF Buccaneer S2Bs. General Dynamics F-111 Aardvark aircraft (veterans of Operation Eldorado Canyon, the American air

Above: The C-17 Globemaster is the airlift lifeline of the Allied forces. This aircraft is pictured at Bagram in central Afghanistan.
Right: An artist's impression of the USAF's future Advanced Tactical Transporter. This tailless aircraft would be able to move rapid reaction forces around the world giving a speedy response to international crises.

strikes against Libya in 1986) were used to hit Iraqi tanks. These ageing swing-wing bombers were fitted with "Pave Tack" laser targeting pods, allowing them to destroy 900 Iraqi tanks with surgical accuracy.

The F-117A is one of the most advanced aircraft to grace the skies. It is not really a fighter, but more a strike aircraft equipped with bombs. Its strange appearance and advanced construction makes the aircraft extremely difficult to see by radar. Development of the aircraft dates back to Lockheed winning a contract to develop the plane in 1978. The first prototype flew on June 18, 1981, a mere 31 months later. By October 1983 the aircraft had entered service with the USAF's 4450th Tactical Group, now the 49th Tactical Fighter Wing.

In Desert Storm, veteran Lockheed U-2 spy planes were supplemented by their more recent Lockheed TR1-A variant and state-of-the-art Joint Surveillance Target Radar System (JSTAR) aircraft—an advanced radar system squeezed into a Boeing 707 and known as the Northrop-Grumman E-8. This aircraft could watch all vehicle movements on the battlefield, directing aircraft to attack new targets as they appeared.

By the time a ceasefire was declared on February 28, 1991, more than 20 Iraqi army divisions had been damaged or destroyed and thousands of Iraqi troops had deserted, been taken prisoner or killed. Around 80 percent of Iraq's oil distribution system lay in ruins, as did 30 percent of its armaments industry. Only 10 percent of the weapons used in the air campaign were "smart," but their importance outstripped their numbers. A couple of bombs from an F-117A could now destroy a factory—a task that could have taken hundreds of aircraft dropping thousands of bombs in World War II. The era of precision warfare, long-heralded, had finally arrived.

Stealth bomber

Two years before the storm in the desert, on July 17, 1989, the Northrop Grumman B-2A Spirit

Left: *The most advanced helicopter gunship in current service, the Apache AH-64D Longbow.*
Right: *F-117s on the ramp. The development of this aircraft was one of the most secretive projects ever undertaken by the USAF.*

stealth bomber made its first flight. The first aircraft was delivered to the USAF on December 17, 1993. This bat-like flying wing can deliver either smart bombs or nuclear weapons unseen and undetected, thanks to the aircraft's shape and the radar-absorbent materials used in its construction. The aircraft is highly automated, and although subsonic and lacking any defensive armament, boasts an impressive array of electronic countermeasures to ensure that any enemy missiles or radar systems are jammed.

Electronics also help to reduce the crew's workload, and numbers: just two pilots are required to fly the B-2A as opposed to a crew of five for the B-52. The B-2A made its combat debut in Operation Allied Force in Yugoslavia in the spring of 1999, when it flew record-breaking missions from its home at Whiteman AFB, Missouri, to the Balkans. Two aircraft each dropped 16 satellite-guided Joint Direct Attack Munitions (JDAM) bombs onto Podgorica Airport in Montenegro on March 24—the first

Left: *By the time the Boeing B-52 is predicted to leave service in 2040, the design will be almost 90 years old.*

Above: *A KC-135 sits on the tarmac while a B-2A Spirit stealth bomber soars overhead. This hugely costly aircraft allows the USAF the ability to hit almost any target in the world without detection.*

night of the war—before returning non-stop, receiving several drinks of fuel from USAF tankers along the way.

War in the Balkans

NATO launched Operation Allied Force in an attempt to protect ethnic Albanians in the province of Kosovo from repression by the governments of Serbia and Montenegro. As with Operation Desert Storm, Allied Force saw several older aircraft using the latest in bomb and missile technology. But the technology was to show its limitations as well as its capabilities. Serbian air defences were stronger than initially anticipated by NATO, and on March 25 Serbian MiG-29 "Fulcrum" fighters took off to meet incoming NATO warplanes. Serbia lost three Fulcrums that day, but their intervention meant that for a time NATO could only operate at night. Furthermore, the poor weather over the Balkans meant that some of the laser-guided bombs often had their targeting disrupted by the heavy rain. Finally, the smart munitions were only as intelligent as the people using them. On April 6, a civilian building was bombed when NATO warplanes were attempting to hit the headquarters of the Serbian army's 203rd Mixed Artillery Brigade. A second attack went awry on April 12 when NATO aircraft accidentally hit a passenger train during an attack on a bridge. Perhaps the most embarrassing incident occurred on May 7 when the Chinese Embassy was bombed by a B-2A. It is thought that communications equipment mounted on top of the Embassy was being used to transmit commands from Belgrade to the Serbian army and Special Police units operating in Kosovo. The Swedish, Swiss and Angolan Embassies suffered accidental damage on May 20 during a NATO air raid (the Swiss ambassador was holding a reception at the time). Even the famed F-117A was not invulnerable. Despite its state-of-the-art protection against radar and air defences, the Serbs were successful in shooting one down near Belgrade on May 28. The air campaign in the Balkans ended on June 10. NATO aircraft had flown 38,000 missions, two NATO aircraft had been lost and no NATO combat facilities were damaged during the operation. Just over one third of the bombs and missiles used by NATO were "smart."

New fighter development

It is not just the Americans who have made progress in the design and construction of advanced combat aircraft. On March 27, 1994, the pan-European Eurofighter Typhoon took to the skies for the first time. With advanced aerodynamics and a pair of powerful, advanced EJ200 turbofans, the Typhoon is able to fly above Mach 1 for long periods without the need for an afterburner. Previously combat aircraft could only maintain supersonic speeds for a short time using their afterburners—known as supersonic dash—due to the large amount of fuel that this required.

As the technological sophistication of warplanes has leapt forward, so has their cost. Previously independent nations are being forced to develop new combat aircraft in collaboration with other countries to share the astronomical costs. The Eurofighter is no exception, and companies from the United Kingdom, Italy, Spain, Norway and Germany are involved in the program. Costs are high because of the advanced materials used in construction, including titanium, aluminum-lithium alloys, and carbon fiber. The design, with small canard foreplanes

and a delta wing, makes the aircraft inherently unstable but very agile. Advanced fly-by-wire technology stabilizes the aircraft while keeping it highly maneuverable and controllable by a single pilot. Thirteen weapons positions, known as "hardpoints," are distributed underneath the fuselage and wings, while an internally-mounted Mauser 1.06in (27mm) cannon gives an added punch.

In 1995, the same year that the mighty C-17 took to the skies, Boeing also introduced the considerably smaller but more deadly F/A-18E/F Super Hornet, which made its maiden flight on November 29. Based on the highly successful McDonnell Douglas F/A-18C/D Hornet, the Super Hornet is 25 percent larger, allowing it to carry greater payloads, and features more powerful engines. The aircraft made its combat debut in Operation Iraqi Freedom, the US-led campaign against the regime of Iraqi President Saddam Hussein in the spring of 2003. The air campaign to remove the Iraqi dictator was ideally suited to aircraft such as the Super Hornet. Whereas Operation Desert Storm in 1991 had seen a large proportion of "dumb" ordnance being used against Iraqi targets, with a smattering of "smart" weapons much publicized in the media, Iraqi Freedom saw a huge increase in the use of precision weapons. The consequence was a notably smaller, but more focused and precise, air campaign.

It is possible that the US Navy may develop an electronic warfare version of the Super Hornet, known as the EF-18G, to replace the ageing carrier-based Grumman EA-6B Prowler.

As the Super Hornet enters service, another McDonnell Douglas design is in need of replacement. The F-15 Eagle has been in service since the early 1970s, and despite its impressive speed and versatility it is nearing the end of its service life. It will eventually be replaced by the Lockheed F-22 Raptor. The first prototype YF-22 flew on September 7, 1997. Plastics and composites make up 56 percent of the Raptor's airframe, along with hi-tech titanium and aluminium components. These materials will give the aircraft stealthy characteristics, while making it highly maneuverable and aerodynamic. Like its Typhoon counterpart it will be capable of supercruise. Although primarily designed as an air superiority fighter, the Raptor will be able to deliver a

Right: *An operator surveys an electronic picture of the battlefield onboard a USAF E-8C JSTARS aircraft which can simultaneously track enemy vehicles and aircraft.*
Below: *Mikoyan-Gurevich MiG-29s were operated by Serbia during the Balkan conflict. The MiG-29 was much feared during the Cold War, but it was no match for NATO warplanes in the 1990s.*

powerful mix of weapons including six AIM-120C and two AIM-9C air-to-air missiles (AAMs) and six 1000lb (453kg) JDAM bombs on underwing hardpoints and in an internal weapons bay. It is thought that the USAF will purchase 339 Raptors.

Entering service a year before the Raptor's maiden flight, the Gripen is the latest in a long line of aircraft from the Swedish Saab manufacturer. This hi-tech fighter was built to replace the Saab Viggen and Draken in Swedish service. Two hundred and four of them will equip the Royal Swedish Air Force, and the aircraft will also be exported to South Africa. Hungary will also buy 14.

France's new generation fighter, the Dassault Rafale, entered French naval service in 2001. In total, the Air Force will purchase 234 aircraft and the Navy 60. Three variants of the aircraft are in production: the "M" single-seat naval variant, the "B" two-seat air force variant and the "C" single-seat air force variant. A two-seat naval variant will enter service in 2008. A plethora of missiles and munitions can be attached to the aircraft's 14 hardpoints (13 for the naval version). These will include air-to-air and air-to-surface missiles in addition to the nuclear ASMP missile.

The Russian aviation industry is also continuing its tradition of designing innovative warplanes. Unveiled in 1997, the Sukhoi S.37 Berkut (Royal Eagle) featured a highly unusual forward-swept wing planform. The wing design provides a high lift-to-drag ratio, improving the aircraft's performance and maneuverability. Furthermore,

Right: *A B-2A refuels from a tanker. This aircraft is not only expensive, but it also requires careful handling. It must be stored in special climate-controlled hangars to protect its anti-radar paint.*
Below: *The crew of a B-2A Spirit review their flight plan prior to a training exercise.*

this design makes the aircraft highly resistant to stalling or spinning out of control, and gives shorter take-off and landing distances. The design utilized much of the technology that was developed for the Sukhoi Su-27 "Flanker," including the undercarriage, cockpit canopy, avionics, and vertical tail. Inside the cockpit, the pilot's seat is tilted back to an angle of 60 degrees to improve the pilot's tolerance of high G-forces during extreme maneuvers, an idea also utilized in the General Dynamics F-16 Fighting Falcon. Although a remarkable technology demonstrator, the S.37 did not enter production.

Another advanced Russian design, Sukhoi's Su-37 "Flanker" made a heart-stopping performance at the 1996 Farnborough Air Show, where the aircraft demonstrated its outstanding maneuvrability. The aircraft can carry up to 14 AAMs, and around 17,636lb (8000kg) of weaponry. A single 1.18in (30mm) 1500 rounds-per-minute cannon is also included.

In the same year another aircraft in the Flanker family, the Sukhoi Su-34 (formerly the Su-32FN), made its first flight. This aircraft, with an unusual side-by-side seat configuration in the cockpit and a rear-facing radar in the tail, was designed as a fighter-bomber in a similar role to America's F-111 and will replace the Sukhoi Su-24 "Fencer" strike aircraft. Deliveries of the Su-34 are expected to begin in 2005.

Above: *An F/A-18E Super Hornet takes off on its maiden flight on November 29, 1995.*
Right: *The Lockheed Martin F-22 Raptor. This stealthy air superiority fighter could be integrated with B-2 stealth bombers to provide a rapid, almost invisible strike force.*
Previous: *The Eurofighter Typhoon was developed to intercept Soviet bombers over northern Europe. Its role had to be extensively redefined following the end of the Cold War.*

Left: *The Gripen is a collaborative venture between BAE Systems of the UK and Saab of Sweden. The aircraft is a state-of-the-art air defence platform designed to counter present and future air threats.*

Two years after the Su-32/34's maiden flight, MiG unveiled what is arguably the zenith of Russian fighter aircraft design to date. On January 12, 1999, the MiG MFI (*Mnogofunksionalni Frontovoi Istrebiel*—"Multi-Role Fighter") was shown to the public for the first time. Although weighing 35 tons (35.5 tonnes), the aircraft is said to be capable of a top speed of 1553mph (2500km/h). MiG are confident that their aircraft will outperform both the Eurofighter and the F-22 Raptor. Furthermore, like several new generation fighters, the MFI uses thrust vectoring technology, which allows the engine's exhausts to be deflected from their normal axes, adding to the aircraft's performance. Carbon fiber and low-observable materials will also give radar operators a hard time as they attempt to detect the aircraft. These materials will also reduce the aircraft's heat signature, helping to protect it from heat-seeking missiles. Although the aircraft is highly impressive, it is not certain whether the Russian Air Force will be able to afford it, given Russia's dire economic fortunes.

By far the most advanced aircraft in this crop of future warplanes is the Lockheed F-35 Joint Strike Fighter (JSF). The F-35 is destined for production in three variants: the standard F-35A, the carrier-capable F-35B, and the Vertical/Short Take-Off and Vertical Landing (VSTOL) F-35C. The aircraft will equip the USAF, US Navy and the US Marine Corps, and is also likely to be purchased by Britain's Royal Air Force and Fleet Air Arm.

Although the rationale for the F-35 was to develop an affordable, low-observable, highly advanced warplane, the F-35 program is already the most expensive defence contract in history. The low-observable characteristics of this aircraft will allow it to operate over dangerous enemy territory, while sophisticated electronics will enable it to perform its mission at any time of the day in all weathers. Lockheed is leading the program but several other countries, including the United Kingdom, Italy, the Netherlands, Turkey, Canada, Denmark, Norway, and Australia are participating in the contract and may purchase the aircraft.

Left top: *Sukhoi's S.37 Berkut is an experimental technology demonstrator, and is unlikely to be developed into a production aircraft.*
Left bottom: *The Lockheed Martin X-35 Joint Strike Fighter development aircraft.*
Below: *MiG's "fifth-generation" fighter prototype, the 1.42, or MFI, pictured at an air base near Moscow.*

Rotary-wing aircraft

As the United States boasts the Apache, Russia the Hind, Italy the Mangusta, and South Africa the Rooivalk, Europe is soon to introduce its own helicopter gunship into the fray. By no means a new project, the Eurocopter Tiger began life as a joint Franco-German venture in the 1970s with work beginning in 1984. Considerable delays, mainly caused by uncertain commitment from the two participant governments, meant that the helicopter was only given the go-ahead at the 1999 Paris Air Show. The first test flight took place in August 2002 and deliveries to the German Army Flying Corps for training commenced in early 2003. At present, only France, Germany, and Australia have made firm orders for attack helicopter and anti-tank variants, but it is intended to market the Tiger to Turkey and Poland, among other nations.

The attack helicopters of the future may be just as advanced as the conventional warplanes. In 1996 the prototype Boeing Comanche performed its first flight. Designed as a replacement for the US Army's Apache gunships, it was the world's first "stealth" helicopter. The aircraft was constructed from composite materials and could evade radar by using similar technologies to the F-117A and the B-2A. A tail rotor enclosed in the rear fuselage of the helicopter also improved its speed and cut down on its radar signature. Much like its USAF stealth cousins, the Comanche's weapons were enclosed in an internal weapons bay to further reduce radar visibility and cut drag.

Inspired by the V-22 Osprey, the designers at Boeing's Phantom Works are looking at another hybrid aircraft named the Canard Rotary Wing (CRW), or Dragonfly. Other than the ability to transform from a rotary to a fixed-wing aircraft,

Above: *The Boeing RAH-66 Comanche attack helicopter could be the most advanced military helicopter that the world has ever seen. The project was canceled in February 2004.*
Right: *The Franco-German Eurocopter Tiger prototype on its first flight.*
Bottom right: *The Agusta Mangusta ("Mongoose") is the first attack helicopter to be designed and built wholly in Europe.*

Above: *The Canard Rotary Wing (CRW), also known as the Dragonfly, is another hybrid aircraft developed by Boeing's Phantom Works.*

the Osprey and Dragonfly share very few characteristics. The Dragonfly takes off as a conventional helicopter, but when it reaches approximately 135mph (217kmh), the turbofan engine that was previously driving only the rotors distributes thrust to both the rotary-wing and rear jet nozzles. As forward momentum moves air over the two sets of wings in front of and behind the main rotor, extra lift is provided as the rotary-wing is locked in place to take the shape of the main wing. This configuration will allow the Dragonfly to access remote areas while having the speed of a high-speed fixed-wing jet. At the moment, Boeing and the Defense Advanced Research Projects Agency (DARPA) are jointly funding the $24 million assembly of two prototypes for extensive research into the future of the design.

UAVs

Despite the additions of stealth technology and sophisticated electronics, the aircraft of the future might lack one important component, namely the pilot. Unmanned Aerial Vehicles (UAVs) are coming of age, and have participated in many recent conflicts. Their obvious attraction lies in the fact that they place no pilots at risk from being shot down while over the battlefield. They can also fly for a long time without having to

Above: *The Global Hawk high-altitude Unmanned Aerial Vehicle (UAV) uses its long, slender wings like a glider.*
Right: *Scan Eagle is a long-range, long-endurance UAV. It can send real-time data and television pictures as it flies over the battlefield.*

Above: *A Predator UAV is operated from the tactical control station onboard the USS* Carl Vinson *aircraft carrier. UAVs are able to undertake many of the missions of manned aircraft.*

worry about pilot fatigue. On April 23, 2001, a Northrop Grumman RQ-4A Global Hawk UAV flew non-stop from Edwards AFB to Edinburgh AFB in Australia in 23 hours and 20 minutes. The Global Hawk has been designed as a reconnaissance aircraft to fly high above the battlefield at altitudes of 60,000ft (18,288m) while watching the ground below.

However, UAVs may have far more deadly uses. On November 3, 2002, a General Atomics RQ-1 Predator UAV launched AGM-114 Hellfire missiles at a car believed to contain members of the al Qaeda organization in Yemen. The Predator had been in action three years earlier during Operation Allied Force, when it was used to find targets for NATO warplanes. The Predator system is controlled by a mobile ground station with commands being transmitted to the UAV via satellite. When not in use, the Predator can be disassembled into six parts and packed into a box known as the "coffin."

Six inches long and deadly

It appears that the military have found an application for a plane that is smaller than the average model kit. Micro Unmanned Aerial Vehicles (MUAVs) are designed to be used by the individual soldier to conduct reconnaissance and surveillance or to detect chemical or biological (chem/bio) weapons. A typical MUAV is less than 6 inches (15.2cm) in length, height and wingspan, and carries a tiny payload of reconnaissance camera, sensors, or other military equipment. They are intended to be simple to operate, and will be able to transmit information back to their operator in real time.

MUAVs are designed to be used by the soldier in the field, who could conduct reconnaissance by unpacking a MUAV from his kit, throwing it into the air by hand, and then flying it by remote control over the surrounding area, while watching the television pictures that the MUAV sends back to see if the enemy is nearby.

One of the smallest military air vehicles is the "Sender," a UAV with a 4ft (1.2m) wingspan and a weight of 9.9lb (4.5kg). It has been developed by the US Naval Research Laboratory and, despite its small size, it boasts a range of almost 100 miles (160km). It may soon be used as a reconnaissance aircraft for US warships, and can be configured to undertake several different missions, from directing anti-ship missiles to searching for hostile vessels.

However, it is not just the United States that is working in the MUAV field. British firm BAE Systems, in conjunction with Lockheed Martin, is developing "Microstar," which weighs under 10oz (300g) and can fly at altitudes of up to 300ft (91m). A small electric propeller motor can generate speeds over 30mph (48km/h). It will be

Below: *Boeing's X-45A is a stealthy, tailless UAV constructed from composite materials and aluminum. The aircraft has two weapons bays which can carry up to 3000lb (1350kg) of munitions.*

Above: *The X-31 was constructed to test "thrust-vectoring" techniques which provide control of the airframe at very low speeds and very high angles of attack.*

Below: *Looking more like a plastic model than a combat aircraft, this prototype Microflyer MUAV could also be used to explore Mars.*

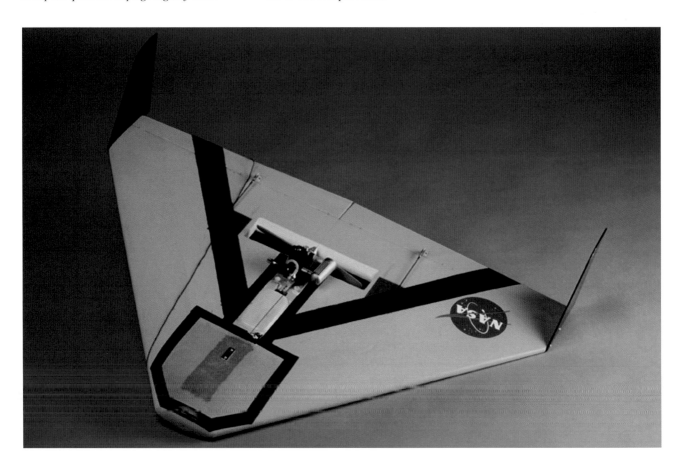

Above: *An artist's impression of a future long-range UAV.*
Right: *The F-35 Joint Strike Fighter is the most expensive military aircraft project ever undertaken.*

Above: *The V-22 Osprey tilt-rotor can take off and land vertically like a helicopter, but can travel much faster over a longer distance.*
Left: *The Boeing X-40A Space Maneuver Vehicle could be the reusable space vehicle of the future. This unmanned aircraft has already performed a number of sub-orbital flight tests.*

The International Space Station

When completed it will be around four times bigger than the Russian Mir space station, weighing 1,040,000lb (471,744kg) and measuring 356ft (108.5m) by 290ft (88m). The International Space Station (ISS) is in effect a space laboratory that will conduct research into medicine, materials, human physiology, and physics. It will be possible to perform long-lasting experiments on proteins, enzymes, and viruses in prolonged weightless conditions. A centrifuge will also be installed on the ISS, which will be used to simulate a range of gravitational strengths, ranging from that of Earth to those of planets such as Mars. In addition to the long stays in space that will be made by the crews, this research will help to explore the possibility of humans surviving for long periods away from Earth or on other worlds, furthering the human exploration of deep space.

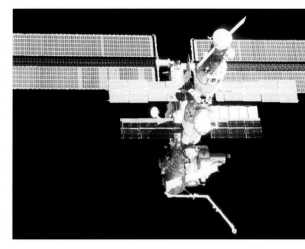

Responsibility for the ISS is being shared out among several countries. The United States is building a living area, solar panels, and the centrifuge module in addition to power systems, life support equipment, communications, and navigational systems. Meanwhile, Canada is building a 55ft (16m) robot arm, similar to those it previously had constructed for the Space Shuttle. The European Space Agency will build a laboratory, as will the Japanese, while ESA's Ariane 5 rocket will be used to ferry supplies to this extra-terrestrial building site. One of the biggest contributing nations is Russia. Having amassed years of experience from its Salyut and Mir space stations, it will provide two research modules, living quarters, solar panels, and a Soyuz transporter to take occupants and supplies to and from the ISS. Brazil and Italy will also supply additional components.

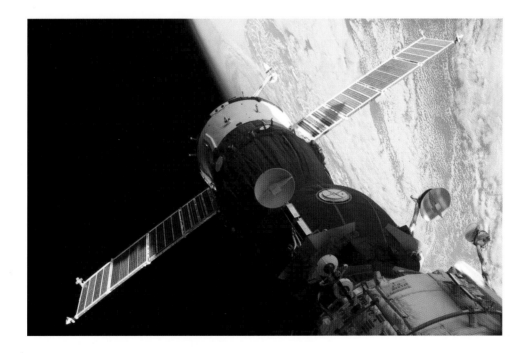

Top: *The International Space Station will be the largest space station yet constructed.*

Above: *A Soyuz spacecraft is docked to the Pirs docking compartment on the International Space Station.*

able to stay aloft for over 20 minutes, and carry miniature TV cameras, communications relays, or chem/bio weapons sensors. Microstar is designed for the individual soldier to operate. All they will need to do is unpack it from their kit, create a flight plan using a digital map, hit the load button, and hand launch. It will be almost as easy as throwing a paper airplane. The advantage of the MUAV is that they are small and almost inaudible, making them almost undetectable at altitudes of 100ft (30m).

But it is not just the military that will benefit from MUAV development; there could be several important civilian spin-offs. BAE Systems believes that Microstar will have significant commercial applications, including traffic monitoring and border surveillance. A MUAV with cameras and sophisticated sensors could be ideal for detecting trapped people in burning buildings.

Both the Predator and the Global Hawk were also used during Operation Enduring Freedom, the US-led military campaign against the Taliban regime in Afghanistan and the al Qaeda guerrilla organization, in retaliation for the terrorist attacks on the United States on September 11, 2001. Air power was crucial to this operation. B-2A Spirit and B-1B Lancer bombers dropped smart bombs on Taliban and al Qaeda sites while Grumman F-14 Tomcats and McDonnell Douglas F/A-18 Hornets flew Combat Air Patrols, guarding the bombers as they attacked. In this war, the majority of weapons used were "smart" and this trend seems set to increase in future conflicts involving western air power.

The future of aviation will be wonderfully varied, and just as the Wright brothers would scarcely recognize a Boeing 747 as an airplane, we would find it hard to comprehend how the massively large and minutely small aircraft of tomorrow get airborne. We have seen the end of just the first century of powered flight—there will be a lot more surprises to come.

Left: *The X-43 Hyper-X, pictured here with its B-52 and Pegasus rocket launch vehicles, was designed for hypersonic research. The aircraft made its first flight in March 2004, reaching speeds in excess of Mach 7.*

Right: *The X-40A also doubles up as an 80 percent scale test-bed for the X-37 Reusable Spaceplane pictured here in concept form.*

index

picture credits